Cases in Health Care Management

SECOND EDITION

JONES & BARTLETT
LEARNING

Cases in Health Care Management

SECOND EDITION

Sharon B. Buchbinder, RN, PhD

Professor and Program Director
MS in Healthcare Management
Dean, Brown School of Business and Leadership
Stevenson University
Owings Mills, Maryland

Nancy H. Shanks, PhD

Emeritus Professor
Department of Health Professions
Health Care Management Program
Metropolitan State University of Denver
Denver, Colorado

Dale Buchbinder, MD, FACS

Clinical Professor of Surgery
The University of Maryland Medical School
Baltimore, Maryland

Bobbie Kite, PhD, MHS

Professor and Director of Healthcare Programming
Associate Dean of Academic Operations and Affairs
MS in Healthcare Management and Health Informatics Programs
University College, University of Denver
Denver, Colorado

JONES & BARTLETT
LEARNING

World Headquarters
Jones & Bartlett Learning
25 Mall Road
Burlington, MA 01803
978-443-5000
info@jblearning.com
www.jblearning.com

Jones & Bartlett Learning books and products are available through most bookstores and online booksellers. To contact Jones & Bartlett Learning directly, call 800-832-0034, fax 978-443-8000, or visit our website, www.jblearning.com.

53751-2

Production Credits
Vice President, Product Management: Marisa R. Urbano
Vice President, Content Strategy and Implementation: Christine Emerton
Director, Product Management: Matthew Kane
Product Manager: Sophie Fleck Teague
Director, Content Management: Donna Gridley
Content Strategist: Tess Sackmann
Director, Project Management and Content Services: Karen Scott
Manager, Program Management: Kristen Rogers
Program Manager: Alex Schab
Senior Digital Project Specialist: Angela Dooley
Senior Marketing Manager: Susanne Walker
Content Services Manager: Colleen Lamy
Vice President, Manufacturing and Inventory Control: Therese Connell
Product Fulfillment Manager: Wendy Kilborn
Composition: Straive
Cover Design: Michael O'Donnell
Text Design: Michael O'Donnell
Media Development Editor: Faith Brosnan
Rights & Permissions Manager: John Rusk
Rights Specialist: James Fortney
Cover Image (Title Page, Part Opener, Chapter Opener): © Willyam Bradberry/Shutterstock
Printing and Binding: McNaughton & Gunn

Library of Congress Cataloging-in-Publication Data
Names: Buchbinder, Sharon Bell, author. | Shanks, Nancy H., author. | Buchbinder, Dale, author. | Kite, Bobbie J., author.
Title: Cases in health care management / [edited by] Sharon B. Buchbinder, Nancy H. Shanks, Dale Buchbinder, Bobbie Kite.
Description: Second edition. | Burlington, Massachusetts : Jones & Bartlett Learning, [2023] | Includes bibliographical references and index. |
Summary: "The new Second Edition of Cases in Health Care Management is a collection of over 100 new and cutting-edge case studies designed to help illustrate the challenges related to managing the health care services. Organized into nine content areas, from Leadership, Management, and Quality/Patient Safety; to Health Disparities and Cultural Competence, Ethics, and more, these realistic scenarios span the full spectrum of issues that can arise in a variety of health care services settings. Appropriate for all levels of higher education, this text engages students in active learning through lively writing and storytelling techniques that pull them into the story while giving them fresh, provocative real-world scenarios to analyze and critique. Furthermore, the authors have incorporated diversity, equity, and inclusion (DEI) and cultural competency throughout to encourage greater cultural awareness, sensitivity, and fairness. Key features : more than one hundred new cutting-edge cases written by experts in the field, new matrix (Appendix B) highlights topic areas related to each case and helps instructors assess the suitability of each case for different student audiences (community college, undergraduate, or graduate students), discussion questions and additional resources for students are provided for each case. Case study guidelines and instructions, with rubrics for evaluation of student performance are provided in Appendix A. Instructors' case study guides to facilitate class and online discussions are part of the instructor resources-available to qualified instructors"– Provided by publisher.
Identifiers: LCCN 2022013916 | ISBN 9781284180398 (paperback)
Subjects: LCSH: Health services administration–Case studies. | Hospitals–Administration. | Health facilities–Administration.
Classification: LCC RA971 .C335 2023 | DDC 362.11076–dc23/eng/20220401
LC record available at https://lccn.loc.gov/2022013916

6048

Printed in the United States of America
26 25 24 23 22   10 9 8 7 6 5 4 3 2 1

Contents

PART 1 Leadership   1

PART 2 Management/Customer Service   37

PART 3 Quality/Patient Safety

PART 4 Finance 125

PART 5 Health Care Professtionals/Human Resources   157

PART 6 Health Disparities/Cultural Competence   181

PART 7 Ethics/Law/Conflict of Interest   221

PART 8 Crossing the Line/Fraud   255

PART 9 Health Policy   279

Foreword

As a health care executive for over 30 years, I experienced uncertainty nearly every day. I often sat with colleagues reflecting on those experiences and opining about the whys and ways to mitigate them next time. In many cases, we scratched our heads, struggling to find root causes, protocol breakdowns, and human error leading to each incident.

In the U.S., medical errors are the third-leading cause of death after heart disease and cancer. Most are system related, due to staffing shortages, technology failures, and the like. For me, the most challenging issues involved human error. These errors take a toll on patients' families and care providers alike.

Despite the challenges, health care is the most rewarding career I can imagine. Healthcare workers impact lives every day. They offer care and hope to the community and compassion to those afflicted. We are blessed to be part of a healthcare environment that incorporates technology, law, spirituality, inventiveness, ethics, epidemiology, and inclusiveness. We have a sacred trust to do what is right each day and must acknowledge the importance of our work and prepare exceptionally. Helping others lead a meaningful life is our mission.

Health care offers amazing opportunities across a wide variety of professions. In addition to roles you have come to expect, like physicians and nurses, it also offers positions you would typically see in traditional corporate structures, like accounting, information technology, marketing, sales, and human resources. And some you would not expect, like physicists, dosimetrists, linear accelerator technicians, data scientists, and even clergy.

Healthcare expenditures in the U.S. represent nearly 18% of the Gross Domestic Product, or $3.6 trillion. Of that, hospital care expenditures are 32.7%; physician and clinical services, 19.9%; and prescription drugs, 9.2%. Another 4.6% goes to nursing care facilities and retirement communities. With so many lives and so much money at stake, it is imperative that managers and leaders run healthcare facilities as efficiently as possible, while delivering superior clinical outcomes.

Cases in Health Care Management, Second Edition, offers a real-world glimpse into the vast, ever changing healthcare environment. Instead of focusing solely on theory, case studies explore the experiences, practices, and daily operations of best-in-class organizations, along with pulling back the curtain on the organizational and personal practices that failed. Students actively engage in figuring out the principles of healthcare theory by abstracting them from examples. Case studies simplify complex concepts by presenting real life situations that would be nearly impossible to replicate in a classroom environment.

Healthcare managers and leaders must be prepared for the unexpected. For instance, how do you move patients from a storm ravaged facility to a safer environment? What is the impact of an active shooter incident on the healthcare system?

How do honesty and integrity play a role in the physician/patient contract? And what is the ethical argument for ensuring all citizens are protected from pandemics and epidemics? No two events are the same. Many of these we are convinced could never happen to us, yet they are the very issues we will encounter.

The cases presented in this book will challenge your skills in analysis, problem solving, decision making, and your ability to cope with ambiguity. I believe it is time well spent because these are precisely the skills needed to be an effective healthcare manager and leader. Take time to reflect and learn. Be honest with yourself and your colleagues as you experience the issues along the way. Unfortunately, we do more learning from those issues we may not fully understand or miss on our first review. Consider it a blessing and an opportunity for your growth.

Thank you for continuing your journey and accepting this sacred trust. All the best!

Kenneth Feiler, MA
Retired President and CEO of Rose Medical Center
Denver, CO
Adjunct Faculty, Healthcare Management
University of Denver
Denver, CO

Preface

The idea for *Cases in Health Care Management* came about 10 years ago just after Sharon and Nancy completed the second edition of *Introduction to Health Care Management*. Little compares with the elation authors feel when they hold their new "baby" in their hands. We marveled at its beautiful cover and gloried in the expanded case study section. Every instructor we had ever spoken to begged us for more case studies in that text. As we looked at the 106 pages of 35 case studies, it occurred to us that while this was an abundance of cases to include in an introductory textbook, many instructors wanted a case study book to accompany different courses and textbooks, not just one course. At that moment, while high on the buzz of a new book, and still drinking coffee, we decided what we really needed to do next was an *entire* book of case studies. Questions percolated in our conversation: Who would write the cases? How many should we have? What should they cover? What settings should they take place in?

We had lots of stories to tell that would help to create excellent teaching/learning experiences. A surgeon and department chair, Dale Buchbinder was excited at the prospect of offering his clinical and administrative experiences to a new generation of clinical and administrative health care managers. Colleagues, friends, and even family members had stories and teachable moments they wanted to share. Another phone call to our publisher, Mike Brown, encouraged us to write a proposal for the new book. He suggested 50 cases would be a suitable number. Originally conceived as a combination of the existing cases from our second edition and a few new ones, it was Dale who pressed for 100% new cases. After much thought and debate about who would write on what topics and how to organize the book, we decided to include at least 100 new cases that were value-added to the health care management literature: we produced 101.

That first edition turned out to not be enough. Over time we realized that, with the changes in health care and the world, new cases were needed. What you now hold in your hands is a second edition of our cases book containing 102 never before published cases in health care management, a virtual buffet of short stories of thought-provoking health care management scenarios that will engage students and instructors alike.

Bobbie collaborated with us on the fourth edition of our *Introduction to Health Care Management* textbook. Because that collaboration was so successful, we invited her to join our writing and editing team on this book, too. She brings new perspective and content areas that make this second edition even better.

Whether your institution is a traditional "bricks and mortar" school or a fully online one, *Cases in Health Care Management* is formatted for your ease of use and adoption, not just for one course, but for an entire curriculum. Instructors of management, law, ethics, human resources, finance, leadership, and other courses will find an array of up-to-date cases from which to choose. With a history of publishing books together and listening to our readers and instructors about what did or did not work in the classrooms and online, we created this book to be student and professor friendly. In addition, we were ever mindful of diversity, equity, and inclusion as we wrote and edited each case study. We are grateful to all our authors for their insightful, well-written, thought-provoking case studies.

As with our other publications, this textbook will be useful to a wide variety of students and programs. Undergraduate students in health care management, nursing, public health, human services, family studies, and allied health programs will find the writing to be engaging. Students in graduate and professional programs in discipline-specific areas, such as business administration, law, medicine, nursing, pharmacy, occupational therapy, public administration, and public health will find the materials both theory based and readily applicable to real-world settings. In particular, many scenarios reflect problems that clinician managers will confront in their day-to-day activities.

With over eight decades of combined experience in higher education, we know that first and foremost, teaching/learning is *not* a solo sport; it is a team effort—a *contact* sport. There must be a give and take between the students and the instructors for deep learning to take place. This text uses active learning methods to achieve this goal. Along with lively writing and the use of creative writing and fiction techniques to pull readers into the story, this book provides fresh, provocative, real-world scenarios for students to analyze and critique.

Cultural competency is a critical component to the delivery of health care and is a crucial part of providing diversity, equity, and inclusion (DEI). One way we incorporated cultural competency and DEI throughout the book was to ask the readers to keep three topics in mind as they review each case or instructor guide. The first is to pay attention to any assumptions they may be drawing on in terms of race, ethnicity, gender or gender identity, sexual orientation, socioeconomic status, culture, or any other protected classes. The second is to ask whether these assumptions are related to the individual/staff level, the clinical or program level, or the organizational or administrative level. Many times, we draw on these assumptions and they unintentionally influence our actions. Lastly, we ask that readers think about how these assumptions impact cultural awareness, cultural knowledge, behaviors, and/or skill development. Cultural competency is an evolving skill for everyone, and we intentionally increased the focus on DEI throughout the book through this framework. Cases that are especially focused on cultural competency have dedicated discussion questions included to further examine these topics.

Cases are organized into nine content areas: Leadership, Management/Customer Service, Quality/Patient Safety, Finance, Health Care Professionals/Human Resources, Health Disparities/Cultural Competence, Ethics/Law/Conflict of Interest, Crossing the Line/Crime/Fraud, and Health Policy. As clinicians and health care managers who live and breathe these scenarios, we purposely chose content areas that reflect flashpoints in health care management.

Specifically, *Cases in Health Care Management* contains:

- One hundred two brand new, cutting-edge cases written by experts in the field.
- A new matrix provided as part of a separate instructor resource package* that highlightss topic areas related to each case is available online. The matrix also includes:

- Complexity scores for each case to determine the audience for whom it is best suited;
- A chart showing the distribution of cases by complexity scores to assist instructors with selecting cases for their students; and,
- Trigger warnings to identify cases with content that may cause negative reactions for readers.
- Discussion questions for each case.
- Additional resources to assist students with exploring the content of the case.
- Case study guidelines and instructions, with rubrics for evaluation of student performance in Appendix A.
- Instructors' case study guides to facilitate class and online discussions are available from the publisher.*

Never underestimate the power of a good cup of joe—or the thrill of holding a new book in your hands. We hope you enjoy this text as much as we enjoyed writing and editing it. As always, our wishes for you are as follows: may your classroom and online discussions be filled with active learning experiences, may your teaching be filled with good humor and fun, and may your coffee cup always be full.

Sharon B. Buchbinder, RN, PhD
Nancy H. Shanks, PhD
Dale Buchbinder, MD, FACS
Bobbie Kite, PhD, MHS

Acknowledgments

Cases in Health Care Management is the result of an ongoing process that involved many of the leaders in excellence in undergraduate health care management education. We continue to be deeply grateful to the Association of University Programs in Health Administration (AUPHA) faculty, members, and staff for all the support, both in time and expertise, and in giving us extensive feedback on the first edition of this book and four editions of our textbook, *Introduction to Health Care Management.* One of the most consistent requests we had for all editions of that text was the call for more case studies. In the first edition, we had 15 case studies and rubrics, and were quite proud of that accomplishment. We heard "More, more, more!" The second edition included 35 more cases, and we thought we had really met the needs of instructors and students. (Insert hysterical laughter here.) And yet, we kept hearing the same call for "More, more, more!" which led to the first edition of *Cases in Health Care Management*, a stand-alone textbook of 101 case studies. The first edition was well-received and used by programs all over the world. However, the field of health care management is dynamic, and it was time for a whole new set of case studies to meet the needs of our student. Thus, we offer the second edition of the *Cases in Health Care Management* book to you, our cherished readers. Both editions of *Cases in Health Care Management* can be used not just for one course, but for an entire curriculum in health care management.

In addition to the four co-editors of this text, 43 authors have contributed to this second edition text, making this a one-of-a-kind book. Not only are our contributing authors expert practitioners in their disciplines and research niches, they are also practiced teachers and mentors. As we read each case study, we could hear the voices of each author. It has been a privilege and honor to work with each and every one of them: Ben Barton, Suzanne Beaumaster, Jenn Block, Kevin M. Bush, Jr., Carolyn L. Candiello, Amanda M. Carlson, Robert Casanova, Susan Casciani, Katherine Corchary, Christina Cottrell, Donna M. Cox, Suzana D. Deng, Stephen Duarte, Kristen Dugan, Laura M. Fricker, Sarah Hess, Anna B. Kayes, D. Christopher Kayes, Shirley Knelly, Boyd Loehr, Jihan Mahmoud, Nichole Marksbury, Marguerite McDowell, Kelly Niles-Yokum, Allison O'Grady, Matthias Ojo, Tolulope Oyewumi, Corinne Piccardi, Monika Piccardi, Madison Price, Samantha Read, Rachel Rogers, Louis Rubino, Nancy K. Sayre, Jane H. Schulze, Gregory James Smith, Tiffany Stockebrand, David Stockwell, Eric J. Thomas, Jeffrey Weide, Charisse F. Wernecke, Audrey Williams, and Lauren Zidovsky.

We also appreciate Kenneth Feiler's kind words in the Foreword, as well as others who have endorsed this new book. And, finally, and never too often, we thank our family and friends, especially Rick Shanks and Casey Kite. Sadly, Rick left us in February 2021 after a long battle with cancer. Both Rick and Casey tolerated long zoom calls about the cases and the creation of this book. Additionally, Casey assisted

Bobbie with editing and other work on her cases and reviewed all of the cases for gender neutrality, a huge contribution that was sincerely appreciated. We love you and could not have done this without you.

Authors

Sharon B. Buchbinder, RN, PhD
Dean Brown School of Business and Leadership
Professor and Program Director, MS in Healthcare Management
Stevenson University
Owings Mills, MD

Nancy H. Shanks, PhD
Emeritus Professor
Department of Health Professions
Health Care Management Program
Metropolitan State University of Denver
Denver, CO

Dale Buchbinder, MD, FACS
Clinical Professor of Surgery
The University of Maryland Medical School
Baltimore, MD

Bobbie Kite, PhD, MHS
Professor and Director of Healthcare Programming
MS in Healthcare Management & Health Informatics Programs
Associate Dean for Academic Operations and Affairs
University College
University of Denver
Denver, CO

About the Authors

Sharon B. Buchbinder, RN, PhD

Dr. Buchbinder is now the Dean of the Brown School of Business and Leadership at Stevenson University. A health care management educator with over four decades of progressively responsible experience, Dr. Buchbinder has worked across the entire spectrum of health care from delivery to research and policy to education and training. In addition to her extensive teaching experience in health care management, she has also conducted health care management research, particularly in the areas of health care professionals' job satisfaction and turnover. She is a past Chair of the Board of the Association of University Programs in Health Administration (AUPHA) and presently leads the MS in Healthcare Management Program at Stevenson University in Owings Mills, Maryland. Her most recent notable scholarly achievements include the publication of two best-selling textbooks, *Introduction to Health Care Management*, now in its fourth edition (with Nancy H. Shanks and Bobbie Kite) and *Career Opportunities in Health Care Management: Perspectives from the Field* (with Jon M. Thompson), which won the prestigious Bugbee-Falk Book Award from the AUPHA.

Nancy H. Shanks, PhD

Dr. Shanks has extensive experience working in health care for the last four and a half decades. Starting as a health services researcher and health policy analyst, she later served as the Executive Director of a health care foundation. During the last 20+ years, she has been a health care administration educator at Metropolitan State University of Denver, where she taught a variety of undergraduate courses in health services management, organization, research, human resources management, strategic management, and law. She retired in 2011 after serving as the Health Care Management Program Coordinator for 14 years and as Chair of the Department of Health Professions for 7 years. Dr. Shanks holds the title of Emeritus Professor of Health Care Management and taught online as an affiliate faculty member at the University for another 6 years. Dr. Shanks's research interests have focused on health policy issues, such as providing access to health care for the uninsured.

Dale Buchbinder, MD, FACS

Dr. Buchbinder is a retired Vascular and Endovascular Surgeon and Clinical Professor of Surgery at The University of Maryland Medical School in Baltimore, Maryland. Dr. Buchbinder served as Chair of Surgery for 18 years at the Greater Baltimore Medical Center (GBMC) and as Chairman of the Department of Surgery at Good Samaritan Hospital for 9 years. He also served as GBMC's Medical Director of Inpatient Surgical Services and Medical Director of the GBMC Wound Care Center. His experience as a physician leader and manager in two major community hospitals in Baltimore is augmented by his time spent as Professor and Vice Chair of the

Department of Surgery at the Chicago Medical School in North Chicago, Illinois. Dr. Buchbinder was elected to several surgical societies including the American College of Surgeons and the Society for Clinical Vascular Surgery. He is a Distinguished Fellow of the Society for Vascular Surgery, Past-President of the Baltimore Academy of Surgery, and Past-President of the Maryland Chapter of the American College of Surgeons.

Bobbie Kite, PhD, MHS

Dr. Kite is currently the Associate Dean of Academic Affairs, the Director of the Healthcare Programming including the Healthcare Management and Health Informatics programs, and a Professor at the University of Denver. Prior to the University of Denver, Dr. Kite was at The Ohio State University Wexner Medical Center, where she served as a postdoctoral fellow for the National Library of Medicine and then as a Clinical Assistant Professor in the field of Biomedical Informatics and a consultant with The Ohio State University Health Plan. With an avid interest in teaching, community collaboration, and research, Dr. Kite has a passion for teaching and maintains her research focused on population health. Before entering the field of biomedical informatics, Dr. Kite earned her doctorate degree in Public Health from the University of Texas Health Science Center, with minors in epidemiology and health policy. She also holds a Master's in Health Science with a focus on emergency and disaster management.

Contributors

Ben Barton, BSN, RN, OCN
Clinical Nurse Manager
Centura Health, Penrose-St. Francis
    Healthcare System
Colorado Springs, CO

Suzanne Beaumaster, PhD, MPA
Professor
University of LaVerne
Department of Public Administration
LaVerne, CA

Jenn Block, PhD
Director of Network Quality
University of Denver
Denver, CO

Kevin M. Bush, Jr., EdD, MS, MA, FACHE
Enterprise Director, Shared Surgical
    Services
Emory Healthcare
Atlanta, GA

Carolyn L. Candiello, MA, CPHRM
System VP, Quality & Patient Safety
GBMC HealthCare, Inc.
Baltimore, MD

Amanda M. Carlson, MSW, MS
Senior Policy Associate
Cobalt Advocates
Denver, CO

Robert Casanova, MHS
Adjunct Faculty
Department of Healthcare
    Management
University College
University of Denver
Denver, CO

Susan Casciani, MSHA, MBA, FACHE
Lecturer, Health Sciences
Towson University
Towson, MD

Katherine Corchary, MS
Certified Nursing Assistant
Denver, CO

Christina Cottrell, MS
Marketing and Communications
    Manager
University of Maryland Medical System
UM Upper Chesapeake Health
Bel Air, MD

Donna M. Cox, PhD
Professor Emerita
Department of Health Science
Towson University
Towson, MD

Suzana D. Deng, MBBS, MHCL
Rapid Response Team Lead
Colorado Department of Public
    Health and Environment
Denver, CO

Stephen Duarte, EdD, MHA, FACHE
Associate Professor
California State University, Northridge
Northridge, CA

Kristen Dugan, DEL, RRT, RPSGT
Director, Strategic Leadership Program
University of Charleston
Charleston, WV

Laura M. Fricker, MS, RN, SHRM-CP, RACR
Executive Director Johns Hopkins
  Intrastaff
Lutherville, MD

Sarah Hess, DEL, REEGT, RPSGT, RST
Professor
University of Charleston
Charleston, WV

Anna B. Kayes, EdD
Professor of Management
Department of Business
  Administration
Brown School of Business and
  Leadership
Stevenson University
Owings Mills, MD

D. Christopher Kayes, PhD
Professor of Management
The George Washington University
School of Business
Washington, DC

Shirley Knelly, MS, CPHQ, LCADC
Chief Compliance Officer
Anne Arundel Medical Center
Annapolis, MD

Boyd Loehr, RN, BSN, MSHM
U.S. Veterans Health Administration
Department of Veterans Affairs
Denver, CO

Jihan Mahmoud, PhD, RN, BSN
Assistant Professor
School of Nursing
Florida Gulf Coast University
Ft. Myers, FL

Nichole Marksbury, MSN-BC, RN
Informatics Nurse Specialist
Veteran Affairs Administration
Denver, CO

Marguerite McDowell, JD, BSN-RN, BSBA
Aetna
Arlington, TX

Kelly Niles-Yokum, PhD, MPA
Professor and Chair MS Gerontology
  Program
University of LaVerne
LaVerne, CA

Allison O'Grady, MA
Director Teaching and Learning
Adjunct Faculty
University College
University of Denver
Denver, CO

Matthias Ojo, MS
Infection Preventionist
Kennedy Krieger Institute
Baltimore, MD

Tolulope Oyewumi, MD, MPH
Adjunct Faculty
Department of Healthcare
  Management
University College
University of Denver
Denver, CO

Corinne Piccardi
Fire Chief
Cabin John Park Volunteer Fire
  Department
Bethesda, MD

Monika Piccardi, RN, BSN, MS
Program Chief, Systems Development
Maryland Department of Health
Baltimore, MD

Madison Price, MSHCM
United HealthGroup
Golden, CO

Samantha Read, BS
Baltimore, MD

Rachel Rogers, MS, BSN, RN
Academic Director
Assistant Teaching Professor
Department of Healthcare
  Management
University College
University of Denver
Denver, CO

Louis Rubino, PhD, FACHE
Professor & Program Director
Health Administration Program
Health Sciences Department
California State University,
　Northridge
Northridge, CA

**Nancy K. Sayre, DHEd,
PA, MHS**
Fulbright Senior Scholar
Universidad Politecnica de
　Madrid
Madrid, Spain

Jane H. Schulze, MPS, BA
Adjunct Faculty
Department of Health Informatics
University College
University of Denver
Denver, CO

**Gregory James Smith,
JD, DBE**
Adjunct Faculty
Department of Healthcare
　Management
University College
University of Denver
Denver, CO

Tiffany Stockebrand, JD
Adjunct Faculty
Department of Healthcare
　Management
University College
University of Denver
Denver, CO

David Stockwell, MD, MBA
Associate Professor of Anesthesiology
　and Critical Care Medicine
Johns Hopkins School of Medicine
Baltimore, MD

Eric J. Thomas, MD, MPH
Professor of Medicine
The McGovern Medical School
University of Texas Health Sciences
　Center
Houston, TX

Jeffrey Weide, DBA, FACHE, PMP
Academic Director
Assistant Teaching Professor
Department of Health Informatics
University College
University of Denver
Denver, CO

**Charisse F. Wernecke, PhD, MAS,
CPA**
Assistant Professor
Stevenson University
Brown School of Business and
　Leadership
Owings Mills, MD

**Audrey Williams, MS, CPHQ,
HS-BCP**
Senior Quality Data Analyst
Anne Arundel Medical Center
Annapolis, MD

Lauren Zidovsky, MAS, BSN, RN
Clinical Trials Manager
Medpace
Denver, CO

PART 1

Leadership

CASE 1

Should a Leader Disclose Impending Layoffs?

Jenn Block

You are the Director of Informatics in the ambulatory division of a medium-sized faith-based health care organization. The hospital-based system has been acquiring physician practices for five years and has been experiencing growing pains. This growth has necessitated the expansion of your team to manage the increased volume of data processing and workflow requests. You work in conjunction with the Medical Director of Process Improvement and the Director of Quality and Clinical Operations and their employees, all of whom have developed a cohesive and high-functioning partnership with you. Your team has worked hard under your leadership for over a year. You have challenged them, supported them, and empowered them. You have earned both their respect and their trust through your open communication and honesty.

Recently, there was a change in leadership, including the President of the Medical Group and the Chief Operating Officer (COO), the top two executives of the Ambulatory Division. The change has been difficult, and your team's anxiety is high. You reassure them normalcy will soon return—and it does. The next nine months fly by as the new executives are attending meetings, assessing the business and the infrastructure, and overseeing the daily challenges that typically arise in health care environments. Your team has been focusing on their primary goals: maximize the efficiencies within the electronic medical record (EMR) and assist the quality team in their initiatives to improve outcomes and performance. Your team continues to work hard because you keep them focused on the goals that you developed before the change in leadership.

In response to whispers on the grapevine, two of your employees approach you and ask if there is going to be a restructuring or layoffs. You and your co-leaders use the next team meeting to acknowledge the concerns. You open the discussion and your employees share their individual stories about how the rumors are impacting their morale and performance. In addition, three of your employees have important life events. A layoff without notice would be cataclysmic to them. One employee is preparing to spend a significant amount of savings to travel back home to Africa for three weeks; one is expecting a new baby; and one is in the middle of purchasing a new home. You communicate to the group that you have not heard of any plans to downsize and will let them know as you are able.

Over the next week, the stress in the organization reaches a crescendo pitch. You schedule a meeting with the COO to address your concerns. Rumors are rampant and employee morale is plummeting. The COO shares with you, confidentially, that members of your team are under review for a reduction in force (RIF). This is the first time you are hearing this information, and you leave the meeting unsure of what to do. You are conflicted because transparency and open communication are foundational elements of your leadership, and your employees trust you. It has only been a week since you communicated with them that there were no discussions of which you were aware.

After thinking about it for two days, you meet with your team. You share with them that it "never hurts to have your resume ready" and you would understand if they felt they needed to look for another position. The employees share their continued concerns and thank you for the support and open communication. The next day, one of your employees meets with the Chief Medical Information Officer in the Technology Department and asks if there are currently any openings in the department. Concerns are shared regarding an impending layoff. By the end of day, word gets back to the COO about your team meeting. The next day the President, the COO, and the Director of Human Resources call you into a meeting. They terminate you for disclosing confidential information.

Discussion Questions

1. What are the pros and cons of disclosing layoffs to staff in advance?
2. Did the Director's disclosure to the staff violate confidentiality?
3. What factors helped contribute to the Director's decisions?
4. How could this situation have been managed to have a better outcome for the Director and staff?

Additional Resources

Bates, S. (2018, April 17). *When should employers tell employees that layoffs are looming?* Society for Human Resources Management. https://www.shrm.org/resourcesandtools/hr-topics/talent-acquisition/pages/when-should-employers-tell-employees-that-layoffs-are-looming.aspx

Cascio, W. F. (2020). *Employment downsizing and its alternatives: Strategies for long-term success.* Society for Human Resources Management. https://www.shrm.org/hr-today/trends-and-forecasting/special-reports-and-expert-views/Documents/Employment-Downsizing.pdf

Elder, E. (2020, July 15). *5 ways to keep employees productive before, during and after a layoff.* randstad risesmart. https://www.randstadrisesmart.com/blog/5-ways-keep-employees-focused-during-after-layoff

Managing Nurse and Leadership Relationships

Amanda M. Carlson

You are a Nurse Manager on the intensive care unit (ICU) floor at a hospital in California. Leadership has approached you and informed you that your department has a high rate of supply waste. Your assignment is to identify why the nurses are wasting supplies. In addition, it is your job to implement and enforce new policies to reduce waste and save money. Over the next month, you observe the nurses and see they are taking excess supplies into patient rooms. When the hospital discharges the patients, the nurses dispose of any unused supplies left in the room to reduce contamination with the next patient.

You believe you have identified the problem, so at the next ICU staff meeting, you bring the matter up to the nurses. You tell the nurses that due to new hospital policies, nurses can only take what they need, when they need it, to the patient rooms. The nurses hesitate before one speaks up. He lets you know they understand supplies are costly and not wasting them is important for saving money. However, they feel like they have had to resort to taking more than they need at the time for two major reasons: 1) the nurses feel they are wasting valuable time by running to the supply room to get a single item at a time instead of taking more, reducing the time spent going back and forth for supplies and spending more time caring for the patient, and 2) for the past six months, turnover in the ICU has been high, meaning the nurses have more patients than normal. When they spend time going for supplies, they are away from the patients and have noticed an increase in preventable patient accidents.

The nursing team shares this as a source of frustration. They feel leadership continually asks them to make changes that support the bottom line without paying attention to how these changes affect patient care and the sacrifices these changes force on the nursing staff. They feel if leadership paid attention to and addressed the root issues of unsafe working conditions, outdated equipment, and offered more enticing benefits for overtime and extra shifts, nursing turnover would decrease, leading to reducing wasted supplies.

You let the team know you appreciate them bringing these matters forward and ask them what they feel would be good solutions for taking care of these issues. A brainstorming session brings up the following:

1. Poor working conditions: Due to understaffing, the nurses are taking care of three patients at a time instead of two. This has led to more patient accidents. The solution they see is identifying the patients at the highest risk and ensuring the nurses taking care of them do not have more than two patients to ensure they can monitor them regularly. They also suggest creating strategically-placed supply carts around the floor to lessen the time they have to walk to the supply closet. This strategy will also reduce waste because they do not have to take more than necessary into the patient rooms.

2. Outdated equipment: The patient beds are outdated because they are not auto-mated, which means the nurses are pushing a total of 400-600 pounds on their own when transporting patients. This has led to staff injuries, further contributing to the understaffing issue. The nurses believe if the hospital were to invest in newer beds that are automated, lighter, and easier to move, the number of injuries would decrease, and they would have proper and safe nurse-to-patient ratios.

3. Better rewards for overtime and extra shifts: The leadership team recently implemented a new rewards system that no longer pays for overtime. Instead, they reward nurses with points for overtime hours worked to be used to pur-chase items on the online company store. The staff feels like there is now less of an incentive to come in for extra shifts because they no longer receive the overtime pay. They suggest bringing back the overtime pay.

You thank the nurses for their insights and the willingness to share their feedback.

Discussion Questions

1. Have you identified the actual problem, a wasting of supplies?
2. What processes can you help implement so the leadership team hears the voice of the nurses?
3. What techniques can be utilized to problem solve workplace challenges? [Hint: look up Lean Six Sigma.]
4. How can you and leadership monitor progress to ensure that financial, clinical, and human problems improve? What metrics could they utilize?
5. What are the most effective reward systems for nurses?
6. How could you and leadership share outcomes learned with other managers or floors?

Additional Resources

Cho, S-H. (2001). Nurse staffing and adverse patient outcomes: A systems approach. *Nursing Outlook, (2)*, 78–85.

Cook, M. (1999). Improving care requires leadership in nursing. *Nurse Education Today, (4)*, 306–312.

Tomey, A. M. (2008). Nursing leadership and management effects work environment. *Journal of Nursing Management, 17*(1), 15–25.

Twigg, D., Gelder, L., & Myers, H. (2015). The impact of understaffed shifts on nurse-sensitive outcomes. *Journal of Advanced Nursing, 71*(5), 1564–1572.

Venturato, L., & Drew, L. (2014). Beyond 'doing': Supporting clinical leadership and nursing practice in aged care through innovative models of care. *Journal of Contemporary Nurses, 35*(2), 157–170.

The Simplest Things

Bobbie Kite

Senior Data Analyst Muffin works for a third-party medical scheduling company that contracts with health care organizations worldwide. After the state engaged the company to help with COVID test and vaccine scheduling, Muffin was told to expect some new duties as assigned due to new COVID responsibilities. With expertise in computer science, database skills, a history of health care management, and logistics training, the company decided Muffin would develop and deploy a scheduling system that could be used for COVID test scheduling. The state had made an unlimited amount of money available for this task and the latest and greatest technology was expected.

After successfully standing up the backend of the operation, Muffin ran into one "people" or "technological" issue after another. One of the larger "people" issues was to make the training user friendly enough. Finding the right balance of designing a tool that didn't require a computer science super-user proved difficult.

In addition, there were multiple interoperability challenges due to the tool integrating disparate data sources from multiple health care organizations, complicated by compatibility issues with software.

Lastly, it proved nearly impossible to hire health care managers who could manage the pressure of these high stakes logistics issues, even with the latest and greatest technology. For example, the supply chain of testing supplies, test processing, and demand for testing was constantly changing multiple times a day. Eventually, they were able to overcome these burdens and things started running smoothly.

Analyst Muffin was tasked with modifying the system to now accommodate for scheduling vaccinations. Muffin had worked out so many issues with the original COVID testing system, they were confident in their ability to deliver this modified program.

There was another "people" challenge that almost became their downfall. And, it was the simplest thing. The company left it up to individuals to schedule their follow-up appointment to receive their second dose of the vaccine. As the data rolled in, they realized only 20% of people were scheduling and coming back for their second dose.

This was creating a nightmare backlog of appointments to be rescheduled, drastically reducing the overall number of people being fully vaccinated. In addition, people were scheduling a second appointment at different locations and failing to cancel other appointments made for the second dose at the original locations. This was then compounded by a lack of communication with the facility where people had received their first doses.

Analyst Muffin quickly designed an automated system that could call folks to get them back in for their second dose, but there was another simple problem. No phone numbers were collected for these people when they came to get their first dose.

It took almost a month to catch up on the scheduling nightmare this created. The solution was to auto schedule folks for their second dose when they came to get their first dose. It seemed like a simple solution, but no one thought of it ahead of time. Three months later, they still had less than 50% from the first round of doses fully vaccinated.

Discussion Questions

1. What is going on in this case?
2. Identify the main organizational problem in this case.
3. What are three factors contributing to this problem?
4. Provide three possible solutions to the problem you identified.
5. Provide your reflections and personal opinions as well as your recommendations for addressing this problem.

Additional Resources

Bae, J., Sukumaran, R., Shankar, S., Sharma, A., Singh, I., Nazir, H., Kang, C., Srivatava, S., Patwa, P., Sing, A., Katiyar, P., Pamplona, V., & Raskar, R. (2021). *Mobile apps prioritizing privacy, efficiency and equity: A decentralized approach to COVID-19 vaccination coordination.* arXiv. https://arxiv.org/abs/2102.09372

Buchbinder, S. B., Shanks, N. H., & Kite, B. J. (2021). *Introduction to health care management* (4th ed.). Jones & Bartlett Learning.

Press, V. G., Huisingh-Scheetz, M., & Arora, V. M. (2021, March). Inequities in technology contribute to disparities in COVID-19 vaccine distribution. *JAMA Health Forum, 2*(3), e210264–e210264. doi:10.1001/jamahealthforum.2021.0264

Schoch-Spana, M., Brunson, E. K., Long, R., Ruth, A., Ravi, S. J., Trotochaud, M., Borio, L., Brewer, J., Buccina, J., Connell, N., Hall, L. L., Kass, N., Kirkland, A., Koonin, L., Larson, H., Lu, B. F., Omer, S. B., Orenstein, W. A., Poland, G. A., ... White, A. (2021). The public's role in COVID-19 vaccination: Human-centered recommendations to enhance pandemic vaccine awareness, access, and acceptance in the United States. *Vaccine, 39*(40), 6004–6012. https://doi.org/10.1016/j.vaccine.2020.10.059

Tewarson, H., Greene, K., & Fraser, M. R. (2021). State strategies for addressing barriers during the early US COVID-19 vaccination campaign. *American Journal of Public Health, 111*(6), 1073–1077. https://doi.org/10.2105/AJPH.2021.306241

COVID-19 Related Delays in Care for Cancer

Marguerite McDowell

You are the Chief Operations Officer (COO) for a large community hospital system. Caring for COVID-19 patients has disrupted normal care and operations. Surveys and interviews indicate that the fear of COVID-19 infection is negatively impacting the rate at which people seek care for cancer. Operational reports reveal a significant drop in patients seeking diagnostic and care to prevent and detect cancer, as well as delays in treatment for those with a confirmed cancer diagnosis. A recent study estimates 33,890 excess deaths among U.S. cancer patients over the age of 40 because of treatment delays related to COVID-19 (Maringe et al., 2020). The types of care that are deferred include emergency room visits, clinic visits, laboratory tests, and radiology treatment. It is important to note that in the U.S., one out of every five (20%) cancer discoveries are because of an emergency room visit (Furlow, 2019). Other repercussions include the closure of the hotel-like residential facility designed for loved ones to allow them to be close when a family member is undergoing cancer treatment. Deferred treatment leading to increasing demands on an already constrained health system has been labeled "care debt." Care debt refers to pent up demand for services as well as serious downstream consequences related to providing those services.

You have gathered hospital leadership for a strategic planning session and begin with an assessment of the system's physical property and equipment, staffing, and processes related to cancer care.

The system has three large traditional acute care hospitals where cancer treatment is delivered, nine community clinics located in the most populous areas of the city, three mobile mammography vehicles, and three mobile clinic vehicles providing preventive services including immunizations and treatment for non-emergency conditions.

Chemotherapy drugs must be prepared for infusion in a pharmacy supervised by a pharmacist. Chemotherapy drugs are prepared for patients of the hospital system at each hospital location. There are also numerous retail pharmacies located throughout the city.

Oncology staff are specially trained and include physicians such as oncologists, pathologists and radiologists, pharmacists, nurses, and radiology technicians. There are three primary methods of treating cancer: surgery, chemotherapy, and radiation treatment. All three acute care hospitals have a separate oncology staff structure with the necessary staff and equipment.

The emphasis of the session is on developing creative out-of-the-box solutions. The team is advised that the Board of Directors has empowered hospital leadership to make whatever changes are necessary in staffing and current use of assets to ensure cancer patients receive the required care.

As part of this strategic planning session, the leadership team is reviewing recent research in the U.S. and other countries that examines:

- The impact of the extended deep cleaning required on oncology radiology equipment after that equipment has been used for a COVID-19 patient.
- The impact of designating certain staff members as COVID-19 staff who cannot be assigned to care for non-COVID-19 patients.
- The quarantine period required for hospital staff who either test positive or reside with someone who tests positive.
- The fact that twenty percent of all cancers are discovered during an emergency room visit.

Discussion Questions

1. How would you modify the way hospital system assets are utilized?
2. How would you make the best use of staffing resources?
3. How would you ensure safe use of emergency facilities?
4. Is there any value to exploring relationships with retail pharmacies not affiliated with the hospital system?
5. Does it matter that mobile mammography units can be modified with the lead shielding and other equipment necessary to safely deliver radiation treatment to cancer patients?

Additional Resources

Furlow, B. (2019). What percentage of cancer diagnoses are made in the emergency department? https://www.cancernetwork.com/view/what-percentage-cancer-diagnoses-are-made-emergency-department

Maringe, C., Spicer, J., Morris, M., Purushotham, A., Nolte, E., Sullivan, R., Rachet, B., & Aggarwal, A. (2020). The impact of the COVID-19 pandemic on cancer deaths due to delays in diagnosis in England, UK: A national, population-based, modelling study. *The Lancet Oncology, 21*(8), 1023–1034. https://doi.org/10.1016/S1470-2045(20)30388-0

Mayor, S. (2020). COVID-19: Impact on cancer workforce and delivery of care. *The Lancet Oncology, 21*(5), 633.

Papautsky, E. L., & Hamlish, T. (2020). Patient-reported treatment delays in breast cancer care during the COVID-19 pandemic. *Breast Cancer Research and Treatment, 184*(1), 249–254.

Prinz, C. (2020). When a global pandemic complicates cancer care. *Cancer, 126*(14), 3171–3173. doi: 10.1002/cncr.33043

Richards, M., Anderson, M., Carter, P., Ebert, B. L., & Mossialos, E. (2020). The impact of the COVID-19 pandemic on cancer care. *Nature Cancer, 1*, 565–567.

Shankar, A., Saini, D., Roy, S., Mosavi, J., Alireza, C., Abhijit, B., Bharti, S. J., & Taghizadeh-Hesary, F. (2020). Cancer care delivery challenges amidst coronavirus disease – 19 (COVID-19) outbreak: Specific precautions for cancer patients and cancer care providers to prevent spread. *Asian Pacific Journal of Cancer Prevention, 21*(3), 569–573.

Wosik, J., Fudim, M., Cameron, B., Gellad, Z. F., Cho, A., Phinney, D., Curtis, S., Roman, M., Poon, E. G., Ferranti, J., Katz, J. N., & Tcheng, J. (2020). Telehealth transformation: COVID-19 and the rise of virtual care. *Journal of the American Medical Informatics Association, 27*(6), 957–962.

CASE 5

Crisis of Care: When Your Front Line Disappears

Kelly Niles-Yokum and Suzanne Beaumaster

Daybreak Senior Care (DSC) is a 30-bed nursing home in southern California. DSC provides skilled nursing care for older adults who require assistive care after a major medical event such as a stroke or a serious fall. DSC is well-staffed for the day-to-day level of patient care with six daytime Certified Nursing Assistants (CNAs) and three on the night shift, for a total of nine front-line employees providing assistance. A well-run, well-respected facility with a five-star rating, DSC employee morale is high, and there is a positive, community feel to the organization.

In March 2020, the COVID-19 pandemic began to impact California at unprecedented levels. State mandates were quickly put in place regarding best practices for safety across institutions with health care operations at the forefront of these considerations. Non-essential businesses were closed immediately. Skilled nursing facilities were considered essential businesses and all employees were considered to be essential workers. Unfortunately, this state of affairs did not constitute "business as usual."

Due to the rapid nature of the pandemic onset, almost overnight, supplies of all kinds became scarce. Skilled nursing facilities were left with limited supplies of personal protective equipment (PPE) on hand with extreme challenges in acquiring the necessary equipment for immediate and future needs of both staff and patients. COVID-19 represented a lot of unknowns for health care workers of all kinds. The symptoms of the virus were difficult to pin down and the outcomes for those who contracted the virus were varied and could be as benign as a simple cough or as extreme as respiratory failure and death. It became clear that older adults and those with underlying medical issues were at great risk of not only contracting the virus but also succumbing to it very rapidly.

DSC soon became a place of fear and anxiety. Many patients were terrified they would contract the virus and die. Staff at all levels found themselves in the position of contracting the virus and then passing it along to their patients or family. It became obvious that DSC was ill equipped to support their staff at functional levels with PPE and the additional training necessary. In particular, CNAs who engaged in the highest levels of patient interaction were concerned about the lack of PPE and appropriate training. Many CNAs felt they were not appropriately compensated or protected for the level of risk and additional work they were experiencing.

Monica, a CNA who had been working at DSC for over eight years, was extremely concerned. She worried about bringing the coronavirus home to her family and the possible impact this could have on each of them. Monica had two young children, a husband with asthma, and a mother-in-law who suffered with diabetes and heart disease. Monica took extra precautions in an attempt to keep them safe. These measures included changing clothes before entering the house, taking her belongings in a disposable plastic bag, and wearing gloves and a mask at all times. She did not want her family to live in fear of contracting the virus. Monica and the other CNAs quickly became disillusioned with DSC and their employment situation.

In the first week of the quarantine lockdown, DSC lost two daytime and one nighttime CNA to turnover. The remaining staff were hard pressed to complete their day-to-day activities in caring for their patients. The center administrator asked the remaining CNAs to work extra hours and pick up additional shifts—without overtime pay. It became obvious to many of the staff that patient care was suffering. At about $15.00 per hour, Monica felt she was not being adequately compensated for risking her life and the health of her family. In addition, Monica was angry that the center was not providing the necessary PPE to her and the other CNAs. Supplies were extremely limited, and all of the employees found themselves reusing masks and gowns along with other supply-rationing measures. Morale at the center among the front-line employees was slipping. Nationally, the virus was taking its toll. Every day, the news illustrated the extreme outcomes being experienced by health care front-line workers across the country, especially in California. This caused additional fear and anxiety among the remaining staff.

The situation prompted Monica and her fellow CNAs to ask management for a pay increase, additional hazard pay, and more PPE. Finally, they asked for additional staffing to cover shortages. They also reported the situation and demands to their union. When Monica took her concerns/demands to management, she was met with heavy resistance. In fact, she was threatened with termination if she did not fall into line. The response from management solidified the situation for the CNAs.

By the end of the third week, Monica and the remaining front-line staff had not returned to work. Monica argued that low wages, difficult working conditions, and clear mishandling of the COVID-19 crisis by management made the situation untenable for her. The compensation wasn't worth her health or that of her family. The mass exodus of front-line employees left the critical components of day-to-day care of the patients of Daybreak to a handful of higher-level employees: the registered nurses, licensed vocational nurses, and licensed practical nurses. DSC lost their critical front-line staff at a time when their presence was needed the most.

Discussion Questions

1.   What protections should management put in place for front-line workers who have family health concerns?
2.   What are some of the approaches that leadership should take to help workers deal with pandemic concerns?
3.   What do you consider minimally necessary responses and work adjustments for management given the significant issues presented by the pandemic?
4.   If you were a manager at DSC, what would be your response to Monica's specific concerns?
5.   If you were Monica, what might you have done differently?

Additional Resources

Bielicki, J. A., Duvall, X., Gobat, N., Goossens, H., Koopmans, M., Tacconelli, E., & van der Werf, S. (2020). Monitoring approaches for health-care workers during the COVID-19 pandemic. *The Lancet, 10*(20), e261–267. https://www.thelancet.com/journals/laninf/article /PIIS1473-3099(20)30458-8/fulltext

Misra-Hebert, A., Jehi, L., Ji, X., Nowacki, A. S., Gordon, S., Terpeluk, P., Chung, M. K., Mehra, R., Dell, K. M., Pennell, N., Hamilton, A., Milinovich, A., Kattan, M. W., & Young, J. B. (2020). Impact of the COVID-19 pandemic on healthcare workers' risk of infection and outcomes in a large, integrated health system. *Journal of General Internal Medicine, 9*, 1–9. https://www.ncbi .nlm.nih.gov/pmc/articles/PMC7462108/

Occupational Safety and Health Administration (OSHA). (n.d.). *Covid 19 control and prevention, healthcare workers and employers.* https://www.osha.gov/SLTC/covid-19/healthcare-workers .html

CASE 6

Why Are the Expectations Different?

Monika Piccardi and Corinne Piccardi

Rachel is her fire department's first female Chief. After working her way up through the ranks over the past 20 years to Deputy Chief, she was voted into her new position when the previous Chief died. Since she also is the first female volunteer Chief in her part of the state, she has gotten the attention of media and news outlets in the area. Rachel is known for her hard work, ethics, efforts to confront the status quo of a male dominated organization and culture, initiating change within the department in the area of diversity, and belief that those in positions under her will live up to their full potential if given the opportunity.

As the Chief, Rachel is responsible for over 100 individuals ranging from ages 16 to 75 years. This includes firefighters, emergency medical technicians (EMTs), and paramedics, as well as all employees working in the operational aspects of the department. Historically, the fire service has been male dominated. In more recent times, more women have been volunteering and working their way up through the ranks. Overall, there is a lack of diversity in many departments in the way of gender, age, and people of color. Rachel has worked hard over the years to bring in a more diverse membership and has encouraged the younger members to take an active role in the administration of the department. During her time, several of the younger department members were elected to the Board of Directors (BOD), yet the BOD remains a majority of older members. Along with all of her on-the-job duties come the expectations that people give the department 100% of their effort in-house and when representing the fire service in the community.

After a monthly board meeting, in which Rachel admonished several members for not following up on activities as directed and expressing frustration that this behavior was impacting operations, she is confronted by several board members and administrative staff for an "intervention." Rachel is told they felt she was being "mean" by expressing her frustrations and addressing this during a meeting by directly confronting those individuals.

After the confrontation, Rachel thought to herself, "This would have never happened to the previous Chief."

The previous Chief was well-known and loved by long-time members. He was a large, imposing figure, in short, a *man's man*. Some of his personal behaviors included shouting and cursing at others. In a different organization, his behaviors would have been considered questionable, if not inappropriate. Her predecessor's behaviors were always overlooked by the BOD, who are some of the same people confronting her now. What is she supposed to do?

Discussion Questions

1. What is happening in this situation?
2. If you were Rachel, how would you respond to the intervention?
3. What are two organizational issues or behavioral problems this case represents?
4. How would you create organizational change in this fire department?
5. What leadership skills would be beneficial in this situation?
6. Are there cultural issues represented in this case? Why or why not?
7. Does the President of the Board of Directors have any role and responsibility in this case?

Additional Resources

Buchbinder, S. B., Shanks, N. H., & Kite, B. J. (2021). *Introduction to health care management* (4th ed.). Jones & Bartlett Learning.

Eisen, H. (2019, March 4). *Building towards better: How a male-dominated organization is creating a culture of inclusion and moving towards a more diverse workforce.* Women of Influence. https://www.womenofinfluence.ca/2019/03/04/building-towards-better-how-a-male-dominated-organization-is-creating-a-culture-of-inclusion-and-moving-towards-a-more-diverse-workforce-2/

Ibarra, H., Ely, R., & Kolb, D. (2013). Women rising: The unseen barriers. *Harvard Business Review.* https://hbr.org/2013/09/women-rising-the-unseen-barriers

Piccardi, C. (2021). *Fear factor: Now you're the volunteer fire chief.* IAFC. https://www.iafc.org/topics-and-tools/resources/resource/fear-factor-volunteer-fire-chief#

Rock, D. (2019, May 24). The fastest way to change a culture. *Forbes.* https://www.forbes.com/sites/davidrock/2019/05/24/fastest-way-to-change-culture/?sh=dbe77643d50c

Williams, J. (2019, August 19). Diversity emergency: Women, minorities underrepresented in EMS. *US News and World Report.* https://www.usnews.com/news/healthiest-communities/articles/2019-08-19/diversity-emergency-women-minorities-underrepresented-in-ems

CASE 7

There Is a New Owner at Our Hospital

Louis Rubino

Mo is reflecting on the activities at the hospital over the last six months. After coming out of a Chapter 11 bankruptcy proceeding, Mountain View Medical Center (MVMC), a 350-bed acute care hospital, has been sold to a for-profit group. Having a long 50-year history as a Presbyterian, non-profit hospital and serving the poor in the community, the employees are concerned about the inevitable changes to come with the new mission. Many suitors expressed interest in buying this busy health care center. When it came down to doing forecasts that prove the financial wherewithal to continue to provide the much-needed services, only one company rose from the pack. Unfortunately, its reputation is not stellar.

Mo has been the respiratory therapy services supervisor at MVMC for the last six years. Beginning as a therapist in the respiratory intensive care unit, he was happy his values aligned with this religious-affiliated institution. He was also comfortable with the organizational culture under the old ownership. Now he is concerned the culture will be altered negatively with the transition. The hospital had supported the pursuit of his bachelor's degree in health administration through a generous employee educational assistance program. He hopes to pursue his master's degree, but is unsure if the new owners will offer a similar incentive. At this point, however, he is more concerned about just keeping his job in this tight market.

After only two months, there have been an abundance of changes under the new ownership. The governing body appointed members do not mirror community demographics like previous members. This new Board of Directors (BOD) seems to be getting much more involved in the management of the hospital than it should be, based on administrative principles. The BOD also changed the mission of the medical center from one that honored the ministry of health care for the poor to one that states, unequivocally, that the hospital is physician-led and beholden to the shareholders.

Due to the medical center's conversion from a not-for-profit to a proprietary institution, state and federal laws and regulations required MVMC to conduct a thorough review of promised continued services to the local community. Even though the state attorney general put stipulations on the new owners to keep essential services, like the emergency department and maternity ward, for a set number of years, there was already talk of closing the behavioral health unit and the transitional care unit due to their lack of profitability.

Many of the hospital department managers and Mo's supervisor peers, who had been with the hospital for years, have either left due to the uncertainty of the sale completion or were not rehired by the new company due to their high wages. His boss, a department manager, was just terminated. Mo has been placed in charge of respiratory therapy services as the new interim department manager.

There is ongoing revenue cycle concern even though the inpatient census and outpatient services are at, or above, the same levels as last year. The payer-mix is not what the new company is used to, due to having their facilities typically being in higher socioeconomic neighborhoods. Monthly budgets are not hitting goals, and cost-cutting strategies are being demanded by the new owners. The new administration is issuing demands for lower staffing levels, cutting pay rates, and reducing inventories. Mo is concerned about how these changes will affect the quality of care of the respiratory therapy services, something that always gave him a sense of pride.

Various stakeholders are also concerned. The physicians are getting restless since the employees are complaining to them and are considering admitting their patients to another facility that does not have so much turmoil. The hospital has two unions, one representing the nurses and the other representing the non-clinical staff (e.g., housekeeping, dietary, security). They are having meetings with their employee members to discuss what is going on and are demanding to exercise their bargaining rights before such massive changes can continue. Various long-term stakeholders (e.g., managed care organizations, long-term care partners, community agencies) are getting wind of the mounting strife and are now thinking of questioning their future relationships with the hospital.

Mo is frustrated, concerned, and scared of what is happening. Before the sale, he was able to go to the Chief Executive Officer (CEO) of the hospital and seek her advice on how to manage the challenges that confronted him and his department. Ms. Chan was a servant leader and had a democratic leadership style. She would meet with any employee who made the request. She always provided Mo with sage advice on stressing the importance of being patient-centered in his approach to problem solving. Mo was also impressed with Ms. Chan's demonstrated emotional intelligence when adverse situations occurred in the hospital. She was able to lead her team to workable solutions that ended up improving services. Mo considers Ms. Chan as his mentor, but she is no longer with the hospital. Her contract was not renewed by the new owners.

Mo has never had a one-on-one meeting with the new CEO, Dr. Larson. A trained physician, Dr. Larson obtained his master's in business administration (MBA) in an accelerated program last year. He was appointed in this role after his tenure working as the Chief Medical Officer (CMO) at one of the new owner's other facilities. He has a different leadership style from Ms. Chan and is authoritarian and hierarchal in his way of relating to his followers. Formal meetings with all the department heads are regularly scheduled, but he has not proclaimed an open-door policy, which would make it more comfortable to approach him as issues arise. It is difficult for Mo to adjust to this very different style, especially now in his new managerial capacity.

Discussion Questions

1. How does Mo, as the newly appointed department manager, become motivated to work effectively under these conditions? How does he motivate his employees when these significant changes are occurring?
2. What can be done to ensure patients are not affected by the changes that are happening?
3. Should the BOD do anything to intervene?
4. Are the changes taking place extreme or are they necessary to stabilize the medical center? What measures can be used to determine this?
5. What conditions in an organization might warrant a person to have an authoritarian leadership style? How about a democratic leadership style?

Additional Resources

Bowen, D. (2018). Leading the way to organizational resilience. *Healthcare Executive, 33*(1), 8–9.

Buchbinder, S., & Buchbinder, D. (2020). The physician leader. In L. G. Rubino, S. J. Esparaza, & Chassiakos, Y. (Eds.), *New leadership for today's health care professionals* (2nd ed.). Jones & Bartlett Learning, pp. 259–280.

Dye, C., & Lee, B. (2016). *The healthcare leader's guide to actions, awareness, and perception* (3rd ed.). Health Administration Press.

Garman, A., & Dye, C. (2009). *The healthcare c-suite: Leadership development at the top.* Health Administration Press.

Heifetz, R., Grashow, A., & Linsky, M. (2009, July–August). Leadership in a (permanent) crisis. *Harvard Business Review.* http://hbr.org/2009/07/leadership-in-a-permanent-crisis/ar/1

Hutton, D., & Moulton, S. (2004). Behavioral competencies for health care leaders. *Best of H&HN OnLine*, 15–18.

Kaissi, A. (2017). How to be a "humbitious" leader. *Healthcare Executive, 32*(6), 54–57.

Kornacki, M. J., & Silversin, J. (2012). *Leading physicians through change* (2nd ed.). American College of Physician Executives.

Mintz, L. J., & Stoller, J. K. (2014). A systematic review of physician leadership and emotional intelligence. *Journal of Graduate Medical Education, 6*(1), 21–31.

Sukin, D. (2009). Leadership in challenging times: It starts with passion. *Frontiers of Health Services Management, 26*(2), 3–8.

Walumbwa, F., Avolio, B., Gardner, W., Wernsing, T., & Peterson, S. (2008). Authentic leadership: Development and validation of a theory-based measure. *Journal of Management, 34*(1), 89–126.

Between a Rock and a Hard Place: Overcoming Poor Leadership

Tiffany Stockebrand

"What do I do?" Fred asked his manager, Roberta. One of Fred's employees, Allison, was transferring to another department in the large hospital system, and he needed to write her close-out performance evaluation. Fred continued, "Her performance standards clearly said that she needed to do an individual development plan (IDP) to receive the top rating, but she didn't complete one."

"What's the problem?" Roberta asked. "Why can't you just rate her at the fully successful level per her standards?"

Then the background spilled out. Allison's transfer came nine months into the year-long rating period. Allison received her standards at the beginning of the year and signed for them. She also had a mid-year evaluation with the opportunity to ask questions or clarify concerns about anything in her standards. As noted in the human resources (HR) guidelines, an IDP involved an employee thinking about how they wanted to grow, what actions they would take during the upcoming year to do so, articulating that in writing, and then taking appropriate actions throughout the year. The goal of the criteria supported employee development in the rapidly changing world of health care. However, Allison had not completed her IDP as required to move from the fully successful level to the top rating.

When Fred evaluated Allison, she became upset at her lower rating due to the lack of an IDP. Allison filed a grievance with the union. Compounding the issue, Allison had been out for several weeks mid-year due to surgery. Fred held the perspective that Allison knew about the IDP criteria and still had seven months in which to do an IDP and work on her growth—and yet had done nothing. Fred respected Allison's right to contact the union, no matter how valid or invalid the underlying complaint. However, the situation was complicated by the fact that Allison had a contentious background with a history of complaints against multiple supervisors including previously proposing legal action. Now, Allison once again threatened legal action if the situation wasn't resolved via the union.

Fred sighed and shook his head. "I feel like I'm between a rock and a hard place. The standards have a clear requirement. Allison signed for the standards. She had *months* to complete an IDP, even beyond the time she had to leave for surgery. I offered her the opportunity to complete an IDP *now* based on growth activities she accomplished throughout the year. She even said no to that. I hold all of her team-mates, including another who was out for medical reasons for an extended period of time, to the same standards. How is this possibly fair to them?"

Based on Allison's history and current communications, both Fred and Roberta feared not giving Allison what she wanted: the highest rating. Roberta approached Chris, the hospital administrator, about this thorny problem.

After hearing Roberta out, Chris responded, "Take care of this. Make up an IDP for her and rate her as high as she wants. Make this problem go away."

Discussion Questions

1. Think about issues of equity. Even though it seems like no one would know, the truth has a way of coming out. What would happen if other employees discovered that management held them accountable to standards then let Allison off because she complained?
2. Leadership is not just about leading down—it is also about leading up. Consider how Roberta can serve as an effective leader not just to Fred but to Chris as well.
3. The options seem binary: give Allison what she wants, make up the IDP, and protect the organization, or hold firm and subject the managers and the hospital to a lawsuit. It's your turn to think outside the box: come up with two to three creative and ethical, legal, and effective solutions.
4. Chris, the hospital's leader, not only directs subordinates to do something ethically questionable but he keeps his own hands clean in doing so. How would a true leader, a servant leader worthy of respect, handle this situation? Does this situation demonstrate the difference between a "manager" and a true "leader"?
5. Consider the legal implications. Allison may sue the organization if they do not give her the rating she desires. But could the hospital get sued if other employees found out that management applies standards unevenly?
6. Consider the ethical implications. Essentially lying by making up the IDP is not only ethically questionable, but also extremely questionable that an upper level leader directs his subordinates to do so.
7. What do Roberta and Fred do if Chris holds firm in his instructions, as this likely violates their standards of integrity? Does Roberta have any special responsibility toward Fred, as she is his leader?

Additional Resources

Buchbinder, S. B., Shanks, N. H., & Kite, B. J. (2021). *Introduction to health care management* (4th ed.). Jones & Bartlett Learning.

Guerin, L. (2015). *How to avoid trouble when conducting performance reviews.* Society for Human Resources Management. https://www.shrm.org/ResourcesAndTools/legal-and-compliance /state-and-local-updates/Pages/Reduce-the-Legal-Risks-of-Performance-Reviews.aspx

Johnson, M. (2013, March 7). *Ethics involving performance appraisal.* https://blog4org331.blogspot
.com/2013/03/ethics-involving-performance-appraisals.html
Pozgar, G. D. (2016). *Legal aspects of health care administration.* Jones & Bartlett Learning.
Vranjes, T. (2016, February 19). *Reduce the legal risks of performance reviews.* Society for Human
Resources   Management.   https://www.shrm.org/ResourcesAndTools/legal-and-compliance
/state-and-local-updates/Pages/Reduce-the-Legal-Risks-of-Performance-Reviews.aspx

CASE 9

Aligning Construction Projects with Lean Design

Jeffrey Weide

Wholesome Health (WH) is an academic medical center and community health system that works with underserved populations. WH leadership decided to move forward with planning a new community health clinic. This clinic would incorporate multiple functions within this one location to include the following services: primary care, specialty care, radiology, laboratory, dental, vision/optometry, pharmacy, health education, the county WIC program (the Special Supplemental Nutrition Program for Women, Infants, and Children), financial counseling and insurance enrollment, community and group programs (e.g., diabetic peer groups), and urgent care.

During initial conversations, the Associate Chief Operating Officer (ACOO) over the facility design realized competing priorities plus bringing some programs into the community for the first time (e.g., urgent care) was going to be difficult. Thus, the ACOO brought in two facilitators from the organization's Lean systems improvement (LSI) office to help conduct design. The two main partners with this project included an architect firm and the construction project team.

The ACOO convened a week-long initial Production, Preparation, and Process (3P) design event for this clinic construction project. A 3P design event is where the team is expected to design a new process or space based on three elements: purpose, people, and process. Since it was a new design, purpose is the key focus because it will ground the team members in designing it for the intended purpose to meet patient needs. For people, there is an element to "respect everyone" and ensure all designs are equitable. Finally, the process element focuses on how to standardize work to a point that it reduces errors and waste.

One or two representatives from each proposed clinic function were invited to participate in the 3P design event. The ACOO was the sponsor of the activity; however, he was limited to providing the kick off of the three-day event, clarification on any assumptions or limitations for the building, and scope definition. After the kick off, facilitators conducted walk-throughs with each individual group and reviewed their needs and lessons learned from existing facilities. These functional needs were then brought back to the group to determine priorities, partnerships, synergies, and adjacencies for workspace.

Three main themes came out from this discussion. First, it was apparent that not all functions would be open during the same hours. For instance, the urgent care and pharmacy would be open longer hours and weekends. Second, some functions required adjacencies to ensure safety and ease of staff use. Third, there was a need for flexible space to allow for primary and specialist care in a patient-centered medical home (PCMH) clinical pod design.

One of the strengths of the design event was inter-disciplinary design. However, this strength was also a weakness. For example, a change to needs for financial counseling led to moving the community group space and financial offices. This meant an issue with the location of the group space now being in the area that locked after typical clinic hours. Another change that led to issues was the expansion of the lab that moved it into the daytime clinic area, so there was a need to add a "stat" lab to the urgent care.

One day during discussions with the ACOO, the Lean Facilitator (LF) assigned to the project learned of changes made between only the function, architect firm, and construction project team. This led to secondary design meetings having to re-evaluate adjacencies, space, and other facility needs. Unfortunately, one design change (the laboratory move) had advanced enough where it was too late to make changes to the design.

While there were some challenges, the clinic received a large welcome from the community and government leaders. The urgent care was utilized so well that it reached capacity in six weeks, as opposed to the six-month projection. This success and exponential growth led to a call for a remodel to expand clinical space within three years of opening.

Discussion Questions

1. What opportunities and challenges do you see with bringing in another group (i.e., Lean Facilitators) to lead design of a new clinic?
2. From this case study, did the facilitation team follow the 3 Ps of a 3P project? Explain your rationale for this answer.
3. How would you define the roles of the following leaders/groups involved with this project?
    a. Associate Chief Operating Officer
    b. Architect Firm
    c. Construction Firm/Project Manager
    d. Lean Facilitator
    e. Clinical leader/representative
4. How would you have worked on any changes to the design after the event?

Additional Resources

Buchbinder, S. B., Shanks, N. H., & Kite, B. J. (2021). *Introduction to health care management* (4th ed.). Jones & Bartlett Learning.
Environmental Protection Agency (EPA). (2016). *Lean thinking and methods—3P*. https://19january2017snapshot.epa.gov/lean/lean-thinking-and-methods-3p_.html

Hicks, C., McGovern, T., Prior, G., & Smith, I. (2015). Applying lean principles to the design of healthcare facilities. *International Journal of Production Economics, 170*(Part B), 677–686.

Kahler Slater (2021). *Design intervention: How a Lean 3P event is a catalyst for change.* https://www.kahlerslater.com/insights/design-intervention-how-a-lean-3p-event-is-a-catalyst-for-change

Rever, H. (2008, October 19). *Five key elements to process improvement project success.* [Paper presentation]. PMI® Global Congress 2008—North America: Denver, CO. https://www.pmi.org/learning/library/five-elements-process-oriented-project-6946

Smith, I. (2016). The participative design of an endoscopy facility using Lean 3P. *BMJ Quality Improvement Reports, 5*(1).

CASE 10

Leading Projects for Population Health with a Cross-Functional Team

Jeffrey Weide

The Metro Community Health System (MCHS) is a multi-clinic, federally qualified health center (FQHC) system that serves disadvantaged populations in a major metropolitan area. The services focus on primary care, oral health, and behavioral health, along with ancillary services to include pharmacy, health education, care management, and community outreach programs.

MCHS utilizes regional and national grants to help with various programs and testing. One such program included a state grant program to assist patients with screening for breast and colorectal cancer. This program also tied into the health outcomes required by the regional accountable care organization ([ACO], an organization designated by the state Medicaid program to ensure health outcomes are met).

The requirement for this program is that at least 60% of "qualified" patients must have a colorectal cancer screening completed. The term "qualified" means the patients fall within an established age range and do not have (nor previously had) colorectal cancer. The purpose of this designation is to ensure regular screening to catch any potential cancer earlier to improve health outcomes.

The Director of Quality (DQ) and Associate Director of Care Management (ADCM) meet to address the issues with the health system's screening rate. The system is not meeting the 60% requirement; in fact, they are only at a 42% screening rate. Since neither is an experienced project manager, they enlist the assistance of the Director of Performance Improvement (DPI), a certified project manager, to teach them how to navigate the project to improve outcomes.

The DPI highlights two key steps before moving onto actions. The first is to accurately identify the state's and grant's requirements for screening. The second is to determine the method for tracking and analyzing screening rates for the health system. After these actions are complete, the two leaders will establish a team to help with conducting workflow and gap analysis to develop a solution.

The leaders select seven individuals to be a part of their team. This team includes the following roles:

- Cancer Navigator (CN, helps patients coordinate screening and care through the grant program);
- Mid-level provider (assigned to all cancer programs);
- Medical Assistant (MA);
- Care manager (CM, helps with complex patient care);
- Electronic health record (EHR) specialist;
- Data analyst (DA); and,
- Grants manager (oversees billing the grant).

During the review of the requirements and tracking method for colorectal screening, there are multiple revelations to the DQ and ADCM about the program. These include:

- There is no single designation in the EHR for individuals that have had or currently have colorectal cancer. Instead, it is based on ICD-10 codes.
- There is a significant delay between colonoscopies and results being entered into the EHR, sometimes up to four days after testing is completed.
- There is a low return rate of at-home Quantitative Fecal Immunochemical Tests (QFIT).
- High-risk individuals (e.g., those with a history of bowel cancer) are not designated appropriately. These patients cannot use QFIT.

Based on these findings, the team conducts a half-day rapid improvement meeting to perform the workflow and gap analysis. The team determines four actions must be taken to improve the screening rates:

1. Fix EHR inconsistencies for designation to ensure correct counts are made for screening.
2. Set up follow-up appointments at the clinic to drop-off QFIT tests.
3. The MA could also do a rapid test to determine if it is negative or if the patient needs an appointment with a provider to discuss positive tests.
4. Work with imaging partners to expedite the results of colonoscopies to the health system.

After these actions are implemented, the health system has screening rates of 51%, 61%, and 66% over the next three months. The group meets again for an after-action report and to determine what processes should be standardized and what needs more improvements to keep the rates above the required 60%.

Discussion Questions

1.   Do you think the DQ and ADCM would have been successful with their improvement project without mentoring by the DPI?
2.   Do you think that the correct team was assembled for this project? Would you have made any changes to the team composition? Provide your rationale for your response.
3.   What steps would you take as the DQ and ADCM next year when grant and state requirements are updated for health outcomes?

Additional Resources

Buchbinder, S. B., Shanks, N. H., & Kite, B. J. (2021). *Introduction to health care management* (4th ed.). Jones & Bartlett Learning.

Centers for Disease Control and Prevention (CDC). *Colorectal (colon) cancer: What should I know about screening?* https://www.cdc.gov/cancer/colorectal/basic_info/screening/index.htm

Rever, H. (2008, October 19). *Five key elements to process improvement project success.* [Paper presentation]. PMI® Global Congress 2008—North America: Denver, CO. https://www.pmi .org/learning/library/five-elements-process-oriented-project-6946

The Doctors Laboratory. (2018, October). *Quantitative Fecal Immunochemical Tests (qFIT).* https:// www.tdlpathology.com/media/Multisite8078/tap4170_qfit_test_update_a4_v2.pdf

CASE 11

Speak Up Safely

Audrey Williams and Shirley Knelly

Valley Alliance Hospital (VAH) has administered a safety culture survey to assess staff perspective of patient safety every 18 months. The results from the most recent survey showed that staff did not feel comfortable speaking up when involved in or witnessing a potential patient safety event, especially when there was a perceived hierarchical discrepancy (e.g., environmental services employee and a physician). In addition to the survey, the Chief Patient Safety Officer (CPSO), Janice Jeopardy, had the organization participate in the Joint Commission's Health Risk Screening Tool (HRST) to measure high reliability, which requires a leadership team committed to zero harm, a fully functional culture of safety, and the use of a robust improvement process in the organization. Janice is dismayed at the results of the HRST. The organization scored the lowest under the trust section of the survey. This indicated there was a lack of trust when reporting events and a fear of intimidating behavior.

Around the same time, VAH was also implementing a new event reporting system where anyone in the health system could report patient safety events or concerns. During conversations with colleagues, there was feedback that staff felt reporting was tattling and nothing ever happened when events were reported to leaders in the past. This response distressed Janice, and she felt she must do something to change this concept of *tattling* to one of *reporting* errors and near misses. After all, the Joint Commission urged health care leaders to establish just cultures where "people are encouraged, even rewarded for providing essential safety-related information...while clear lines are drawn between human error and at-risk or reckless behaviors" (The Joint Commission, 2021, p. 2). Janice was in a quandary. How could she implement a real speak up safely/just culture plan when people were afraid to report errors?

Discussion Questions

1. Janice wants to delve into understanding the feelings and opinions of staff before creating an action plan. To do this, she decides to do focus groups. Who should be invited to participate in the focus groups and why?
2. What does this case suggest about the culture in the hospital?

3. Why do you think staff feel uncomfortable speaking up, especially between job classes?
4. What type of leadership style do you think is best to address the issues and provide the training?
5. When contemplating the integration of the reporting system, what is the structure of oversight, and what internal committees are necessary to ensure successful implementation of the system?
6. What key technical components of the reporting system are essential to address the concerns of end users such as fear of reporting, lack of access, lack of feedback, etc.? For example, is the technology accessed on the desktop or from a link in the electronic medical record for ease of use, is there the ability to enter an event anonymously, limited number of mandatory fields, staff available to receive an email acknowledgement and can they track the progress of the event cycle, etc.?
7. What is the roll out strategy for the reporting system in conjunction with the speak up safely/just culture plan?
8. How would the organization measure the success of the integration of a new reporting system and just culture?

Additional Resources

Agency for Healthcare Research and Quality. (2018, July). *Understand just culture*. https://www.ahrq .gov/hai/cusp/videos/07a-just-culture/index.html

Agency for Healthcare Research and Quality. (2019, September 7). *Reporting patient safety events*. https://psnet.ahrq.gov/primer/reporting-patient-safety-events

Boysen, P. G. (2013). Just culture: A foundation for balanced accountability and patient safety. *The Ochsner Journal*, *13*(3), 400–406. https://www.ncbi.nlm.nih.gov/pmc/articles/PMC3776518/

Buchbinder, S. B., Shanks, N. H., & Kite, B. J. (2021). *Introduction to health care management* (4th ed.). Jones & Bartlett Learning.

Pronovost, P. J., Morlock, L. L., Sexton, J. B., Miller, M. R., Holzmueller, C. G., Thompson, D. A., Lubomski, L. H., & Wu, A. W. (n.d.). *Improving the value of patient safety reporting systems*. Agency for Healthcare Research and Quality. https://www.ahrq.gov/downloads/pub/advances2 /vol1/Advances-Pronovost_95.pdf

The Joint Commission. (2021, June 18). *Sentinel event alert. The essential role of leadership in developing a safety culture*. https://www.jointcommission.org/-/media/tjc/documents/resources /patient-safety-topics/sentinel-event/sea-57-safety-culture-and-leadership-final2.pdf

PART 2

Management/ Customer Service

CASE 12

The Sudden Shift in Volume

Ben Barton

Tree is the Nurse Manager on a busy orthopedic unit at Queen Palmer Medical Center (QPMC), a 225-bed faith-based community hospital serving a medium-sized metropolitan area. Volumes have been steadily growing over the past two years along with the population. An aging community means more patients requiring joint replacements as well as increases in hospitalizations after traumatic events such as falls and associated fractures. Things are going well; volumes are high, staffing levels are good, and productivity remains strong. The hospital system to which QPMC belongs is in a strong financial state, thanks to steady volumes and good budgetary management. Suddenly, COVID-19 arrives, and before anyone can blink, elective surgeries are cancelled. Hospital volumes are down by 50-55%, and Tree's unit is closed.

On a normal weekday, Tree's unit would average six registered nurses (RNs) and two certified nursing assistants (CNAs) working the day shift, and five RNs and two CNAs working the night shift. Tree's unit of 45 staff members has been merged with a separate surgical unit with a similar-sized staff. A plethora of challenges are ready to be addressed. Tree's staff members are working in a unit that they don't know, with some of their normal colleagues and an equal number of unfamiliar faces. They are floating to different units more frequently and are being called-off due to low census at an alarming rate, using up their hard-earned paid-time-off (PTO). In addition, many of the patients for whom they are caring are different from the ones they used to see on a regular basis on their home unit.

Virtually overnight, Tree goes from facing complaints about being short-staffed and burned out, to complaints about using too much of their PTO, too much floating, and not being on their home unit. Everyone is facing the frustrations and fears of an unprecedented pandemic, along with fears of job security, and a change from the norm. Topping off the list of anxieties is the fear that an acute outbreak could occur. If that occurs, staff will be forced to care for a population consisting primarily of COVID-19 patients. The dearth of work would shift back to overwork, short-staffing, and potentially greater volumes than they've ever seen. Will the next surge drown Tree, the staff, and the hospital?

Discussion Questions

1. What are some innovative ideas to preserve PTO, create engagement, and salvage associate satisfaction?
2. How would you go about hitting a productive target in the setting of plummeting patient volumes?
3. What options are there to stave off layoffs?
4. If the Chief Financial Officer (CFO) came to Tree and indicated the staffing matrix (the grid used to determine how many staff are needed for a certain number of patients) would be changing, what are some things to consider related to this change?
5. What steps can be taken to ensure Tree's team is able to manage the inevitable eventual return of normal operations?

Additional Resources

Dukes, T. (2021, September 9). Latest COVID surge stressing hospital staff, space across North Carolina. *The News and Observer.* https://www.newsobserver.com/news/coronavirus/article254099708.html

Harte, J., & Bernstein, S. (2021, September 17). Some U.S. hospitals forced to ration care amid staffing shortages, COVID-19 surge. *Reuters.* https://www.reuters.com/world/us/some-us-hospitals-forced-ration-care-amid-staffing-shortages-covid-19-surge-2021-09-17/

Marcozzi, D. E., Pietrobon, R., Lawler, J. V., French, M. T., Mecher, C., Baehr, N. E., & Browne, B. J. (2021). The application of a hospital medical surge preparedness index to assess national pandemic and other mass casualty readiness. *Journal of Healthcare Management, 66*(5), 367–378.

Masson, G. (2021, September 30). Cleveland health system implements new staffing strategies amid COVID-19 surge. *Becker's Hospital Review.* https://www.beckershospitalreview.com/hospital-management-administration/cleveland-health-system-implements-new-staffing-strategies-amid-covid-19-surge.html

Medina-Craven, M. N., & Ostermeier, K. (2021). Investigating justice and bullying among healthcare workers. *Employee Relations, 43*(1), 31–44. https://doi.org/10.1108/ER-04-2019-0195

Perry, N. (2021). When telehealth went viral: How the COVID-19 pandemic influenced the rapid move to virtual medical treatment, and what non-rural providers not treating COVID-19 patients should do about it. *Journal of Health Care Finance, 47*(4). https://www.healthfinancejournal.com/index.php/johcf/article/view/254

Schumaker, E. (2021, August 13). Short-staffed hospitals battling COVID surge after opting not to staff up. *ABC News.* https://abcnews.go.com/US/short-staffed-hospitals-battling-covid-surge-opting-staff/story?id=79360422

Toner, E., & Waldhorn, R. (2020, February 27). What US hospitals should do now to prepare for a Covid-19 pandemic. *Clinicians' Biosecurity News.* https://centerforhealthsecurity.org/cbn/2020/cbnreport-02272020.html

Upstate Medical University. (n.d.). *Four phases of emergency management.* https://www.upstate.edu/emergencymgt/about/phases.php

U.S. Department of Health & Human Services, Health Resources & Services Administration. (2021, January 28). *Medicare payment policies during COVID-19.* https://telehealth.hhs.gov/providers/billing-and-reimbursement/medicare-payment-policies-during-covid-19/

How Important Is a Problem List?

Jenn Block

You are the Manager of Clinical Quality. You also oversee electronic health record (EHR) training for a major national hospital system. Upper management has tasked you to maximize the use of the EHR. You came up the ranks starting as an EHR specialist, so you know what a system gets out of its EHR depends on the practice, the EHR, and the capabilities within the system and of the providers themselves. Many hospital-based systems have acquired physician practices, therefore one system may have different approaches to using the same tools within an EHR.

You decide to focus on one tool within the EHR that can be quite valuable and powerful: the problem list tool. This tool allows providers and other members of the care team to see a snapshot of a patient's current acute diagnoses and their chronic conditions. The problem list tool snapshot is pivotal to identifying and addressing the patient's current needs for care. Your research informs you that there have been barriers to achieving the optimal use of the problem list in other large hospital systems, including, but not limited to:

- Primary care providers use them in diverse ways;
- Input and upkeep of the problem lists can be time consuming; and,
- Problem list etiquette isn't typically taught to providers during training.

Because the problem list is integral to the maximization of the EHR, developing a policy that outlines a shared approach will allow users to maximize its use.

With the evolution of reimbursement models from fee-for-service to value-based care, the coordination of the patient's team can determine success. This change has been the impetus to increase communication among the various members of the care team. Effective communication hinges on the sharing of complete and timely information. However, primary care providers (PCPs) often have limited time due to increased caseloads and decreased appointment times. PCPs are already overburdened, and it is difficult to create time and engagement for projects that may not immediately increase provider satisfaction. One way to achieve this is through a sense of duty to the care and outcomes of the patient, which relies on this technology to work effectively. In addition, new value-based contracts for Medicare Advantage plans are contingent upon accurately reflecting the complexity of the patient. Standardizing the problem list can assist providers in maximizing financial reimbursement by using a preference list with each patient, along with their documented Hierarchical Condition Category codes, "a risk-adjustment model originally designed to estimate future health care costs for patients" (American Academy of Family Physicians, n.d., para. 1). This standardization permits more efficiency for the provider, potentially overcoming the argument that maintaining the list is time consuming.

Lastly, with multiple acquired practices within a large system, managers must delineate expectations in advance, and independent cultures must merge with the larger organizational culture. If administrators do not take these steps ahead of time, complications will arise in projects and physician engagement can be more difficult. A successful and sustainable change can only occur when managers understand the complexities of physician culture. They must also be adept at using techniques to inspire passion and team-based resolutions to issues. The culture of an organization is analogous to having an elephant in the room. Everyone knows the elephant is there, but many don't want to acknowledge its presence. Managers must talk about the cultural pachyderm in the organization and work to overcome obstacles to change. Even when physician champions make plans for change, they can become frustrated by the barriers they experience. These impediments often lead to the forfeiture of those plans due to the inability to engage others in their practice on an emotional level (Johnson & Stewart, 2008).

With all of these things in mind, how do you proceed?

Discussion Questions

1. What is the importance of leveraging the problem list in an EHR?
2. How can you and upper management effectively use change management practices to recommend standardization of the problem list in their EHR?
3. What steps do you recommend for building the case for standardization of the problem list in their EHR?
4. What barriers might you encounter throughout this process and what tools could you use to overcome them?

Additional Resources

American Academy of Family Physicians (AAFP). (n.d.). *Hierarchical condition category coding.* https://www.aafp.org/family-physician/practice-and-career/getting-paid/coding/hierarchical -condition-category.html

Health Catalyst. (2019). *Five action items to improve HCC coding accuracy and risk adjustment with analytics.* https://www.healthcatalyst.com/insights/5-ways-improve-hcc-coding-accuracy -risk-adjustment

Holmes, C. (2011). The problem list beyond meaningful use. Part I: The problems with problem lists. *Journal of AHIMA, 82*(2), 30–33. http://journal.ahima.org/wp-content/uploads/JAHIMA -problemlists.pdf

Hummel, J., & Evans, P. (2012, December). *Standardizing the problem list in ambulatory electronic health record to improve patient care.* Agency for Healthcare Research and Quality. https://www .ahrq.gov/sites/default/files/wysiwyg/evidencenow/tools-and-materials/ehr-problem-list.pdf

Johnson, B. C., & Stewart, E. E. (2008). The key to implementing change in your practice. *Family Practice Management, 15*(8), A5–A8. https://www.aafp.org/fpm/2008/0900/pa5.html

Service Dogs as a New Presence in Ambulatory Clinics

Jenn Block

Jem was a new Practice Manager at the Sumner Primary Care Clinic in Sumner, Colorado. Previously, Jem had worked at a much smaller pediatric office on the other side of town. Prior to being hired, Jem interviewed with the owner of the practice, Dr. Joss, who seemed serious. Dr. Joss was also a provider at the practice and made it clear during the interview the expectation that Jem would take care of all issues that arose in the practice so that all the providers could focus solely on seeing patients. Dr. Joss explained that Jem would be directly overseeing the two front desk staff, the billing manager, and the 10 medical assistants to the providers. Jem's career started in health care as a medical assistant, one of the things Dr. Joss praised during the interview.

Fast forward three weeks, and Jem was surprised there was no formal on-boarding. During the first week at work, it became clear this would be a busy practice with a range of patients from newborn babies to the elderly. Jem decided to work in each of the areas to better understand their processes. This week started with the front desk staff. Jem had just finished checking in a patient when another one walked through the front door with a large dog. The patient walked over to the front desk to check in for a scheduled appointment with one of the doctors. Jem had only seen one patient with a service dog previously, but that patient was blind, and it was a guide dog. This patient seemed young and healthy which surprised Jem, not to mention the dog was huge. The canine wore no vest or tags identifying it as a service dog, but calmly stayed at the patient's left side during check-in. Visibly distressed and trembling, the front desk clerk checked-in the patient and pointed in the direction of the waiting area. Once seated, the front desk clerk asked to speak to Jem privately.

"This patient has never brought in a dog before and has been coming here for about a year." Still shaking from the encounter, "That dog is enormous, just like my neighbor's dog who bit a child down the street. I bet it could really hurt someone. Even the other patients looked concerned when they walked in. I saw one patient' get up and change seats. We have never had a situation like this before. This patient is really nice, but I have heard stories from my friends in other clinics that patients are trying to bring their dogs in with them, claiming they need them for emotional support. What should we do?"

Jem considered what was said and became worried other patients would complain, or worse, the dog might endanger them, so Jem decided to have a discussion with the patient back up at the front desk.

Jem explained to the patient that there was concern about the large the dog and that other patients and staff might fear the animal because of its size. The patient seemed to be getting upset but listened as Jem spoke. Next, Jem politely asked the patient to put the dog into the car for the remainder of the visit.

Face flushed, hands opening and closing, voice tense, the patient said, "My case worker told me I'm allowed to have my dog with me."

Jem was trying to be sympathetic but was becoming anxious with the change of affect—and the impact it might have on the other patients. Jem tried to think of a solution that would make everyone happy, since the dog appeared to be calmly laying at its owner's feet. Jem asked the patient if there was a vest in the car that could be put on the dog while in the office.

"No, my dog is too big, I can't find a vest anywhere that fits, and honestly, I can't afford one," the patient said. "I told my case worker, who assured me I could have my dog with me while I was doing service dog training."

This revelation was surprising to Jem considering most service dogs are trained by a professional. The patient's story raised further suspicion.

The patient was now yelling in front of the other patients. Jem decided that the best thing to do was to ask the patient to leave and reschedule the appointment. The patient started screaming to see the doctor right away for the appointment and that there were several prescriptions to be refilled. Staff started trickling out to the front desk to see what the commotion was, including the doctor. The patient now had a face full of tears, and was still yelling at Jem, who was shaking and unsure of what to do.

The doctor immediately guided the patient and dog back to an exam room and looked at Jem in a disapproving manner.

Jem's heart sank. *Am I am going to get fired my first week on the job for not being able to manage that situation?*

Later, the doctor found Jem eating lunch in the break room.

"If you would have just come and asked me, I would have told you that the patient is a disabled veteran who has been trying to get approved for a service dog." The doctor continued, "Finally, the patient found a non-profit that will help with training a service dog. You should never hesitate to ask me if you have a question. This incident was really upsetting just when I've been making great progress in gaining the patient's trust."

Jem vowed never to allow this type of incident happen again.

Discussion Questions

1.   What are the applicable laws that apply to this scenario?
2.   What is the difference in the law as it applies to an emotional support dog and a service dog?

3. What cultural and procedural issues played a part in how this situation was managed?
4. What would have been a more appropriate way for Jem to manage the situation to decrease the risk of it escalating?
5. What type of training would you recommend for Jem and the staff?
6. Did you make any assumptions while reading this case regarding race, ethnicity, gender or gender identity, sexual orientation, socioeconomic status, culture, or other protected class? Were these assumptions focused at the individual/staff level, clinical/program level, or organizational/administrative level? How do these assumptions affect cultural awareness, cultural knowledge, behaviors, and/or skill development?

Additional Resources

Center for Substance Abuse Treatment. (2014). *Improving cultural competence.* Substance Abuse and Mental Health Services Administration. https://www.ncbi.nlm.nih.gov/books/NBK248428/

U.S. Department of Justice, Civil Rights Division. (2010). *ADA requirements: Service animals.* https://www.ada.gov/service_animals_2010.htm

U.S. Department of Justice, Civil Rights Division. (2010). *Frequently asked questions about service animals and the ADA.* https://www.ada.gov/regs2010/service_animal_qa.html

Wisch, R. F. (2019). Table of state service animal laws. *Michigan State University, Animal Legal & Historical Law Center.* https://www.animallaw.info/topic/table-state-assistance-animal-laws

CASE 15

Telehealth in a Rural Clinic

Jenn Block

You are the Practice Manager of the Liberty Family Practice (LFP) clinic in a rural factory town outside of Philadelphia, Pennsylvania. The clinic has three providers: two physicians and an advanced practice nurse (APRN) who care for over 12,000 patients from the town and surrounding area. The providers see 30-34 patients per day. In addition to the three providers there are two front desk staff, one billing clerk, six medical assistants, and one scheduler. The patient population consists of families with commercial coverage from the local employer (49.8%), Medicare Advantage patients (28.6%), and Medicaid patients (9.9%). Over half of your patients have one or more chronic condition, and the counties your practice serves have more mental health and substance abuse disorders than other counties within the state. Some patients have had a challenging time meeting their deductibles with the high cost share plans they have, while others have struggled to get to appointments at LFP due to transportation challenges.

Last year, LFP transitioned to an electronic medical record (EMR), but has not made all the modules operational. The transition was difficult for the senior physician, who had been in the practice for over 30 years using paper records. The physician has learned how to use the EMR but has decreased the number of patients seen daily in order to work with it. The other providers have had an easier time with the technology and use it more efficiently. In the middle of spring, a pandemic hits and chaos ensues. The LFP patient volume drops to less than 10 patients per day because people are limiting their exposure to others and are skeptical about the safety of coming into the office. This continues for over two weeks, along with a realization that there is no relief in sight. The owner of LFP is anxious they will not be able to make payroll if the volumes remain low for more than a few weeks, and shares their concerns with you and the other staff.

You have heard from your payer partners that telehealth is a fantastic way to see patients during this time. However, you have not yet enabled the telehealth application connected to the patient portal within your EMR. The Department of Health and Human Services has announced a temporary new rule that allows providers to utilize other applications such as Zoom and Facebook Messenger to conduct telehealth visits, although these allowances may not be permanent. In addition, your payer partners have announced that they are waiving copays and cost-sharing amounts for telehealth visits for the remainder of the year. You become concerned that your patient population's health will worsen if they don't receive routine care from their providers.

You read an article stating that anxiety and depression may increase with the fear of the pandemic and the social isolation from patients staying at home, especially the elderly. You want to help save the practice, but you have no experience in implementing a new program such as telehealth. You're concerned the challenges you experienced during the transition to the EMR will influence the owner's decision whether to pursue it. However, you also know that with the new uncertainty that the pandemic has created, it may be a while before patients will want to return to the clinic in person.

Discussion Questions

1. What are the current federal and state rules and regulations regarding telehealth?
2. In this scenario, how will you convince the owner that a new telehealth program can save the practice?
3. For which patients and for what type of appointments would you recommend implementing telehealth first?
4. What are potential barriers to implementing telehealth visits in this scenario? For the clinic? For the patients?

Additional Resources

American Medical Association. (2020). *Telehealth implementation playbook*. https://www.ama-assn
     .org/system/files/2020-04/ama-telehealth-playbook.pdf
California Telehealth Resource Center. (2020, November 30). *CTRC telehealth program developer kit*.
     https://telehealthresourcecenter.org/resources/toolkits/ctrc-telehealth-program-developer-kit/
Rural Health Information Hub (RHIhub). (2021). *Barriers to telehealth in rural areas*. https://www
     .ruralhealthinfo.org/toolkits/telehealth/1/barriers

CASE 16

Big Brother Is Watching: Part I

Sharon B. Buchbinder

Bob Bartleby feels like he's being watched. He and his wife, Ella, a free-lance technical writer, live in an apartment with good security. They lock their doors and keep their blinds down at night. Since the beginning of the pandemic, they have had food delivered and seldom venture out.

He isn't normally paranoid, so why does he feel like everything he does is being scrutinized? He stares at his computer and thinks about his employer, Durable Health, Inc. This privately held, for-profit, multistate organization serves the Delaware, Maryland, and Virginia region distributing respiratory supplies. They pay their employees well and have an excellent health benefit plan. It is a good company to work for—except for his micro-managing boss, Jerry Jupiter.

When the pandemic forced all non-essential employees to work from home, Bob had been thrilled to be free from Jerry. Before the COVID-19 pandemic, the guy had stalked the building each morning to see who was late, then had made a note of each occurrence. At annual performance reviews, he'd pull out his little notebook, where he had noted how often someone had been late—and lowered their appraisals accordingly.

When not behaving like a human time clock, Jerry had lurked behind employees to see what was on their computer screens. If it wasn't a spreadsheet with data, the man had tapped the hapless person on the shoulder and asked what they were doing. Employees with other job opportunities had left as fast as they could. Last year, over half of Jerry's direct reports had left Durable Health, Inc. Like Bob, most of those who had stayed needed the health benefits.

When Bob complains to Ella that he feels like he's being observed, she teasingly suggests it's because he misses his "favorite stalker," Jerry. Her joke gives Bob an idea. He conducts some Internet research and discovers there are software programs employers could deploy to employees' computers—without their knowledge or consent. He also learns this is illegal in the European Union, but not in the United States. Only two states—Connecticut and Delaware—have laws against this. Bob works in Maryland, but lives in Delaware.

On his day off today, Bob decides to do something about this creeping feeling and calls his friend Tim, an independent computer forensics consultant. Tim conducts a thorough forensic investigation of Bob's home computer and discovers a program is taking photographs of his screen as he works. In addition, the program counts his key strokes and mouse movements, and provides a report of his productivity. Tim tells Bob he's not being paranoid. He is being watched—and it appears the spy in the machine is his employer.

Bob is upset and feels violated. A high performer by Durable Health's own key performance indicators, Bob worries there is some new secret corporate metric he is not achieving. He can't lose this job, he needs the health benefits. His wife has diabetes and he has asthma. Bob is thinking about getting a lawyer—and is also afraid he'll get fired.

Discussion Questions

1. What is going on in Part I of this case?
2. Identify the main organizational problem in Part I of this case.
3. What are three factors contributing to this problem?
4. Provide three possible solutions to the problem you identified.
5. Provide your reflections and personal opinions as well as your recommendations for addressing this problem.

Additional Resources

Buchbinder, S. B., Shanks, N. H., & Kite, B. J. (Eds.). (2019). *Introduction to health care management* (4th ed.). Jones & Bartlett Learning.

Connolly, R. (2020, December 14). The pandemic has taken surveillance of workers to the next level. *The Guardian*. https://www.theguardian.com/commentisfree/2020/dec/14/pandemic-workers surveillance-monitor-jobs

Finnegan, M. (2020, October 29). The new normal: When work-from-home means the boss is watching. *Computer World*. https://www.computerworld.com/article/3586616/the-new-normal-when-work-from-home-means-the-boss-is-watching.html

Gershgorn, D. (2020, November 12). Welcome back to the office. Please wear this tracking device. *Medium*. https://onezero.medium.com/welcome-back-to-the-office-please-wear-this-tracking-device-98747a66750f

Rodriguez, K., & Windwehr, S. (2020, September 10). Workplace surveillance in times of Corona. *Electronic Frontier Foundation*. https://www.eff.org/deeplinks/2020/09/workplace-surveillance-times-corona

Satariano, A. (2020, May 7). How my boss monitors me while I work from home. *New York Times*. https://www.nytimes.com/2020/05/06/technology/employee-monitoring-work-from-home-virus.html

U.S. Department of Health and Human Services. (2017, June 16). *HIPAA for professionals*. https://www.hhs.gov/hipaa/for-professionals/index.html

CASE 17

Big Brother Is Watching: Part II

Sharon B. Buchbinder

Hyacinth Higgins woke up at six in the morning, took a shower, and dressed for work as a customer service supervisor for We Care Health Insurance—at home. At seven in the morning, she woke her two elementary school children, Hetta and Henry, aka Junior, rushed them through their morning ablutions and urged them to finish their milk and cereal. They made it to class on time—at home.

By eight in the morning, Hyacinth's husband, Henry (Senior), had already been at work for eight hours of his 12-hour shift. An essential worker, Senior works in a large warehouse for an enormous online shopping company. From the moment Senior walked through the door of the warehouse and had his temperature taken remotely until the moment he clocked out for the day, his manager monitored his productivity via a tracker on his belt. In addition, the social distancing tool alerted his manager if he strayed from the six foot mandate and got too close to co-workers.

Hetta and Junior had three breaks from their school tablets; two were for exercise and bathroom breaks, and one was for lunch. After stopping at the grocery store and pharmacy on the way home, Senior walked in the door at noon and joined the family for a bite to eat at a do-it-yourself sandwich buffet. Hyacinth ate, ran to the bathroom, and was back to her computer within the 30 minutes allotted for her meal break. If she was late, her manager would be texting her, asking why she wasn't working, and sending her screen shots of her empty seat.

Over lunch, the kids asked for permission to play Internet video games with their friends after school, but Hyacinth said no. She needed the bandwidth for work until five in the evening. Before he went to bed, Senior reminded the children they had homework to do. "Work first, then play your games—after dinner."

Hyacinth slid into her desk chair just as her boss's face popped up on her screen.

Horatio Hornblower frowned. "I noticed your recorded phone calls are down today. Is there a problem?"

Hyacinth shook her head. "Take a look at my keystrokes and my mouse movements, along with the regular snapshots of my screen in the monitoring program.

You'll see I've been researching a customer complaint. We might be open to a law suit."

"Explain yourself," Horatio harumphed. "Legal matters require in-house counsel review."

"Mrs. Doubtfire is concerned someone in our company may have provided her HIPAA personal health information (PHI) to her ex-husband. We do not have written consent from our customer to release her PHI to him. Upon further investigation, it appears one of our junior customer service employees may have breached HIPAA. I was about to listen to her recorded phone calls."

"Send me everything you have," Horatio snapped. "I'll look into this myself. If it's true, this is a terrible invasion of privacy."

Discussion Questions

1. What is going on in this case?
2. Identify the main organizational problem in this case.
3. What are three factors contributing to this problem?
4. Provide three possible solutions to the problem you identified.
5. Provide your reflections and personal opinions as well as your recommendations for addressing this problem.

Additional Resources

Buchbinder, S. B., Shanks, N. H., & Kite, B. J. (Eds.). (2021). *Introduction to health care management* (4th ed.). Jones & Bartlett Learning.

Connolly, R. (2020, December 14). The pandemic has taken surveillance of workers to the next level. *The Guardian*. https://www.theguardian.com/commentisfree/2020/dec/14/pandemic-workers-surveillance-monitor-jobs

Finnegan, M. (2020, October 29). The new normal: When work-from-home means the boss is watching. *Computer World*. https://www.computerworld.com/article/3586616/the-new-normal-when-work-from-home-means-the-boss-is-watching.html

Gershgorn, D. (2020, November 12). Welcome back to the office. Please wear this tracking device. *Medium*. https://onezero.medium.com/welcome-back-to-the-office-please-wear-this-tracking-device-98747a66750f

Rodriguez, K., & Windwehr, S. (2020, September 10). Workplace surveillance in times of Corona. *Electronic Frontier Foundation*. https://www.eff.org/deeplinks/2020/09/workplace-surveillance-times-corona

Satariano, A. (2020, May 7). How my boss monitors me while I work from home. *New York Times*. https://www.nytimes.com/2020/05/06/technology/employee-monitoring-work-from-home-virus.html

U.S. Department of Health and Human Services. (2017, June 16). *HIPAA for professionals*. https://www.hhs.gov/hipaa/for-professionals/index.html

CASE 18

Pay Before You Park!

Sharon B. Buchbinder

After getting up at 4 AM, taking care of herself, her husband, and her pets, 70-year-old Mrs. Banner drove her 72-year-old husband, Bruce, to the Cancer Center of Central Maryland (CCCM) for the fourth time that week. She pulled up to the designated patient drop off point, climbed out of her car, removed his walker and set it up, and then assisted him to the curb. After making sure her husband was safely inside, she drove to the parking garage adjacent to CCCM. Due to the pandemic, she was not permitted to accompany her husband into the center. While convenient, the garage was poorly lit. She found a spot close to the exit in a handicapped space. She then waited in the dark garage for her husband to complete his radiation therapy.

On days one through three, her parking time was from 7:30 AM to 8:30 AM, when she would pick him up at the same place she dropped him off. Each of those times she had her credit card ready to pay at the exit. Each time the machine accepted the parking ticket without requesting additional money and lifted the gate. The fourth day was different.

On day four, her husband's radiation session and meetings with doctors were two hours long. At 9:30 AM, she headed for the exit with her credit card in hand. The machine said *CARD EXPIRED* and it would not accept her credit card. She pressed the button labelled *HELP* for assistance and no one responded, there was only static. She pressed the button a second time.

A woman in a blue uniform shirt and black trousers threw open the door to the parking office and screamed, "WHAT DO YOU WANT?"

Mrs. Banner replied, "The machine says my ticket is expired and it won't take my credit card."

The parking attendant screamed, "YOU'RE SUPPOSED TO PAY *BEFORE* YOU PARK."

Mrs. Banner said, "I didn't know that."

She continued to yell. "GET OUT OF YOUR CAR, GET OVER TO THAT MACHINE AND *PAY*."

She did as the uniformed woman instructed. As Mrs. Banner waited in line to pay, the man in front of her in line had difficulty with his ticket which he had pre-paid.

The parking lot attendant then yelled at him, "GO INTO THE LOBBY AND TAKE CARE OF IT THERE."

Mrs. Banner paid her parking fee, took the ticket, got back into her car, and the machine accepted her exit pass, at last. Grateful she would not be screamed at again, Mrs. Banner decided to write a letter of complaint to CCCM.

Discussion Questions

1.   What is going on in this case?
2.   Identify the main organizational problem in this case.
3.   What are three factors contributing to this problem?
4.   Provide three possible solutions to the problem you identified.
5.   Provide your reflections and personal opinions as well as your recommendations for addressing this problem.

Additional Resources

Buchbinder, S. B., Shanks, N. H., & Kite, B. J. (Eds.). (2021). *Introduction to health care management* (4th ed.). Jones & Bartlett Learning.

Gilbert, D. (2015). Car parking is a clinical quality issue. *BMJ, 350,* h1312. https://www.bmj.com /content/350/bmj.h1312

Kennedy, D. M. (2017). Creating an excellent patient experience through service education: Content and methods for engaging and motivating front-line staff. *Journal of Patient Experience, 4*(4), 156–161.

CASE 19

The Awful Allergist

Sharon B. Buchbinder

Sixty-five-year-old Super Sneezy was referred to an allergist at Happy Valley Medical Center (HVMC) for the evaluation of an allergic reaction to the sea bass family, which gave her hives and blisters inside her lips. Since Super Sneezy had a large number of allergies, when she met with Dr. Snooty, a man who towered over her by a foot and never sat during the patient encounter, she agreed to the complete skin testing panel, as well as blood tests.

As she left her patient encounter, she requested a print copy of her medical information.

The administrator frowned. "I don't know what you're talking about. I don't even know how to use the electronic medical record (EMR) system. You're going to need to talk to Dr. Snooty."

Dr. Snooty was nowhere to be seen.

When she returned, due to concerns about anaphylaxis, her husband accompanied her for the skin testing. Super Sneezy had been told the procedure(s) would take 90 minutes. In fact, it took four hours, and the arrogant allergist was clearly annoyed to see her husband with her in the exam room.

After the tests were completed, Mrs. Sneezy requested her printed medical records. Once again, the administrator told her she would need to talk to the doctor.

Again, he was nowhere to be seen.

When Mrs. Sneezy returned for a review of the findings and recommendations, Dr. Snooty did not sit down. He stood, lectured, and did not permit her to ask questions or to respond to his comments. At one point, he said she had to get rid of the feathers in her bed. She responded, "I have NO feathers in my bed!"

Ignoring her response, Dr. Snooty continued to talk over Mrs. Sneezy. "You're anxious and your anxiety makes you breathe rapidly and that's why you *think* you have asthma. I'm going to prescribe lorazepam."

Mrs. Sneezy opened her mouth to protest, but he just kept talking.

"It's very safe. You take it whenever you feel twitchy. It's so safe, I prescribe it to children. I'm also going to give you this migraine medicine. All the girls in my office take it and they feel better in thirty minutes."

Mrs. Sneezy finally got a word in. "I've had asthma since I was three years old. It's not in my head."

He waved his hand as if swatting away a fly. "We'll do spirometry testing to see if that's true. And begin a series of desensitization shots for all your inhalant allergies."

Frustrated, she said, "I need to think about all of this."

He frowned. "What did you say?"

"I *said*, I need to think about all this." He glared at her, and she repeated herself a third time.

Dr. Snooty flung the door open. "We're done here."

Mrs. Sneezy followed him out the door and said, "I would like my medical documentation."

At that point, they were at his administrator's desk. He snapped, "Give Mrs. Sneezy her paperwork!"

The administrator who had stated she didn't know how to use the EMR printed out the documents and thrust them into Mrs. Sneezy's open hand saying, "You know your way out."

Discussion Questions

1. What is going on in this case?
2. Identify the main organizational problem in this case.
3. What are three factors contributing to this problem?
4. Provide three possible solutions to the problem you identified.
5. Provide your reflections and personal opinions as well as your recommendations for addressing this problem.

Additional Resources

Buchbinder, S. B., Shanks, N. H., & Kite, B. J. (Eds.). (2021). *Introduction to health care management* (4th ed.). Jones & Bartlett Learning.

Ha, J. F., & Longnecker, N. (2010). Doctor-patient communication: A review. *The Ochsner Journal, 10*(1), 38–43.

Kennedy, D. M. (2017). Creating an excellent patient experience through service education: Content and methods for engaging and motivating front-line staff. *Journal of Patient Experience, 4*(4), 156–161.

Massachusetts Medical Society. (2018). *What it means to be a monitor.* Physician Health Services, Inc. https://www.massmed.org/Physician_Health_Services/Helping_Yourself_and_Others/What_it_means_to_be_a_Monitor/

Mueller, P. S. (2015). Teaching and assessing professionalism in medical learners and practicing physicians. *Rambam Maimonides Medical Journal, 6*(2), e0011. https://doi.org/10.5041/RMMJ.10195

Spiritus, E. (2011, December 8). Ten signs it might be time to fire your doctor. *Forbes.* https://www.forbes.com/sites/deborahljacobs/2011/12/08/10-signs-it-may-be-time-to-fire-your-doctor/?sh=205bb8c82b25

Vozoris, N. T., Fischer, H. D., Wang, X., Stephenson, A. L., Gershon, A. S., Gruneir, A., Austin, P. C., Anderson, G. M., Bell, C. M., Gill, S. S., & Rochon, P. A. (2014). Benzodiazepine drug use and adverse respiratory outcomes among older adults with COPD. *European Respiratory Journal, 44,* 332–340. https://erj.ersjournals.com/content/44/2/332

CASE 20

The Super Stressful Stress Test

Sharon B. Buchbinder

Mrs. Banner, who is 70 years old, has a history of asthma, chronic obstructive pulmonary disease (COPD), and atrial fibrillation (AF). Her cardiologist, Dr. Rhythm, informed Mrs. Banner that she needed an echo stress test to assess her current cardiac status.

Upon arrival at the cardiac test suite at 3:15 PM for her 3:30 PM appointment, Mrs. Banner was already short of breath. Her husband had dropped her off at the address on the appointment letter, but the entrance was barricaded due to COVID. She walked up a hill and then up a flight of stairs, in the rain, to get to the main entrance. Once inside the main entrance, she was given poor directions. She walked through the warren of buildings only to be told in another building that she was in the wrong place.

When Mrs. Banner checked in at the suite, between gasps, she told the receptionist that in the future when they book appointments, they should tell patients they need to come to the main entrance to the hospital, not the address on the letterhead.

The receptionist snapped, "I didn't send that to you."

Mrs. Banner replied, "The *practice* needs to inform patients. I have COPD and asthma, and this was a challenge."

The receptionist pointed to a hard plastic chair. "Take a seat."

Mrs. Banner waited 45 minutes. No one spoke to her. Mrs. Banner texted her husband and told him if no one communicated with her by 4:15 PM, she was leaving. As she finished the text at 4 PM the EKG technician called her name and the stress test proceeded as planned.

The next day, Mrs. Banner emailed Dr. Rhythm and told him that he almost lost her as a patient.

Discussion Questions

1. What is going on in this case?
2. Identify the main organizational problem in this case.
3. What are three factors contributing to this problem?

4. Provide three possible solutions to the problem you identified.
5. Provide your reflections and personal opinions as well as your recommendations for addressing this problem.

Additional Resources

Buchbinder, S. B., Shanks, N. H., & Kite, B. J. (Eds.). (2021). *Introduction to health care management* (4th ed.). Jones & Bartlett Learning.

Kennedy, D. M. (2017). Creating an excellent patient experience through service education: Content and methods for engaging and motivating front-line staff. *Journal of Patient Experience, 4*(4), 156–161.

CASE 21

Who Will Care for the Caregivers?

Sharon B. Buchbinder

Jane Viola has just graduated from nursing school at the state university when the COVID-19 pandemic hits her rural city of 100,000 people. An excellent student, Jane has accepted a job at the only hospital in the city. She was promised a mentor for her first year on the job. The pandemic, however, has other plans for her. Thrown onto a floor with little experience and a national shortage of personal protection equipment (PPE), Jane is terrified she will get COVID-19—or worse. Even though she completed her clinicals at the same hospital, being on her own was different from having a professor to go to with concerns and questions. Now she is *it!*

Every hospital bed is taken, the Emergency Department (ED) has patients in the halls, and she is working 12- to 14-hour shifts without a bathroom or meal break. She lives at home with her parents and doesn't want to infect them. When she goes home, she strips in the garage, puts her scrubs in a bag outside, and cleans her shoes with bleach. She even has a microwave, a cot, sleeping bag, and heater in the garage so she can minimize their exposure. She goes into the house only to shower and use the toilet and when her parents are in their bedroom with the door closed. Despite all her efforts, her mother becomes infected with COVID-19. With the help of the same hospital where Jane works, her mother survives. At last, the long-awaited vaccines arrive, and life begins to return to normal.

Over a year later, however, Jane's mother has side effects from the disease: shortness of breath, difficulty thinking, fatigue, and daily headaches. To compound matters, Jane's father has aged badly over the last 14 months, the toll of the pandemic and his wife's illness. Formerly an active man who walked five miles a day, he retired early just before the pandemic. He and Jane's mother had planned to travel and enjoy their "golden years." Now he has difficulty getting out of bed and is unable to care for himself or his wife. When he does get up, he stares at the news on TV all day long. He refuses to see a doctor because he says there is nothing wrong with him. He tells Jane he's ready to "meet his Maker." Now, in addition to her full-time nursing job, Jane has two frail parents to care for—and no idea where to find help.

When she describes her homelife to a co-worker, Jane's friend, also a nurse, suggests she should go to human resources (HR) to ask for their assistance. While sympathetic, the Director of HR says their employee assistance plan (EAP) covers only psychological, alcohol, and substance abuse issues that impact employee performance, not elder care. The Director of HR states he cannot help her and suggests she reach out to the County Department on Aging.

Discussion Questions

1. What is going on in this case?
2. Identify the main organizational problem in this case.
3. What are three factors contributing to this problem?
4. Provide three possible solutions to the problem you identified.
5. Provide your reflections and personal opinions as well as your recommendations for addressing this problem.

Additional Resources

Auerbach, D. I., Levy, D. E., Maramaldi, P., Dittus, R. S., Spetz, J., Buerhaus, P. I., & Donelan, K. (2021, September). Optimal staffing models to care for frail older adults in primary care and geriatrics practices in the U.S. *Health Affairs, 40*(9), 1368–1376. https://www.healthaffairs.org/doi/abs/10.1377/hlthaff.2021.00401

Buchbinder, S. B., & Kite, B. J. (2021). Special topics and emerging issues in health care management. In S. B. Buchbinder, N. H. Shanks, & B. J. Kite (Eds.), *Introduction to health care management* (4th ed.) (pp. 411–453). Jones & Bartlett Learning.

Centers for Disease Control and Prevention (CDC). (2021). *Post-COVID conditions.* https://www.cdc.gov/coronavirus/2019-ncov/long-term-effects/index.html

Hoffman, P. B. (2021, September/October). Why unpaid caregivers matter. *Healthcare Executive*, 24–26.

Schabacker, E. (2021, October 3). As burnout deepens nursing shortage, nursing schools struggle to add more students. *Billings Gazette.* https://billingsgazette.com/news/state-and-regional/as-burnout-deepens-nursing-shortage-nursing-schools-struggle-to-add-more-students/article_767f2e6f-8190-5bb8-b803-6c2487830975.html

Schwartz, R., Sinskey, J. L., Anand, U., & Margolis, R. D. (2020). Addressing postpandemic clinician mental health: A narrative review and conceptual framework. *Annals of Internal Medicine, 173*(12), 981–988. https://doi.org/10.7326/M20-4199

Society for Human Resource Management. (2021). *General: What is an employee assistance program (EAP).* https://www.shrm.org/resourcesandtools/tools-and-samples/hr-qa/pages/whatisaneap.aspx

Sukut, J. (2021, January 30). Early career nurses and students cope with learning during a pandemic. *Billings Gazette.* https://billingsgazette.com/news/local/early-career-nurses-and-students-cope-with-learning-during-a-pandemic/article_cff22e3f-f703-50ea-9f59-50fa5771fe04.html

CASE 22

Dr. Oldschool Is Thinking of Quitting

Suzana D. Deng

Downtown Health Systems (DHS) is a busy 450-bed, safety net hospital in a densely populated part of town. The computer systems used for keeping medical records are outdated. The Board of Directors (BOD) approved a substantial budget for the installation of a new health information technology (HIT) system for physicians, clinicians, physician assistants, and nurses. It took the team more than six weeks to produce an HIT system for DHS. The team agreed that, at least in the initial stages, the system will only be used for electronic medical records/electronic health records (EMR/EHR). The information technology (IT) department has trained providers. Part of the training required providers to sign documents requiring them to log details of every encounter with their patients within 8-12 hours afterwards. They were "strongly" encouraged to use the system in real time, i.e., during the encounter.

Within two weeks of launching, calls and complaints from physicians and nurses inundated the IT department. The Chief Information Officer (CIO) expressed his concern to the Chief Operating Officer (COO) that a significant number of physicians and nurses get busy and end up updating these records days later. The legal department warned the COO that updating the records many days after patients' encounters could have legal repercussions for these providers and the hospital.

The Chief Medical Officer (CMO), Dr. Jonathan Oldschool, was spearheading a near revolt. He was a beloved, 60-year-old geriatrician, who had worked at DHS for more than 34 years. He knew the hospital in and out and had mentored many other physicians. He and some of his colleagues insisted the system was not user friendly. The fee structure of the hospital is fee-for-service and requires providers to adhere as much as possible to the 15-minute per visit rule. The COO called a meeting for all stakeholders. The meeting immediately went off the rails; many providers had grievances and complaints.

Dr. Oldschool said, "I start seeing patients at 8:30 AM. Fifteen minutes is, already, not enough time to connect with my patients. Now, I'm supposed to log in and type all the information real-time! I'm not able to focus and give patients my full attention. Sometimes, they tell me something while I am typing a different complaint. I find myself asking patients to repeat themselves. One of my patients asked the receptionist if I was feeling ill, telling her that I don't seem to be my old self. I don't remember the last time I had lunch in this hospital. I routinely use lunch time to catch up but that is even not enough. By the time I get home I am so exhausted. I dread entering the hospital every day. Something's gotta give."

Similar anecdotes were bitterly recounted by other providers. Dr. Diligent complained, "Last week, I had a complicated case. I decided to take a few minutes to keenly listen to my patient before I logged in the data. The system kept on logging me off. I don't remember how many times I had to log in. When I called the IT department, they told me the system will log me out every three minutes if I am not actively using it. Now I must sleep in a wrist brace because my carpal tunnel syndrome has gotten worse. I am literally typing more than taking care of my patients. I agree with Dr. Oldschool. Something's gotta give."

Discussion Questions

1. What are the facts and challenges of this situation?
2. What are the drivers of health information technology? What are the benefits of HIT?
3. What are the main problems facing physicians and providers in relation to this new HIT system?
4. Why is it important for Dr. Oldschool and his colleagues to adopt this HIT system? How does the COO convince physicians of the benefit of HIT?
5. What are the potential financial implications of extending the patients' visits from 15 to 20-25 minutes?
6. What are the ethical and legal implications of logging patients' data hours after an encounter/procedure?

Additional Resources

Borkowski, N. (2012). *Organizational behavior in health care*. Jones & Bartlett Learning.

Centers for Disease Control and Prevention. (2016). *Public health 101 series: Introduction to public health informatics*. https://www.cdc.gov/training/publichealth101/informatics.html

Institute of Medicine Committee on Quality of Health Care in America. (2001). *Crossing the quality chasm: A new health system for the 21st century*. National Academies Press. https://doi.org/10.17226/10027

Melnick, E. R., Dyrbye, L. N., Sinky, C. A., Trockel, M., West, C. P., Nedelec, L., Tutty, M. A., & Shanafelt, T. (2020). The association between perceived electronic health record usability and professional burnout among US physicians. *Mayo Clinic Proceedings, 95*(3), 488–503. https://www.mayoclinicproceedings.org/article/S0025-6196(19)30836-5/fulltext

Ward, R., Stevens, C., Brentnall, P., & Briddon, J. (2008). The attitudes of health care staff to information technology: A comprehensive review of the research literature. *Health Information & Libraries Journal, 25*(2), 81–97 https://doi.org/10.1111/j.1471-1842.2008.00777.x

Management of Morale: Turbulent Times at Tree Star Health

Anna B. Kayes

Aida's 30-minute commute early Friday morning was filled with anxiety. "I didn't sleep. I am worried about work. How am I going to function today?" she asked, replaying what had led to this state of panic. Aida had been promoted recently to a supervisor role within the human resources department at a large urban hospital, Tree Star Health. Her promotion was the result of a rapid restructuring at the hospital that moved and merged departments, based on a plan for the hospital to focus less on outpatient surgery and more on inpatient care. Several key leaders within the hospital system had been replaced, a layer of middle management had been eliminated, and supervisors and employees found themselves with new tasks and responsibilities almost overnight. What had started as a rewarding role in her new position had turned into a nightmare, or at least an overwhelming set of problems—all in one week. Aida recalled the week in vivid detail. It all started with a staff meeting on the hospital's medical-surgical floor.

The Staff Meeting

Monday's staff meeting was supposed to be fun. Aida had looked forward to teaching conflict resolution techniques to the managers and staff on the large medical-surgical floor. Tree Star had been encouraging collaboration with human resources staff and nurse educators in training on topics the nurse managers identified as important. Armed with handouts and a PowerPoint, she had smiled when she pictured all the conflict scenarios that she was going to address. Instead, the meeting had spiraled into a tense exchange between two staff members over their workload. Callouts, where nursing staff call in and do not show up to work their scheduled shift, were at an all-time high, and they were arguing over why they were so short-staffed.

The general lack of civility in the discussion was troubling. Aida knew civility was often tied to other outcomes such as patient safety and employee morale, and this conflict-ridden communication was not helpful. One of the nursing team members pulled Aida aside and complained that all the Generation Z nurses were competitive and tech savvy but would often gossip about each other's performance. The team member relayed the experienced nurses who were older would often use more direct and open communication and address feedback directly. The way the staff meeting dissolved into an argument between two staff members was representative of this tension in communication styles. "I was not prepared for this," thought Aida.

Job Engagement Results

Opening her email Wednesday morning, she saw the message she was waiting for. The results were in! Aida had distributed a job engagement survey to nurses on two of the largest floors of the hospital with the most turnover. She looked at the results several times, and it confirmed her worst fear: engagement was the lowest it had been in the 10 years of conducting the survey. Many categories were low compared to previous years, particularly in the areas of supervisor relationship quality, supervisor support, workload, peer relationships, and motivation. She remembered the national research report from the Society for Human Resource Management (SHRM) had noted that employee morale in health care organizations was at an all-time low across the country. That report had indicated that two-thirds of health care employers considered maintaining morale a huge challenge. Knowing other employers were experiencing the same difficulty did not make the situation any better. "There has to be a solution to this," Aida thought.

Another Initiative

"I love tea!" Aida exclaimed Thursday morning. In her latest publication on health care human resources, she read about a stress reduction solution that some hospitals implemented to help with job engagement and reduce stress among employees. In this novel solution, the hospital chaplain would rotate through hospital units with a cart that had healthy snacks, tea, and aromatherapy items. Conversation with the chaplain was designed to augment engagement and lower stress in conjunction with the tea and snacks. This initiative was designed to provide a pleasant interlude for staff and help with job engagement. "I wonder if this would work in our hospital," reflected Aida. She knew that there was a lot of work to be done based on the engagement survey results.

"What Are You Going to Do?"

Aida looked at her email inbox Thursday night. An 11:30 PM message from the Director of Human Resources had the subject line "What are you going to do?" Knowing it was probably not a good idea to continue working so late and that she needed more work-life balance, Aida had opened the email anyway. The Director outlined the staff morale problems, the job engagement survey results, and the anonymous complaints that had been coming in on employee web forms. Aida knew she needed a plan to tackle these problems and would be asked about it when she came to work on Friday.

Friday morning had arrived and Aida's reflection on the week ended. She pulled into the parking lot and gave herself one more stern order. "I am almost there; I need to focus!"

Discussion Questions

1. What are some motivational and engagement strategies that Aida should suggest to the Director?
2. What strategies might improve civility at work?
3. How might generational and religious differences impact the strategies?
4. Do you think employees who are already overextended will appreciate a tea break? Why or why not? Are there other strategies that you would suggest?
5. Provide your reflections and personal opinions as well as your recommendations for addressing these problems.

Additional Resources

Bruce, A. (2003). *Building a high morale workplace.* McGraw-Hill Professional.

Buchbinder, S. B., Shanks, N. H., & Kite, B. J. (2021). *Introduction to health care management* (4th ed.). Jones & Bartlett Learning.

Conner Black, A. (2019). Promoting civility in healthcare settings. *International Journal of Childbirth Education, 34*(2), 64–67.

Keogh, M., Marin, D. B., Jandorf, L., Wetmore, J. B., & Sharma, V. (2020). Chi time: Expanding a novel approach for hospital management. *Nursing Management, 51*(4), 32–38.

Society for Human Resource Management (SHRM). (2020). *Covid-19 research: How the pandemic is challenging and changing employers.* https://www.shrm.org/hr-today/trends-and-forecasting/research-and-surveys/documents/shrm%20cv19%20research%20presentation%20release%202.pdf

Loyalty in the Health Care Delivery System

Bobbie Kite

Ricky Rockwell recently retired and began taking care of his elderly mother, Mrs. Ladybird. She was in her late 80s and had several minor medical issues, but overall was in good health. One day she was out grocery shopping, alone, as was her routine. Grocery shopping was the one thing she still did by herself. She only needed a few items and liked to get out every once in a while. This time would turn out to be different though, as the impatience of another shopper combined with a crowded aisle caused an avoidable situation.

As Mrs. Ladybird looked down at her phone while she walked down a narrow aisle, another shopper pushed past her with a full cart in an attempt to push her out of the way. Startled, Mrs. Ladybird stumbled, and fell into the shelves. The shelves cut her arm open. Ricky was called and Mrs. Ladybird was taken to their local doctor to be checked out and have her wound dressed.

It seemed there was no real damage, other than the gaping wound, and she rested for a couple of days to recover. About a week later, she started experiencing great pain in her knee, to the point where she was not able to walk. "Mom, it feels like you have a goose egg behind your knee!" Ricky said with a shaky voice. She was immediately seen by her family doctor, who assured her that this was just inflammation from her fall and prescribed her anti-inflammatory medication.

After several trips to the doctor, an x-ray, a sonogram, and blood work, they still had no idea what was causing the swelling and pain in the knee. When Mrs. Ladybird's son inquired about an MRI, he was told that due to insurance "red tape," these were the only tests they were allowed to do at that time. When pressed, the physician suggested that it might have been Mrs. Ladybird's shoes, she had recently bought a new pair and that *must* be the culprit.

Neither Ricky nor Mrs. Ladybird desire a second opinion. After all, they have been going to this doctor for over 30 years. They have their doubts about the diagnosis, but don't want to disturb her long-term relationship with her doctor. Over two months have passed, and Mrs. Ladybird remains in pain. Her son, who has been at her side and watching all of this unfold, finally asks another provider at the office to review his mother's case.

Discussion Questions

1. What is going on in this case?
2. If you were the one to receive the son's complaint, what would your course of action be?
3. What are three factors contributing to this problem?
4. Provide three possible solutions to the problem you identified.
5. Provide your reflections and personal opinions as well as your recommendations for addressing this problem.

Additional Resources

Buchbinder, S. B., Shanks, N. H., & Kite, B. J. (2021). *Introduction to health care management* (4th ed.). Jones & Bartlett Learning.

Goetz, K., Jossen, M., Rosemann, T., Hess, S., Brodowski, M., & Bezzola, P. (2019). Is patient loyalty associated with quality of care? Results of a patient survey over primary care in Switzerland. *International Journal for Quality in Health Care, 31*(3), 199–204.

Huang, C. H., Wu, H. H., Lee, Y. C., & Li, L. (2019). What role does patient gratitude play in the relationship between relationship quality and patient loyalty? *Inquiry: The Journal of Health Care Organization, Provision, and Financing, 56,* 0046958019868324.

Pozgar, G. D. (2016). *Legal aspects of health care administration.* Jones & Bartlett Learning.

CASE 25

Tele-NO

Matthias Ojo

You are a family care physician at Springfield Medical Center (SMC), a longstanding medical center in Springfield with community members whose families have lived there for at least three generations. Members of this community have been receiving care from SMC for multiple generations, which has helped the primary care physicians and health care providers build relationships with their patients. Four months ago, SMC started undergoing renovations to update the facility, equipment, and technology with modern standards. As a result of the renovations, SMC has started to provide medical care to its patients through telemedicine and telehealth to minimize the impact on the ability of you and other health care providers to see patients on site. Although it's a change for you, it is clear the benefits outweigh the disadvantages.

Patients have been complaining about the new telemedicine and telehealth care delivery system and expressing their dissatisfaction and preference to have on-site appointments. In addition, many are resistant to change, prefer traditional health care delivery, and are not confident in their ability to navigate the technology required to engage in these new health care delivery modalities.

This morning Gladys, an experienced 35-year-old medical clerk, received an emergent call from Ms. Tracy, a reputable lawyer and single mother of Jackson, a seven-year-old who had a persistent five-day cough and a fever of 100.6 degrees.

Ms. Tracy had been on the phone with Gladys for 45 minutes demanding that a physician see her son immediately or she would be filing a patient neglect lawsuit. You hear some commotion but figure they will involve you if the need arises. Gladys repeatedly informed Ms. Tracy that SMC was only seeing emergent cases on site, but they could schedule a virtual appointment with a health care provider. Unsatisfied with Glady's response, Ms. Tracy demanded to speak with a physician. She was referred to Mark, a Physician Assistant (PA), who also informed her that SMC was only seeing emergent cases, and they would gladly schedule a telehealth video call that afternoon.

Mark informed Ms. Tracy that her son's condition was probably viral and was most likely a cold or flu. After a thorough but unyielding conversation with Ms. Tracy, Mark calls you in the middle of another telehealth appointment and tries to inform you of the situation at hand.

You inform Mark that you will call Ms. Tracy after your current appointment. Upon ending your telehealth appointment, you call Ms. Tracy, who explains her frustration and her son's history of bronchitis and his underlying symptoms. After hearing Ms. Tracy's concerns and reports, you schedule an on-site appointment with her later that afternoon.

Discussion Questions

1. What are the facts of the case?
2. How could the above scenario have been avoided?
3. Is there anything Springfield Medical Center could have done differently to address the impact renovations could have on patient care? If yes, what? If no, why?
4. As a physician, what must you do to ensure this issue is addressed?
5. Do you think Ms. Tracy has grounds for a neglect lawsuit? Why or why not?
6. Based on Jackson's condition and medical history, was Mark correct in determining that Jackson's condition was not emergent? Who should have been responsible for determining whether Jackson's condition was emergent?

Additional Resources

9 News Perth. (2015, March 18). *Whooping cough death.* https://www.youtube.com/watch?v=Q79xt1rj3gk

American College of Surgeons. (2020, March 17). *COVID-19: Guidance for triage of non-emergent surgical procedures.* https://www.facs.org/covid-19/clinical-guidance/triage

Buchbinder, S. B., Shanks, N. H., & Kite, B. J. (2021). *Introduction to health care management* (4th ed.). Jones & Bartlett Learning.

Centers for Disease Control and Prevention (CDC). (2021). *Managing healthcare operations during COVID-19.* https://www.cdc.gov/coronavirus/2019-ncov/hcp/facility-planning-operations.html?CDC_AA_refVal=https%3A%2F%2Fwww.cdc.gov%2Fcoronavirus%2F2019-ncov%2Fhcp%2Fframework-non-COVID-care.html

Eschner, K.(2020, August 4). Older adults have a hard time accessing virtual health care. *Popular Science.* https://www.popsci.com/story/health/telemedicine-older-adults-pandemic/

Wu, K., Smith, R. C., Lembcke, T. B., & Ferreira, B. D. T. (2020). Elective surgery during the Covid-19 pandemic. *The New England Journal of Medicine, 383*(18), 1787–1790.

Data Analytics in an Academic Medical Center

Rachel Rogers

City Medical Center (CMC), a large academic medical center in a mid-sized urban setting, recently implemented a new electronic health record (EHR). The EHR selected was a leader in the market, and the medical center hired a new team of directors, analysts, designers, and trainers to support the implementation, optimization, and the maintenance of the record. Super-users were sent for training and an ambitious training plan was developed and deployed. The new team joined the IT staff and almost doubled the numbers of employees reporting up to the chief information officer (CIO). Much of the clinical staff believed the new record would bring all good things including access to real-time, accurate, and useful data to make better clinical decisions and improve outcomes across the facility.

The head of the obstetrics and gynecology department, Dr. Renee Fielding, was particularly excited to have access to data about the numbers of patients cared for in the three specialty clinics, as well as all the patients in 17 family medicine clinics. As soon as the new EHR was up and running, Dr. Fielding entered a data request through the analytics portal. The request stated the following, "I need a weekly report of pregnant patients cared for at CMC."

The data analyst assigned to the request had a few questions, consulted with Dr. Fielding, then created and sent a report. The doctor didn't think the numbers in the report were correct, and reached out to the Director of Analytics to complain. The report was reviewed at the next staff meeting and a good portion of the meeting was spent on discussing how the analytics team could not possibly have this report correct, that no decisions could be made with the data, and that they would have to go back to manually counting their pregnant patients using a shared spreadsheet.

About the same time, a nurse manager (NM) of one of the specialty women's care clinics under Dr. Fielding's leadership started learning about the analytics package that came integrated with the new EHR and was open for use by clinical and administrative staff. The NM had gone to an hour-long training session on the tool and was curious to try it out. It had the ability to sort for all patients with a visit at the clinic, and then isolate patients with a positive pregnancy test from the lab within the last 90 days. The number queried was very small though, and the NM began to worry. An on the spot decision was made to contact the marketing department to have more patient brochures printed up and sent out to community centers in hopes of drumming up more business.

Discussion Questions

1. What are the advantages and disadvantages of an electronic health record (EHR)?
2. Identify the main problems with how Dr. Fielding and the NM are using the analytics tools within the EHR.
3. Define how "big data" may be used in an academic medical setting.
4. List four examples of how an analytics tool can be used in a clinical setting to improve patient care.

Role-Based Questions

CIO Role:
1. You are the chief information officer (CIO). What is your role in implementing an analytics strategy at CMC?
2. As the CIO, what is your leadership strategy?

Director of Analytics Role:
1. What is the responsibility of the director in this situation?
2. How can the director create a strategy to help clinicians effectively use the analytics tools available in the EHR?

Additional Resources

Eddy, N. (2020, January 13). *Too many providers are failing to meaningfully integrate data analytics.* Healthcare IT News. https://www.healthcareitnews.com/news/too-many-providers -are-failing-meaningfully-integrate-data-analytics

Felmlee, J. (2018, September 28). *The best clinical data management strategy to reduce waste, clutter, and inefficiency.* Health Catalyst. https://www.healthcatalyst.com/insights/improve-clinical -data-management-healthcare-reduce-waste/

Ginsburg, P., de Loera-Brust, A., Brandt, C., & Durak, A. (2018, November 1). *The opportunities and challenges of data analytics in health care.* Brookings. https://www.brookings.edu/research /the-opportunities-and-challenges-of-data-analytics-in-health-care/

St. James, E., Ferguson, J., & Casazza, N. (2018, November 21). *Clinical data analytics: Why setting goals is the key to success.* Health Catalyst. https://www.healthcatalyst.com/insights /clinical-data-analytics-why-setting-goals-key-success

CASE 27

Dr. Neighsayer

Nancy H. Shanks

Like many young women, Janie thinks of her obstetrician gynecologist (OB-GYN), Dr. Neighsayer, as her primary care physician (PCP) and has been going to this same female doctor for several years. She has always felt they had a good patient-physician relationship, and Janie has always felt comfortable discussing any issues with her. Since it's time for her annual pap smear and check-up, she makes an appointment. They are having a good visit, when Janie decides she wants to mention a new concern that has come up in the last couple of months and she has been having trouble dealing with.

Janie says, "Dr. Neighsayer, I have been having some issues with premenstrual syndrome (PMS) before I get my period. I've had lots of bloating, and I've also been craving certain foods. This also seems to be related to my becoming depressed and experiencing some rather significant mood swings. My significant other (SO) doesn't really understand and finds all of this annoying. What suggestions do you have that can help me with these concerns?"

Dr. Neighsayer doesn't hesitate and curtly replies "No, no, no. I can't recommend anything; that's really not something that I deal with. If you're having mental health issues, I think you need to see a psychiatrist or psychologist."

Janie is shocked that this topic is off limits for her doctor. After looking online for information about PMS, Janie had assumed that Dr. Neighsayer would know about this and be able to advise her as she had done in the past with other issues relating to her female health care.

Without further discussion Janie leaves and realizes that she is now confused about the physician she has chosen, as well as the relationship she thought they had. That evening she and her SO meet you and several other gal pals and their SOs for drinks and supper. The topic of the appointment comes up and Janie explains what transpired. She then asks for your help in deciding what to do next.

Discussion Questions

1. Are you also shocked that Dr. Neighsayer would not help Janie with this concern?
2. What is PMS?

3.   Why would you expect an OB-GYN to be willing to address this?
4.   How does this incident impact the physician-patient relationship?
5.   Do you think it is good PR for Dr. Neighsayer's practice?
6.   What do you think Janie should do next?
7.   Do you have recommendations for Dr. Neighsayer and her practice about how she might change her position on this issue?

Additional Resources

Buchbinder, S. B., Shanks, N. H., & Kite, B. J. (2021). *Introduction to health care management* (4th ed.). Jones & Bartlett Learning.

Chipidza, F. E., Wallwork, R. S., & Stern, T. A. (2015). Impact of the doctor-patient relationship. *The Primary Care Companion for CNS Disorders, 17*(5), 1–15.

Johnson, T. (2019, March 11). *The Importance of physician-patient relationships communication and trust in health care.* Duke Center for Personalized Health Care. https://dukepersonalizedhealth.org/2019/03/the-importance-of-physician-patient-relationships-communication-and-trust-in-health-care/

WebMD. (2021, January 20). *What is PMS?* https://www.webmd.com/women/pms/what-is-pms

CASE 28

The Patient Experience: Medication Side Effects

Audrey Williams and Samantha Read

Maryland's Health Services Cost Review Commission's (HSCRC) quality program aims to reward hospitals for quality of care to protect against hospitals restricting expenses that can result in a decline of quality. The HSCRC's Quality Reimbursement Program (QBR) is a pay-for-performance initiative to incentivize hospitals to improve quality and value of patient care. Part of that initiative is "Patient and Community Engagement," which includes results from a hospital's patient experience survey. Calculations are done to determine if a hospital performs above or below the QBR threshold (national average) or benchmark (top 5% of performers). Points are awarded based on how a hospital performs. Anything below threshold receives zero points. The number of points a hospital earns determines whether it is financially rewarded or penalized (Health Services Cost Review Commission, n.d.).

Casey Walker is the Director of the Service Excellence Department (SED) at a large 400-bed, 12-inpatient unit Maryland hospital. A large part of Casey's responsibility is to ensure the hospital performs well in the "Patient and Community Engagement" section, especially the measures related to the patient experience survey. The hospital is not meeting the threshold for the communication about medication domain for QBR by 1%, placing the hospital at risk to be penalized. Patients receive a patient experience survey after discharge and are asked questions regarding communication about medications given during their admission. During review of the question level data, Casey finds less than half of the patients (48%) are answering that side effects of new medications were *always* explained in a way the patient could understand. The hospital is a quarter of the way through the year, leaving Casey with nine months to improve the performance before the end of year when final data are reported.

It is important to Casey to not only improve this question for the financial impact on the hospital, but also to ensure that patients understand their new medications. Ensuring understanding of medication side effects allows patients to be engaged in their own care, communicate how they are feeling appropriately, and improve safety outcomes. To understand the current state of this issue, she learns the nursing units vary in their approach to the improvement process, if they have a process at all. Casey decides to put together a taskforce charged with improving patients' experience on side effects *always* being explained with new medications.

Discussion Questions

1. Casey must present the taskforce proposal to executive leadership for budget approval. Discuss three pivotal items she should include in her project proposal and the value of those items.
2. Identify key departments and stakeholders who should be involved in the medication side effects taskforce.
3. The management of effective teams is important for the success of large taskforces. Discuss three management strategies you would use to organize and guide the group.
4. Determine a strategy for rolling out your improvement changes, either starting with the lowest performing nursing unit or the nursing unit with the historically highest volume of returned surveys. Determine the strategy Casey should suggest and why.
5. Did you make any assumptions while reading this case regarding race, ethnicity, gender or gender identity, sexual orientation, socioeconomic status, culture, or other protected class? Were these assumptions focused at the individual/staff level, clinical/program level, or organizational/administrative level? How do these assumptions affect cultural awareness, cultural knowledge, behaviors, and/or skill development?

Additional Resources

Buchbinder, S. B., Shanks, N. H., & Kite, B. J. (2021). *Introduction to health care management* (4th ed.). Jones & Bartlett Learning.

Center for Substance Abuse Treatment. (2014). *Improving cultural competence.* Substance Abuse and Mental Health Services Administration. https://www.ncbi.nlm.nih.gov/books/NBK248428/

Health Services Cost Review Commission. (n.d.). *Quality based reimbursement (QBR).* https://hscrc.maryland.gov/Pages/init_qi_qbr.aspx

Planetree. (2017). *HCAHPS improvement brief: Communication about medications.* https://resources.planetree.org/wp-content/uploads/2017/11/Planetree-Communication-about-Medications-HCAHPS-Improvement-Brief-v2-11.28.17.pdf

Scales, D. (2017). Taking medications correctly requires clear communication. *Harvard Health Blog.* https://www.health.harvard.edu/blog/taking-medications-correctly-requires-clear-communication-2017013011043\

Secemsky, B. (2017, December 6). How should clinicians discuss the side effects of medications? *Huffington Post.* https://www.huffpost.com/entry/how-should-clinicians-discuss-the-side-effects-of-medications_b_8059876

A Small Hospital Prepares for a Surge of Patients During a Pandemic

Lauren Zidovsky

Mark Bishop is the chief executive officer (CEO) of United Hospital (UH), a full service, acute care, not-for-profit hospital in Colorado. Mark's hospital is part of a local health care network, United Health Care (UHC). Mark transitioned into the CEO position after a promotion through the financial ranks within the organization. The 2018 revenues for his hospital totaled $153,670,000. As of December 2019, Mark has been busy preparing for the local health care needs and financial strategies. Cross-analyzing the finances of UH, the CEO focused primarily on outpatient services and inpatient capacity, as well as surgical and ancillary services. Mark determined that all revenues were adequately reinvested with internal strengths on surgical service lines followed by ancillary services. However, this organization's financial health was about to be challenged. The coronavirus pandemic was on the horizon.

In mid-January 2020, health care officials and systems began to receive increased information regarding the novel coronavirus, COVID-19. This novel respiratory virus was soon infiltrating communities countrywide. By March 2020, the UHC network was rapidly impacted by this crisis. Local challenges started with the lack of personal protective equipment (PPE). Gowns and N95 masks were already on back order before the first confirmed case of COVID-19 was even diagnosed at UH. In these first frantic weeks, federal agencies such as the Centers for Disease Control and Prevention (CDC) and the Occupational Safety and Health Administration (OSHA), as well as international organizations like the World Health Organization (WHO), issued everchanging recommendations and guidelines on PPE and testing on a daily basis, and, in some cases, an hourly rate. While the system providers and nurses experienced a surge of cases, enormous pressure built on the administrative staffs.

Mark identified you to lead the hospital's COVID-19 task force. You have worked for UH for more than 10 years and for the last four you have been the director of quality (DQ). You had several years of experience on emergency planning focused on management of the hospital's guidelines. You worked with the director of supply management, director of the emergency department, and the infectious disease specialists to decide changes moving forward. The COVID-19 task force worked through resource planning within the hospital's network.

You identified four phases of emergency planning: preparedness, response, mitigation, and recovery.

Preparedness occurred through improving supply chain access to increase PPE and respiratory supplies. The navigation of the supplies came with some coordination from federal agencies, local channels in UH, as well as local donors and government municipalities. The supply management team recognized that it was prepared for two weeks of supply and could not adequately resolve the slow down. They also articulated a large gap in specimen collection kits.

One *response* planning protocol focused on when to test staff and how to manage testing or screening sites. The executive, supply chain management, and infectious disease teams largely disagreed on criteria and the cost of staff testing.

Mitigation preparation was incorporated with the use of virtual visits for patient care. Telehealth was established as a critical tool to assist the health care providers in addressing urgent needs, triage, and patient treatments. Telehealth was a concern for Mark, as he acknowledged that insurance companies may not adjust these visits in a fiscally similar way as in-person care. In early April, within weeks of transitioning patients to telehealth visits, the federal government issued a protocol for full reimbursements for these visits. Promotion of patient scheduling became a financial objective.

Lastly, *recovery*, as a late phase of emergency planning, added mental and social work counselors to assist staff burn-out, anxiety, and post-traumatic stress. There had been cases of staff experiencing "nervous" breaks while on shift in the outpatient clinic. You realized that support and intervention were critical to navigate this mounting pressure.

In May 2020, UH experienced another surge of COVID-19 through its emergency department (ED). Information sharing was occurring through local jurisdictions. The county, with a population of just over 360,000 residents, saw more than 150 new, symptomatic cases daily that required medical attention. In response, Mark asked for a second emergency preparedness phase with service line mitigation. UH had experienced huge losses in revenues since early March, when elective procedures and services were placed on hold. This was an extremely stressful decision process.

With the rising numbers of infected individuals, the COVID-19 task force implemented several structural and organizational changes to the hospital. It estimated a daily ED influx of 20 COVID-19 cases, with a 50% increase in hospital admissions. You introduced 12 newly-designed single-patient pods for observational cases in the ED. A 38-bed telemetry floor was converted to a COVID-19 floor. Two cardiac catheterization suites and four operating rooms (ORs) (all with negative pressure, HEPA air filtration, and respiratory equipment) were re-allocated as a COVID-19 intensive care unit (ICU). While these altered rooms increased the ICU capacity, they significantly reduced the number of available ORs and ancillary services, which were the two highest earning areas of the hospital.

The COVID-19 task force made the tough recommendation to change the hospital staffing model. Along with the loss of revenue, UH decided it needed to furlough approximately 8% of its employees, in particular the agency-contracted and per-diem staff. A proportion of staff were reassigned to other areas. For example, the OR nurses were directed to cover urgent care clinics and the employee health clinic. Employees faced continuous pressure and worried about their safety on the job. You understand how staffing changes can alter quality outcomes in patient care and will look to address this with the team.

As the numbers of COVID-19 positive cases rise to the highest seen in this region of Colorado, diversion of patients to other hospitals in and out of the UHC system may need to happen. The task force continues daily focusing on financial health, quality outcomes, safety, and staffing challenges during this pandemic. All the rule books were tossed out with this novel virus, and you created new policies every day. Will they be enough?

Discussion Questions

1. What additional emergency planning strategy could be added to preparedness, response, recovery, and mitigation?
2. As a DQ, is there a way to integrate a more comprehensive emergency coordination plan during an ongoing pandemic?
3. How would a change in practice protocols and treatment guidelines get communicated to the staff, especially given the daily changes or lack of resources that may require diversion?
4. With the increased numbers of COVID-19 positive cases rising in the county, what local and state stakeholders should be sitting on the emergency planning board and why? What additional internal leaders should be considered stakeholders?
5. How does the current pandemic provide insight or tools for future preventative planning?
6. The disruptive innovator, telehealth, has a platform of full reimbursement and use during the pandemic. In your opinion, will it progress further, for example with the use of artificial intelligence (AI), in the health care field? Provide a rationale for your response.
7. What type of tools can the hospital quality manager implement to continue to monitor quality and safety practices, specifically during a surge in cases?

Additional Resources

Dukes, T. (2021, September 9). Latest COVID surge stressing hospital staff, space across North Carolina. *The News & Observer.* https://www.newsobserver.com/news/coronavirus/article 254099708.html

Harte, J., & Bernstein, S. (2021, September 17). Some U.S. hospitals forced to ration care amid staffing shortages, COVID-19 surge. *Reuters.* https://www.reuters.com/world/us/some-us -hospitals-forced-ration-care-amid-staffing-shortages-covid-19-surge-2021-09-17/

Marcozzi, D. E., Pietrobon, R., Lawler, J. V., French, M. T., Mecher, C., Baehr, N. E., & Browne, B. J. (2021). The application of a hospital medical surge preparedness index to assess national pandemic and other mass casualty readiness. *Journal of Healthcare Management, 66*(5), 367–378.

Masson, G. (2021, September 30). Cleveland health system implements new staffing strategies amid COVID-19 surge. *Becker's Hospital Review.* https://www.beckershospitalreview.com/hospital

-management-administration/cleveland-health-system-implements-new-staffing-strategies -amid-covid-19-surge.html

Perry, N. (2021). When telehealth went viral: How the COVID-19 pandemic influenced the rapid move to virtual medical treatment, and what non-rural providers not treating COVID-19 patients should do about it. *Journal of Health Care Finance, 47*(4). https://www.healthfinancejournal. com/index.php/johcf/article/view/254

Schumaker, E. (2021, August 13). Short-staffed hospitals battling COVID surge after opting not to staff up. ABC News. https://abcnews.go.com/US/short-staffed-hospitals-battling-covid-surge -opting-staff/story?id=79360422

Toner, E., & Waldhorn, R. (2020, February 27). What US hospitals should do now to prepare for a Covid-19 pandemic. *Clinicians' Biosecurity News.* https://centerforhealthsecurity.org/cbn/2020 /cbnreport-02272020.html

Upstate Medical University. (n.d.). *Four phases of emergency management.* https://www.upstate.edu /emergencymgt/about/phases.php

U.S. Department of Health & Human Services, Health Resources & Services Administration. (2021, January 28). *Medicare payment policies during COVID-19.* https://telehealth.hhs.gov/providers /billing-and-reimbursement/medicare-payment-policies-during-covid-19/

PART 3

Quality/Patient Safety

CASE 30

SnappyQuikMedCare: Part I

Sharon B. Buchbinder

Mrs. Banner is not having a banner year. Between her 72-year-old husband's cancer, grueling treatments for cancer, and the pandemic, she has not had been able to schedule her own health care. Her last gastroenterologist disappeared without notice, and it has taken her a year to find another. Her colonoscopy is a year overdue, and with a history of bowel carcinoma in situ, she cannot put the procedure off any longer.

She has heard her new gastroenterologist, Dr. Happy, is a lovely woman and has an excellent reputation as a physician in the community. Dr. Happy has an excellent support staff. In addition, her office is connected to the corporate electronic health record (EHR) in which Mrs. Banner has all of her medical records. When Mrs. Banner sees Dr. Happy, she is pleased with her experience. Dr. Happy is warm, funny, and answers all her questions.

Mrs. Banner leaves the doctor's office with a thick packet of materials and an appointment for her colonoscopy. Lucky for her, there has been a cancellation and she can have the procedure in a month, rather than three months. Before she leaves, a staff member makes a strong point of reviewing the bowel regimen. It is a four-day preparation with extensive dietary restrictions. On days three and four, she is only allowed to drink clear fluids and the bowel medicine. Mrs. Banner pays close attention to the instructions and tucks everything into her organizing folder for future reference.

The week approaches for her procedure and Mrs. Banner pulls out the materials only to discover she has not had the required pre-op COVID test. She must have it, despite the fact that she has been vaccinated. In a panic, she rushes to get the COVID test, then returns home to review the folder to see if she missed anything else. The bowel preparation is uppermost on her mind. She follows it to the letter knowing that if she doesn't do it right, they will cancel the surgery, and she will be forced to start all over again and wait several more months. She *cannot* get this wrong.

The preparation is not fun, but Mrs. Banner knows she must adhere to this critical phase of the medical treatment. She pushes through and, at last, the day arrives. Mr. Banner, who is now in remission, drives her to the SnappyQuikMedCare Ambulatory Center, which is owned by the same medical corporation as

Dr. Happy's office. When she arrives, she feels she is a good patient who has done everything required. She cannot wait for the procedure to be over.

The receptionist greets her with a thermometer and COVID checklist, which they go through quickly, followed up with driver's license and insurance cards. All is going smoothly until the receptionist says, "Did you bring the rest of the documents with you?"

Mrs. Banner says, "What documents? I just gave you my insurance information."

The receptionist says, "You were *supposed* to fill these out and bring them with you. Have a seat over there and fill them out now."

Embarrassed, Mrs. Banner takes a seat and fills out the first two pages. The third one asks for ALL 50 of her medications—which Mrs. Banner knows for a fact are listed in the EHR. She returns to the front desk and says, "I'm not filling this form out. All my medications are in my electronic health record."

The receptionist takes the clipboard and says nothing.

Mrs. Banner texts her husband, who is waiting outside in the car, and tells him what has occurred. She is afraid they won't take her, and all that preparation will have been for naught.

A nurse comes out and calls her name and invites her back into the pre-op area. Nurse Nancy is pleasant and invites Mrs. Banner to take her clothes off and to put on a hospital gown in bay number five. After she undresses, Nurse Nancy returns with a printout of all Mrs. Banner's meds and points to the sheet. "Which of these do you take?"

Mrs. Banner says, "All of them. Those are my medications."

"No," the nurse sighs. "We need to know *exactly* when you took what on this list. That's why the carbonless form was in the packet Dr. Happy's office sent home with you. Now Nurse Connie will have to transcribe all of this onto that form *for* you."

Mrs. Banner shook her head. "I don't understand. Dr. Happy's office has this in her files—and no one told me this before."

"Corporate bought SnappyQuikMedCare last year," Nurse Connie interjected. "This side is still all on paper, not on the electronic health record system. Everything has to be handwritten."

Mrs. Banner is mortified. She's always organized and careful. How had she missed that paperwork? Now these poor nurses were going to have to do all this work. She apologizes profusely to both nurses and is near tears.

Discussion Questions

1. What is going on in this case?
2. Identify the main organizational problem in this case.
3. What are three factors contributing to this problem?
4. Provide three possible solutions to the problem you identified.
5. Provide your reflections and personal opinions as well as your recommendations for addressing this problem.

Additional Resources

Bear, J. (1996). *Send this jerk the bedbug letter: How companies, politicians, and the mass media deal with complaints and how to be a more effective complainer.* Ten Speed Press.

Buchbinder, S. B., Shanks, N. H., & Kite, B. J. (Eds.). (2021). *Introduction to health care management* (4th ed.). Jones & Bartlett Learning.

Definitive Healthcare. (2019, April 18). 2018's priciest outpatient procedure: The colonoscopy. https://blog.definitivehc.com/priciest-outpatient-procedure-colonoscopy

Gordon, S. (2020, November 26). *Is your doctor bullying you during your appointments? Discover how bullying doctors impact patient care.* https://www.verywellhealth.com /is-your-doctor-a-bully-4152017

Kennedy, D. M. (2017). Creating an excellent patient experience through service education: Content and methods for engaging and motivating front-line staff. *Journal of Patient Experience, 4*(4), 156–161.

Melnick, E. R., Sinsky, C. A., & Krumholz, H. M. (2021). Implementing measurement science for electronic health record use. *JAMA, 325*(21), 2149–2150.

Nanji, K. C., Patel, A., Shaikh, S., Seger, D. L., & Bates, D. W. (2016). Evaluation of perioperative medication errors and adverse drug events. *Anesthesiology, 124*, 25–34 doi: https://doi .org/10.1097/ALN.0000000000000904

Reed, M., Huang, J., Brand, R., Graetz, I., Jaffe, M. G., Ballard, D., Neugebauer, R., Fireman, B., & Hsu, J. (2020). Inpatient-outpatient shared electronic health records: Telemedicine and laboratory follow-up after hospital discharge. *American Journal of Managed Care, 26*(10). https://www.ajmc .com/view/inpatient-outpatient-shared-electronic-health-records-telemedicine-and -laboratory-follow-up

Reed, M., Huang, J., Brand, R., Graetz, I., Neugebauer, R., Fireman, B., Jaffe, M. G., Ballard, D., & Hsu, J. (2013, September 11). Implementation of an outpatient electronic health record and emergency department visits, hospitalizations, and office visits among patients with diabetes. *JAMA, 310*(10), 1060–1065. doi:10.1001/jama.2013.276733

Robertson, L. (2008, July 23). *Managing customer service: An outpatient approach.* AMN Healthcare. https://www.amnhealthcare.com/latest-healthcare-news/managing-customer-service -outpatient-approach/

Sarasin, D. S., Brady, J. W., & Stevens, R. L. (2019). Medication safety: Reducing anesthesia medication errors and adverse drug events in dentistry part 1. *Anesthesia Progress, 66*(3), 162–172. https://doi.org/10.2344/anpr-66-03-10

The Joint Commission (TJC). (2014, November). *Sentinel event policy and procedure.* http://www .jointcommission.org/sentinel_event_policy_and_procedures/

The Joint Commission (TJC). (2021, June). *Sentinel event alert 40: Behaviors that undermine a culture of safety.* http://www.jointcommission.org/sentinel_event_alert_issue_40_behaviors _that_undermine_a_culture_of_safety/

CASE 31

SnappyQuikMedCare: Part II

Sharon B. Buchbinder

Nurse Connie starts an intravenous drip in Mrs. Banner and gives her a warm blanket. Meanwhile, Nurse Nancy reviews a pre-op checklist and consent form and tells her where she is in the queue. "You're up next. Dr. Happy and Dr. Snoozy, the anesthesiologist, will be in shortly to do their consent forms."

Dr. Snoozy is a tall woman who reviews everything in a cold, professional tone without even acknowledging Mrs. Banner's joke about looking forward to a good nap.

Dr. Happy pops in, and although masked, her tone is upbeat and chirpy. "How was the prep?"

"Horrible," Mrs. Banner gags. "Would be nice if they could make it cherry flavored, take the edge off."

"Let's see how you did," Dr. Happy responds and reviews the consent form, again.

In the freezing cold operating room, Mrs. Banner rolls into position for the procedure. She gives her name, date of birth, repeats the name of her surgeon, the procedure she is expecting, and even adds the name of the anesthesiologist for a laugh. "Did I get it right?"

At length, Dr. Happy says, "Yes, you did."

Dr. Snoozy pushes the propofol and says, "You're going to feel a stinging sensation."

A while later, a groggy Mrs. Banner wakes up in the freezing cold bay and a different nurse, who does not introduce herself, asks what her pain level is. Mrs. Banner says three. The nurse tells her that it will pass and leaves. Mrs. Banner wishes someone would offer her one of those nice warm blankets, but she is unable to initiate a verbal request. It is as if she's in a horror movie: she can see and feel everything, but not advocate for herself. When the nurse returns, she has a post-op discharge list and removes the IV needle. There is a large lump under the tape and gauze, which means it has infiltrated the subcutaneous tissue. Mrs. Banner is going to have a huge bruise. The nurse without a name tells her she can get dressed and that they are calling her husband to come pick her up.

Mrs. Banner dresses with some difficulty, nearly falling when putting on her sweatpants, but she's in a hurry to get warm and get out of there. Mrs. Banner texts her husband to turn the heat up in the car full blast.

The nurse with no name walks her to the exit, opens the door, and points. "Is that your husband?"

Mrs. Banner says, "Yes."

"Okay," the nurse says and closes the door behind Mrs. Banner. She does not assist a legally intoxicated patient to the car. Despite the exit's proximity to the vehicle, there is a curb, and Mrs. Banner clutches the side of the car to get to the passenger door. When Mrs. Banner arrives at home, she goes to bed, turns on a heating blanket, and slowly gets warm.

The next morning, Mrs. Banner recounts her experience at SnappyQuikMed-Care to her husband. He has had a lot of procedures over the last year, and he compares his experiences to hers, saying he never felt dismissed by the health care providers where he went.

Mrs. Banner replies, "You know what? I've had better experiences getting my car's oil changed than I did at SnappyQuikMedCare."

Discussion Questions

1.   What is going on in Part II of this case?
2.   Identify the main organizational problem in Part II of this case.
3.   What are three factors contributing to this problem?
4.   Provide three possible solutions to the problem you identified.
5.   Provide your reflections and personal opinions as well as your recommendations for addressing this problem.

Additional Resources

Bear, J. (1996). *Send this jerk the bedbug letter: How companies, politicians, and the mass media deal with complaints and how to be a more effective complainer.* Ten Speed Press.

Buchbinder, S. B., Shanks, N. H., & Kite, B. J. (Eds.). (2021). *Introduction to health care management* (4th ed.). Jones & Bartlett Learning.

Definitive Healthcare. (2019, April 18). 2018's priciest outpatient procedure: The colonoscopy. https://blog.definitivehc.com/priciest-outpatient-procedure-colonoscopy

Gordon, S. (2020, November 26). *Is your doctor bullying you during your appointments? Discover how bullying doctors impact patient care.* https://www.verywellhealth.com/is -your-doctor-a-bully-4152017

Kennedy, D. M. (2017). Creating an excellent patient experience through service education: Content and methods for engaging and motivating front-line staff. *Journal of Patient Experience, 4*(4), 156–161.

Melnick, E. R., Sinsky, C. A., & Krumholz, H. M. (2021). Implementing measurement science for electronic health record use. *Journal of the American Medical Association, 325*(21), 2149–2150.

Nanji, K. C., Patel, A., Shaikh, S., Seger, D. L., & Bates, D. W. (2016). Evaluation of perioperative medication errors and adverse drug events. *Anesthesiology, 124,* 25–34. doi: https://doi .org/10.1097/ALN.0000000000000904

Reed, M., Huang, J., Brand, R., Graetz, I., Jaffe, M. G., Ballard, D., Neugebauer, R., Fireman, B., & Hsu, J. (2020). Inpatient-outpatient shared electronic health records: Telemedicine and laboratory follow-up after hospital discharge. *American Journal of Managed Care, 26*(10). https:// www.ajmc.com/view/inpatient-outpatient-shared-electronic-health-records-telemedicine-and -laboratory-follow-up

Reed, M., Huang, J., Brand, R., Graetz, I., Neugebauer, R., Fireman, B., Jaffe, M. G., Ballard, D., & Hsu, J. (2013, September 11). Implementation of an outpatient electronic health record and emergency department visits, hospitalizations, and office visits among patients with diabetes. *Journal of the American Medical Association, 310*(10), 1060–1065. doi:10.1001 /jama.2013.276733

Robertson, L. (2008, July 23). *Managing customer service: An outpatient approach.* AMN Healthcare. https://www.amnhealthcare.com/latest-healthcare-news/managing-customer-service -outpatient-approach/

Sarasin, D. S., Brady, J. W., & Stevens, R. L. (2019). Medication safety: Reducing anesthesia medication errors and adverse drug events in dentistry part 1. *Anesthesia Progress, 66*(3), 162–172. https://doi.org/10.2344/anpr-66-03-10

The Joint Commission (TJC). (2014, November). *Sentinel event policy and procedure.* http://www .jointcommission.org/sentinel_event_policy_and_procedures/

The Joint Commission (TJC). (2021, June). *Sentinel event alert 40: Behaviors that undermine a culture of safety.* http://www.jointcommission.org/sentinel_event_alert_issue_40 _behaviors_that_undermine_a_culture_of_safety/

SnappyQuikMedCare: Part III

Sharon B. Buchbinder

It takes Mrs. Banner four days to completely recover from the effects of the anesthesia. She writes a formal grievance to the SnappyQuikMedCare Corporate Office. It is a lengthy, explicitly detailed email. She sends it to the CEO of SnappyQuikMedCare because she knows to get a grievance resolved, you start from the *top,* not the bottom of the organization. The CEO says he's not in charge of that outpatient facility, but he gets her connected with the person who is: the Nurse Manager of the SnappyQuikMedCare Ambulatory Center.

In the meantime, while Mrs. Banner awaits a response, she gives Dr. Happy a courtesy call to tell her personally about the grievance she has filed. Dr. Happy turns into Dr. Angry the moment Mrs. Banner completes her story.

Dr. Happy/Angry snarls, "If you were cold, why didn't you *ask* for a blanket?"

Mrs. Banner replies, "Because I could not initiate conversation. I felt like I was in a strait jacket."

Dr. Happy/Angry says, "What did you *expect* when you left the building?"

Mrs. Banner replies, "I expected the nurse to assist a legally intoxicated patient to the vehicle and to ensure they were safe. There was a curb, my balance was off. I could have fallen."

Sarcasm dripping from her words, Dr. Happy/Angry says, "Well, I am *so* glad you were here to tell us *all about* how we can improve our processes, because *you are such an expert.*"

Mrs. Banner responds, "The day of my colonoscopy, I had no intention of being your mystery shopper. My intention was to get in, get the procedure done, to get out safely—and to be comfortable."

Dr. Happy/Angry snaps, "Thanks so *much* for your call."

Mrs. Banner, seething from the physician's verbal abuse, picks up the phone and calls her lawyer.

Discussion Questions

1. What is going on in Part III of this case?
2. Identify the main organizational problem in Part III of this case.

3.   What are three factors contributing to this problem?
4.   Provide three possible solutions to the problem you identified.
5.   Provide your reflections and personal opinions as well as your recommendations for addressing this problem.

Additional Resources

Bear, J. (1996). *Send this jerk the bedbug letter: How companies, politicians, and the mass media deal with complaints and how to be a more effective complainer.* Ten Speed Press.

Buchbinder, S. B., Shanks, N. H., & Kite, B. J. (Eds.). (2021). *Introduction to health care management* (4th ed.). Jones & Bartlett Learning.

Definitive Healthcare. (2019, April 18). 2018's priciest outpatient procedure: The colonoscopy. https://blog.definitivehc.com/priciest-outpatient-procedure-colonoscopy

Gordon, S. (2020, November 26). *Is your doctor bullying you during your appointments? Discover how bullying doctors impact patient care.* https://www.verywellhealth.com/is-your-doctor-a-bully-4152017

Kennedy, D. M. (2017). Creating an excellent patient experience through service education: Content and methods for engaging and motivating front-line staff. *Journal of Patient Experience, 4*(4), 156–161.

Melnick, E. R., Sinsky, C. A., & Krumholz, H. M. (2021). Implementing measurement science for electronic health record use. *Journal of the American Medical Association, 325*(21), 2149–2150.

Nanji, K. C., Patel, A., Shaikh, S., Seger, D. L., & Bates, D. W. (2016). Evaluation of perioperative medication errors and adverse drug events. *Anesthesiology, 124,* 25–34 doi: https://doi.org/10.1097/ALN.0000000000000904

Reed, M., Huang, J., Brand, R., Graetz, I., Jaffe, M. G., Ballard, D., Neugebauer, R., Fireman, B., & Hsu, J. (2020). Inpatient-outpatient shared electronic health records: Telemedicine and laboratory follow-up after hospital discharge. *American Journal of Managed Care, 26*(10). https://www.ajmc.com/view/inpatient-outpatient-shared-electronic-health-records-telemedicine-and-laboratory-follow-up

Reed, M., Huang, J., Brand, R., Graetz, I., Neugebauer, R., Fireman, B., Jaffe, M. G., Ballard, D., & Hsu, J. (2013, September 11). Implementation of an outpatient electronic health record and emergency department visits, hospitalizations, and office visits among patients with diabetes. *Journal of the American Medical Association, 310*(10), 1060–1065. doi:10.1001/jama.2013.276733

Robertson, L. (2008, July 23). *Managing customer service: An outpatient approach.* AMN Healthcare. https://www.amnhealthcare.com/latest-healthcare-news/managing-customer-service-outpatient-approach/

Sarasin, D. S., Brady, J. W., & Stevens, R. L. (2019). Medication safety: Reducing anesthesia medication errors and adverse drug events in dentistry part 1. *Anesthesia Progress, 66*(3), 162–172. https://doi.org/10.2344/anpr-66-03-10

The Joint Commission (TJC). (2014, November). *Sentinel event policy and procedure.* http://www.jointcommission.org/sentinel_event_policy_and_procedures/

The Joint Commission (TJC). (2021, June). *Sentinel event alert 40: Behaviors that undermine a culture of safety.* http://www.jointcommission.org/sentinel_event_alert_issue_40_behaviors_that_undermine_a_culture_of_safety/

CASE 33

The Infusion Center at Mordant Medical Center: Part I

Sharon B. Buchbinder

It has been a difficult year for Mrs. Banner. Between her 72-year-old husband's cancer, grueling treatments for cancer, and the pandemic, she has not had been able to take care of her own medical needs. Recently, there has been a distinct improvement in Mr. Banner's condition, and he is able to complete more activities of daily living than in the previous 10 months. He is even driving now! She seizes this window of opportunity and makes a flurry of doctors' appointments for herself that she has been putting off. Her primary care physician has referred her to an endocrinologist for her osteoporosis and an infectious disease doctor for a recurrent localized infection.

The endocrinologist, Dr. Green, is kind and listens to Mrs. Banner's history, including all the stressors in her life for the last year. Dr. Green recommends an intravenous infusion of zoledronic acid for Mrs. Banner's osteoporosis, orders bloodwork, and advises Mrs. Banner that the Infusion Center at Mordant Medical Center will call her to set up a time for her infusion. Dr. Green also advises her that she may have flu-like symptoms for two to three days after the infusion.

Mrs. Banner's next doctor's visit is with the infectious disease specialist, Dr. Microbe. The appointment is two days before the infusion center appointment. Dr. Microbe listens to Mrs. Banner's history. Mrs. Banner points to the abscess on her leg, and asks what to do about the infection. Dr. Microbe asks how long she's had this and Mrs. Banner says one week—then tells her she has an appointment with the infusion center in two days to receive the zoledronic acid. Dr. Microbe looks at the site of infection and tells Mrs. Banner she should reschedule the infusion, as the infection could worsen with the osteoporosis drug.

Using the Mordant Medical Center (MMC) patient portal, Mrs. Banner emails Dr. Green, to apprise her of the latest wrinkle. *Should she go or not?* An autoresponder states her doctor is out-of-town, but Dr. Green will get back to her when she returns. Hearing nothing from her endocrinologist for over 24 hours, Mrs. Banner reschedules her appointment to a Thursday before a holiday weekend to avoid using her sick time at work. Finally, Mrs. Banner's abscess resolves with the correct medication. She is glad she delayed the infusion.

The day after her infusion was originally scheduled, Dr. Green calls Mrs. Banner and asks her why she canceled the infusion. When Mrs. Banner explains that Dr. Microbe recommended it and she tried to reach Dr. Green, but couldn't, she rescheduled the procedure. Dr. Green reiterates the importance of the infusion and the potential side effects. Mrs. Banner replies that she understands and all is in place. She is on track.

The evening before the new appointment, at 4:55 PM, Mrs. Banner receives a phone call from Sam, the charge nurse of the infusion center.

He tells her that her appointment on Thursday is being canceled because her bloodwork is "too old." Mrs. Banner tells him Dr. Green never indicated she needed repeat bloodwork. Sam reiterates it's "too old."

Mrs. Banner says, "Dr. Green never mentioned the bloodwork had to be within 30 days. I'm going to call her now."

Sam snaps, "Well you *do* that."

Discussion Questions

1. What is going on in this case?
2. Identify the main organizational problem in this case.
3. What are three factors contributing to this problem?
4. Provide three possible solutions to the problem you identified.
5. Provide your reflections and personal opinions as well as your recommendations for addressing this problem.

Additional Resources

Bear, J. (1996). *Send this jerk the bedbug letter: How companies, politicians, and the mass media deal with complaints and how to be a more effective complainer.* Ten Speed Press.

Buchbinder, S. B., Shanks, N. H., & Kite, B. J. (Eds.). (2021). *Introduction to health care management* (4th ed.). Jones & Bartlett Learning.

Gordon, S. (2020, November 26). *Is your doctor bullying you during your appointments? Discover how bullying doctors impact patient care.* https://www.verywellhealth.com/is-your -doctor-a-bully-4152017

Kennedy, D. M. (2017). Creating an excellent patient experience through service education: Content and methods for engaging and motivating front-line staff. *Journal of Patient Experience,* 4(4), 156–161.

Reed, M., Huang, J., Brand, R., Graetz, I., Jaffe, M. G., Ballard, D., Neugebauer, R., Fireman, B., & Hsu, J. (2020). Inpatient-outpatient shared electronic health records: Telemedicine and laboratory follow-up after hospital discharge. *American Journal of Managed Care,* 26(10). https:// www.ajmc.com/view/inpatient-outpatient-shared-electronic-health-records-telemedicine- and-laboratory-follow-up

Reed, M., Huang, J., Brand, R., Graetz, I., Neugebauer, R., Fireman, B., Jaffe, M. G., Ballard, D., & Hsu, J. (2013, September 11). Implementation of an outpatient electronic health record and emergency department visits, hospitalizations, and office visits among patients with diabetes. *Journal of the American Medical Association,* 310(10), 1060–1065. doi:10.1001 /jama.2013.276733

Robertson, L. (2008, July 23). *Managing customer service: An outpatient approach.* AMN Healthcare. https://www.amnhealthcare.com/latest-healthcare-news/managing-customer-service-outpatient -approach/

The Joint Commission (TJC). (2014, November). *Sentinel event policy and procedure.* http://www .jointcommission.org/sentinel_event_policy_and_procedures/

The Joint Commission (TJC). (2021, June). *Sentinel event alert 40: Behaviors that undermine a culture of safety.* http://www.jointcommission.org/sentinel_event_alert_issue_40_behaviors _that_undermine_a_culture_of_safety/

The Infusion Center at Mordant Medical Center: Part II

Sharon B. Buchbinder

Mrs. Banner calls Dr. Green's office and receives a message to call back "during normal business hours." Reluctantly, Mrs. Banner calls Dr. Green's cell phone and apologizes for using her mobile number. She describes the cancellation and conversation with Sam. She reminds Dr. Green how difficult it is to schedule her own medical appointments while taking care of her husband and working full-time.

Dr. Green says, "I told you the bloodwork had to be within 30 days."

Mrs. Banner says, "I don't recall you telling me that and I don't see that noted in my electronic patient files, nor is it on the print out you provided to me when you saw me."

Dr. Green sighs. "Usually, if a patient's bloodwork is out of date, they can take the sample at the infusion center and send it for a stat reading. It adds an hour to the time—I don't know why he didn't offer you that. Can you do Friday?"

"Yes, absolutely," Mrs. Banner says. "I can get the bloodwork done, too. I live near the lab MMC uses for bloodwork."

"Okay," Dr. Green says. "Do you have the direct number he called you from?"

Mrs. Banner provides Dr. Green with the information.

A few minutes later Mrs. Banner's phone rings.

"Hi, this is your new *best* friend," Sam says. "I understand you can come in on Friday. We are light, so what time works for you?"

Knowing the bloodwork might not be completed for the 8 AM slot, Mrs. Banner selects the 11 AM slot.

Sam says, "Is there an MMC-affiliated lab near you?"

"Yes," Mrs. Banner says. "I could throw a rock and hit several."

"Weeeelllll," Sam replies, "I wouldn't do *that*. I will order the bloodwork. It's your job to get in there."

"Yes, of course," Mrs. Banner says. "So I should schedule an hour and a half for this?"

Sam says, "No, it only takes 15 minutes."

Confused, Mrs. Banner says, "The other person told me it would be much longer."

Sam sighs. "The infusion only takes 15 minutes, but we tell people to plan for more time because this is a *cancer* infusion center and *cancer* patients take priority over *other* patients."

Mrs. Banner thinks, other patients like *me*? Why is my doctor sending me here if the staff don't want to take care of me?

After a breathless pause in the conversation, Mrs. Banner says, "I appreciate this. I understand I'll be having flu-ish symptoms after the infusion, so I planned the time for this so I could be sick."

Sam snaps, "Who told you *that*?"

"Dr. Green."

"*Really*? I guess she knows you better than I do."

Mrs. Banner says, "Well, I'm one of those people who gets the one in one-hundred thousandth side-effects."

Voice dripping with sarcasm, Sam replies, "Well, then sure, you will be the sickest and most *miserable* person ever to receive this drug and you *will* have the flu."

Stunned, Mrs. Banner says, "That's *not* what I meant."

Sam hangs up.

Discussion Questions

1. What is going on in Part II of this case?
2. Identify the main organizational problem in Part II of this case.
3. What are three factors contributing to this problem?
4. Provide three possible solutions to the problem you identified.
5. Provide your reflections and personal opinions as well as your recommendations for addressing this problem.

Additional Resources

Bear, J. (1996). *Send this jerk the bedbug letter: How companies, politicians, and the mass media deal with complaints and how to be a more effective complainer*. Ten Speed Press.

Buchbinder, S. B., Shanks, N. H., & Kite, B. J. (Eds.). (2021). *Introduction to health care management* (4th ed.). Jones & Bartlett Learning.

Gordon, S. (2020, November 26). *Is your doctor bullying you during your appointments? Discover how bullying doctors impact patient care*. https://www.verywellhealth.com/is-your-doctor-a-bully-4152017

Kennedy, D. M. (2017). Creating an excellent patient experience through service education: Content and methods for engaging and motivating front-line staff. *Journal of Patient Experience, 4*(4), 156–161.

Reed, M., Huang, J., Brand, R., Graetz, I., Jaffe, M. G., Ballard, D., Neugebauer, R., Fireman, B., & Hsu, J. (2020). Inpatient-outpatient shared electronic health records: Telemedicine and laboratory follow-up after hospital discharge. *American Journal of Managed Care, 26*(10). https://www.ajmc.com/view/inpatient-outpatient-shared-electronic-health-records-telemedicine-and-laboratory-follow-up

Robertson, L. (2008, July 23). *Managing customer service: An outpatient approach*. AMN Healthcare. https://www.amnhealthcare.com/latest-healthcare-news/managing-customer-service-outpatient-approach/

The Joint Commission (TJC). (2014, November). *Sentinel event policy and procedure*. http://www.jointcommission.org/sentinel_event_policy_and_procedures/

The Joint Commission (TJC). (2021, June). *Sentinel event alert 40: Behaviors that undermine a culture of safety*. http://www.jointcommission.org/sentinel_event_alert_issue_40_behaviors_that_undermine_a_culture_of_safety/

The Infusion Center at Mordant Medical Center: Part III

Sharon B. Buchbinder

Mrs. Banner gets her bloodwork completed in a timely manner and shows up early for her appointment at the infusion center. The receptionist is pleasant and tells her to take a seat, someone will be out shortly.

Nurse Kathy calls Mrs. Banner's name and leads her past a sign that proclaims *Cancer Center at Mordant Medical Center,* then to a large space that has four intravenous infusion sets, one in each corner. Aside from Mrs. Banner, there are two other patients, one male, one female, both receiving infusions. It appears they are cancer patients; the woman has someone with her who seems to be a family member.

Nurse Kathy points to a chair and indicates Mrs. Banner should be seated. Mrs. Banner hands her the printout of her blood work and her current medications. The nurse asks her name, date of birth, and why she's there.

Mrs. Banner responds with the correct answers and tells Nurse Kathy how grateful she is to be squeezed into the schedule.

Nurse Kathy does not react to the thank you and orders the drug to be infused. She replies curtly to some small talk social overtures from Mrs. Banner.

Nurse Kathy proceeds to do a complete verbal history of all of Mrs. Banner's medical conditions in a voice that can be heard by the three strangers in the room—and the next room over. When Nurse Kathy begins to ask for additional information regarding Mrs. Banner's Irritable Bowel Syndrome with Constipation (IBS-C), Mrs. Banner tells her she is seeing a gastroenterologist and makes it clear she won't be answering any more questions about her bowels.

A pleasant medical assistant asks Mrs. Banner if she would like a drink of water and she accepts. The room is freezing, but there appear to be no blankets available—not even for the cancer patients.

The medication arrives, the butterfly needle is inserted without incident, and as predicted, the entire infusion procedure takes approximately 15 minutes.

Mrs. Banner's husband is delayed in traffic, so she goes to the MMC gift shop and finds a warm shawl to wear while she waits for him.

Mr. Banner arrives and asks how she feels.

She responds, "My scalp feels like someone took the top of it and keeps pulling it up."

Mr. Banner says, "Sounds like my chemotherapy."

The next morning, Mrs. Banner wakes up with a splitting headache, along with back, neck, shoulder, groin, and hip pain; sore muscles; shaking chills; and a low-grade fever. She emails Dr. Green and tells her she's in that "20% of people who get the flu side effects" and asks when she should expect to see the benefits of this procedure.

Discussion Questions

1. What is going on in Part III of this case?
2. Identify the main organizational problem in Part III of this case.
3. What are three factors contributing to this problem?
4. Provide three possible solutions to the problem you identified.
5. Provide your reflections and personal opinions as well as your recommendations for addressing this problem.

Additional Resources

Bear, J. (1996). *Send this jerk the bedbug letter: How companies, politicians, and the mass media deal with complaints and how to be a more effective complainer.* Ten Speed Press.

Buchbinder, S. B., Shanks, N. H., & Kite, B. J. (Eds.). (2021). *Introduction to health care management* (4th ed.). Jones & Bartlett Learning.

Gordon, S. (2020, November 26). *Is your doctor bullying you during your appointments? Discover how bullying doctors impact patient care.* https://www.verywellhealth.com/is-your-doctor-a-bully-4152017

Kennedy, D. M. (2017). Creating an excellent patient experience through service education: Content and methods for engaging and motivating front-line staff. *Journal of Patient Experience, 4*(4), 156–161.

Reed, M., Huang, J., Brand, R., Graetz, I., Jaffe, M. G., Ballard, D., Neugebauer, R., Fireman, B., & Hsu, J. (2020). Inpatient-outpatient shared electronic health records: Telemedicine and laboratory follow-up after hospital discharge. *American Journal of Managed Care, 26*(10). https://www.ajmc.com/view/inpatient-outpatient-shared-electronic-health-records-telemedicine-and-laboratory-follow-up

Reed, M., Huang, J., Brand, R., Graetz, I., Neugebauer, R., Fireman, B., Jaffe, M. G., Ballard, D., & Hsu, J. (2013, September 11). Implementation of an outpatient electronic health record and emergency department visits, hospitalizations, and office visits among patients with diabetes. *Journal of the American Medical Association, 310*(10), 1060–1065. doi:10.1001/jama.2013.276733

Robertson, L. (2008, July 23). *Managing customer service: An outpatient approach.* AMN Healthcare. https://www.amnhealthcare.com/latest-healthcare-news/managing-customer-service-outpatient-approach/

The Joint Commission (TJC). (2014, November). *Sentinel event policy and procedure.* http://www.jointcommission.org/sentinel_event_policy_and_procedures/

The Joint Commission (TJC). (2021, June). *Sentinel event alert 40: Behaviors that undermine a culture of safety.* http://www.jointcommission.org/sentinel_event_alert_issue_40_behaviors_that_undermine_a_culture_of_safety/

CASE 36

To Tell the Truth

Carolyn L. Candiello

Carlos and Lorena brought their 5-year-old son, Lucas, to New Hope Community Hospital with breathing difficulty and a fever. He was seen and admitted by Dr. Little, a board-certified pediatrician who had been practicing for 15 years. Dr. Little diagnosed an upper respiratory infection and ordered antibiotics to be given intravenously twice daily. After just a day, Lucas was starting to feel better, and Dr. Little was encouraged with his progress. Before signing off for a three-day holiday weekend, she provided hand-off to Dr. Jarvis, her colleague.

When she returned on day five of Lucas's admission, she was surprised to see him still in the hospital with worsening symptoms. Carlos and Lorena approached her and asked if she knew what she was doing and whether they should bring him to a different hospital. Dr. Little tried to allay their concerns and told them she would assess him immediately.

Upon a close review of the electronic health record, she discovered Lucas hadn't received his antibiotics for two days. She was sure she included that information in the hand-off to Dr. Jarvis and besides, she thought, "Shouldn't the nurses have made sure it happened?" After a call to the pharmacy, Dr. Little discovered that a "stop order" had been placed. At a recent medical executive committee meeting, a policy was approved to automatically stop antibiotics for all patients after three days unless the physician specifically writes an order to the contrary. The pharmacist explained this was a best practice for antibiotic stewardship and was designed to avoid complications from over-use of antibiotics. Dr. Little was alarmed this policy applied to pediatric patients and hadn't been communicated to the pediatricians.

She immediately restarted the antibiotics and wondered what she would tell Carlos and Lorena. She wasn't sure what she should document in the medical record. Above all, she was worried about Lucas, whose oxygen saturations were dangerously low. She hoped he wasn't going to need to be transferred to the specialty hospital 60 miles away. Even though she knew this was something she couldn't have prevented, she still blamed herself. She called the Director of Quality and Safety for guidance.

Discussion Questions

1. What are the failures in this case?
2. Consider the roles of the other caregivers on the team: Dr. Jarvis, nursing, pharmacy.
3. Should Dr. Little try to explain to Carlos and Lorena what happened, or should she just assure them Lucas will get better?
4. If Dr. Little explains what happened, how should she do it? What if she doesn't tell them?
5. How can the hospital avoid a lawsuit?
6. How was a major policy change such as this made without input by the pediatrics department? Were there leadership failures?
7. What are concerns that you might have for Dr. Little in terms of "second victim"? Should Dr. Little be reprimanded?

Additional Resources

Centers for Disease Control and Prevention. (2020a). *Core elements of hospital antibiotic stewardship programs*. https://www.cdc.gov/antibiotic-use/core-elements/hospital.html

Centers for Disease Control and Prevention. (2020b). *Implementation of antibiotic stewardship core elements at small and critical access hospitals*. https://www.cdc.gov/antibiotic-use/core-elements/small-critical.html

Gerber, J. S., Jackson, M. A., Tamma, P. D., Zaoutis, T. E., & Committee on Infectious Diseases. (2021). Antibiotic stewardship in pediatrics. *Pediatrics, 147*(1).

Patient Safety and Goal Setting in a Research Hospital

D. Christopher Kayes, David Stockwell, and Eric J. Thomas

Derek sat down at his desk to review the upcoming patient safety committee meeting agenda. As Director of Patient Safety at a large research hospital, Derek led the committee charged with advising on methods and processes for ensuring patient safety, implementing those methods, and monitoring their success. The committee included people from across the hospital—administrators, nurses, and physicians—and made recommendations to the Medical Director and hospital Chief Executive Officer (CEO). Because they had an interdisciplinary membership from across different functions of the hospital, committee members were also responsible for gathering insights from each different group (for example, nurses and physicians) and getting them "on board" to implement the committee's recommendations.

Derek and the committee were under pressure to improve patient safety. Patients had growing concerns about safety issues, made worse by fears about contracting infectious diseases such as COVID-19 in hospitals. Accreditation and ranking bodies considered patient safety an important part of their overall hospital ranking system, and these rankings were published and widely read. In some cases, upper management even received incentives tied to meeting or exceeding safety goals. Most importantly, as health care professionals they only sought the highest level of care and failures in safety were seen as unacceptable.

Despite some early successes with increasing patient safety, Derek was concerned about the direction of the committee. The hospital had adopted a "SMART" goal process. SMART was an acronym for setting goals that were Specific, Measurable, Attainable, Relevant, and Timely. The SMART goal approach was adopted after hiring a high-priced consulting firm that recommended this approach and had helped implement the system. But this approach had drawbacks.

The SMART goal approach to patient safety created incentives for the health care workers who provided direct care to patients to focus on only a narrow subset of errors. Other types of errors received less attention. Even more alarming, the committee feared the SMART goal system meant many errors were not being reported because they were not defined by the SMART goal system. Derek feared the hospital was spending an increasing number of resources, both time and money, to prevent a small subset of errors. Less attention was being paid to making sure the safety-critical processes were reliable, proactive, and anticipatory of future risks.

Derek was always looking for ways to improve patient safety and improve the goal setting process. Upper management, including the hospital CEO as well as many of his colleagues, were excited about following a "zero-harm" approach. The zero-harm approach focused on eliminating all possible errors. This goal seemed daunting and would take a significant number of resources to achieve. Derek saw this new goal of zero harm as ambitious, but not practical. Depending on the institution's definitions, a zero-harm goal may be no better than a SMART goal. Zero harm often only targeted certain types of harms, typically those described as hospital acquired conditions (HACs), which were predefined by the Centers for Medicare and Medicaid Services (CMS). However, these conditions were narrowly defined as subtypes of preventable harm. CMS definitions often excluded harms that were still viewed by staff and patients as important events. These types of events barely escaped the definition and were outside of any events that occurred once someone was admitted to the hospital. For example, if a patient acquired COVID-19 while in the hospital, it would not be considered an error.

The committee was proud of the work they had done implementing the SMART goal process. However, growing complaints across different functions of the hospital pointed to important issues in patient safety unaddressed by the current system. Derek was skeptical that the zero-harm target would offer greater benefits. Besides, the hospital had already invested a substantial amount of money in the SMART goal system.

The pressure was mounting. Accreditation was coming. In addition, administrators were pushing to improve the hospital's ranking. Improving patient safety was a big part of the ranking.

Discussion Questions

1. Should Derek introduce the possibility of switching to a new set of goals for patient safety?
2. Would he risk offending the committee?
3. Would he risk the support of upper management if he didn't at least mention the new approach to patient safety to the committee?
4. How can Derek continue to refine and improve patient safety, even with an imperfect process?
5. What information should Derek bring to the committee to help them decide next steps?

Additional Resources

Kayes, D. C. (2005). Destructive pursuit of idealized goals. *Organizational Dynamics, 35*(4), 391–401.

Sitkin, S., See, K., Miller, C., Lawless, M., & Carton, D. (2011). The paradox of stretch goals: Pursuit of the seemingly impossible in organizations, *Academy of Management Review, 36*(3), 544–566.

Stockwell, D. C., Landrigan, C. P., Schuster, M. A., Klugman, D., Bisarya, H., Classen, D. C., Dizon, Z. B., Hall, M., Wood, M., & Sharek, P. J. (2018). Using a pediatric trigger tool to estimate the proportion of total harm burden hospital acquired conditions represent. *Pediatric Quality & Safety, 3*(3). DOI: 10.1097/pq9.081

Vincent, C., & Amalberti, R. (2015). Safety in healthcare is a moving target. *BMJ Quality & Safety, 24*(9), 539–540. doi:10.1136/bmjqs-2015-004403

CASE 38

Aww, That's So Sad for You

Bobbie Kite

Merry Contrary went to the doctor for a routine checkup. Suffering from white coat syndrome her whole life, she had become used to telling medical providers not to be alarmed if they saw her pulse and blood pressure far above normal. She had also become accustomed to them taking her pulse and blood pressure four to five times per visit to try to see if they could get the numbers to come down. She always alerted medical providers to this beforehand and thanked them for their patience. She was embarrassed to have such bad white coat syndrome and hoped it would get better as she got older and stayed in therapy. She was also afraid her medical concerns wouldn't be taken seriously as the stigma of being an "emotional" patient had caused her to be treated differently many times previously.

This visit, a particular nurse decided to take on why Merry had such fear of the doctor visits. She removed the cuff and said, "What, your mom didn't know how to be a mother, and every time you brought a problem to her, she rushed you to the doctor so it would be your fault and not hers."

Merry burst into tears, mortified this nurse would say something so callous and unfeeling.

"I give up trying to get your numbers to be normal," she muttered. "The doctor can take it herself."

When the physician entered, Merry was still crying. After her seventh try, the doctor was satisfied this was only a severe case of white coat syndrome.

That acknowledgement, however, didn't stop them from giving her a 15-minute lecture on the long-term effects of high blood pressure and its relation to early death. Merry did not go for another checkup for four years.

Discussion Questions

1. What is going on in this case?
2. Identify the main organizational problem in this case.
3. What are three factors contributing to this problem?

4.   Provide three possible solutions to the problem you identified.
5.   Provide your reflections and personal opinions as well as your recommendations for addressing this problem.

Additional Resources

Buchbinder, S. B., Shanks, N. H., & Kite, B. J. (2021). *Introduction to health care management* (4th ed.). Jones & Bartlett Learning.

Pioli, M. R., Ritter, A. M., de Faria, A. P., & Modolo, R. (2018). White coat syndrome and its variations: Differences and clinical impact. *Integrated Blood Pressure Control*, *11*, 73–79.

Xiang, H., Xue, Y., Wang, J., Weng, Y., Rong, F., Peng, Y., & Ji, K. (2020). Cardiovascular alterations and management of patients with white coat hypertension: A meta-analysis. *Frontiers in Pharmacology*, *11*, 1498.

CASE 39

Dying Enough for Hospice

Bobbie Kite

Mr. Glider was an elderly man in his late 80s living in a northern rural state. He had severe dementia and lived in an assisted living community. He had two sons, one who lived nearby, and one who lived several states away. Both sons checked on Mr. Glider a couple of times a week over the phone; they also checked in with medical staff from the facility regularly. Mr. Glider's extended family called him to check in often as well, but with the severe dementia, the phone call was sometimes an ordeal.

The country was in a pandemic, which meant no one in the family had really seen him in several months. The son who lived close by was able to wave through his window, but nothing more.

Mr. Glider began complaining of general pain to his son who lived nearby. After several days of this, the son was able to get him to the emergency room. He was unable to accompany his father due to hospital restrictions during the pandemic. The son asked the intake staff to let him know what was happening and when he should return.

After two days and no real answers, the son went back to the hospital to pick up his father. Mr. Glider was found standing outside, confused, wearing seven pairs of pants. No one could tell Mr. Glider's son what they had done or what the diagnosis was. Immediately his son decided to take him to a different emergency room, where he was admitted into the hospital for a severe urinary tract infection.

Six days later, Mr. Glider had declined past the point of recovery. The pandemic restrictions were exacting, and no visitors were allowed. Mr. Glider's granddaughter called the hospital repeatedly until she reached the attending physician and begged to be allowed to have some of the family see Mr. Glider since it was evident, he was likely dying. Finally, they were given permission to visit the following day for two hours.

It was clear that he was not going to recover, and the case worker came in to discuss a transition to hospice. Not wanting him to suffer, the family quickly weighed options, toured a selected hospice facility, and went over the insurance and cost specifics with both the hospital and hospice staff, specifically addressing Mr. Glider's coverage with Medicare.

Upon returning to the hospital, the family met with several hospital workers to arrange his transfer and go over details of the transition. With heavy hearts, they left the hospital but were relieved to know he wouldn't suffer for much longer.

About an hour later, the granddaughter received a call from the caseworker mentioning that they weren't going to be able to approve the transfer to hospice for Mr. Glider since they didn't have enough data to justify his transfer. A nurse had documented one of the family members putting a sponge to Mr. Glider's mouth, and the transfer guidelines considered this to be "drinking water," which reset the clock on the required timeframe of no eating and drinking to qualify for a hospice transfer.

After some heated discussions with a case manager and hospital staff, the family was left with no choice but to leave their dying family member and go back to the hotel to wait for the hospital to decide that Mr. Glider was dehydrated enough to be moved to hospice.

Discussion Questions

1. How does dementia affect managing the care of patients across different facilities?
2. How would you manage this situation as the case manager's supervisor?
3. What are three factors contributing to this problem?
4. How do you direct conversation when insurance requirements are influencing the pathways of care?
5. Provide your reflections and personal opinions as well as your recommendations for addressing this problem.

Additional Resources

Aldridge, M. D., Ornstein, K. A., McKendrick, K., Moreno, J., Reckrey, J. M., & Li, L. (2020). Trends in residential setting and hospice use at the end of life for Medicare decedents. *Health Affairs*, 39(6), 1060–1064.

Allen, W. (2020). Medical ethics issues in dementia and end of life. *Current Psychiatry Reports*, 22(6), 1–7.

Buchbinder, S. B., Shanks, N. H., & Kite, B. J. (2021). *Introduction to health care management* (4th ed.). Jones & Bartlett Learning.

Fox, A., MacAndrew, M., & Ramis, M. A. (2020). Health outcomes of patients with dementia in acute care settings—a systematic review. *International Journal of Older People Nursing*, 15(3), e12315.

Mo, L., Geng, Y., Chang, Y. K., Philip, J., Collins, A., & Hui, D. (2021). Referral criteria to specialist palliative care for patients with dementia: A systematic review. *Journal of the American Geriatrics Society*, 69(6), 1659–1669.

Røsvik, J., & Rokstad, A. M. M. (2020). What are the needs of people with dementia in acute hospital settings, and what interventions are made to meet these needs? A systematic integrative review of the literature. *BMC Health Services Research*, 20(1), 1–20.

Wachterman, M. W., & Sommers, B. D. (2021). Dying poor in the US—Disparities in end-of-life care. *JAMA*, 325(5), 423–424.

CASE 40

Half Dead Pancreas: Part I

Bobbie Kite

Ms. Nannu, who is 60 years old, presents to an emergency room in a smaller urban area with severe abdominal pain. She has residual brain damage and mental health issues from traumatic brain injuries when she was young. Her sister gets a call saying she is being taken to a major urban city for emergency surgery since her "pancreas is half dead."

The sister calls Ms. Nannu's daughter to see if she has been contacted or has any further information. The sister discovers the daughter doesn't know either. The sister then calls her own daughter, Dandie, to help. Several hours later, the sister and her daughter have located Ms. Nannu at the county hospital, verified she is still alive, and driven/flown in to see her.

A thought occurs to Dandie as she is en route. "What about her medications? The nice, compliant person the medical providers are interacting with now will be quite different from the person she will become if she misses her medications."

After a couple of hours of questioning, multiple trips to the nurses' station, and attempts to reach *any* doctor, Dandie still had no idea what was happening. Dandie had her mom stop by Ms. Nannu's house on the six-hour drive to the hospital. Ms. Nannu's daughter gave Dandie's mother 43 bottles of medications and a hand-written list to take with her to the hospital.

Several hours later, all medications were finally entered into Ms. Nannu's chart, and she received her evening meds.

A day later she was transferred to a different unit. Dandie came to check on her that evening, and Ms. Nannu mentioned she hadn't had her meds.

Dandie called the nurse and asked, "Can you please verify my aunt had her nightly medications?"

The nurse did not respond.

Dandie inquired an additional three times.

Finally, the nurse said, "We have no record of Ms. Nannu having any medication, it seems the doctors do not want her to have any medications. I hope it works out!"

Knowing this could not be the case, Dandie called in Ms. Nannu's sister to help. After several more hours, they never found the medication list that was entered the day before in the emergency room and all medications had to be reapproved and reentered. Ms. Nannu received her evening medications around midnight.

Discussion Questions

1. What is going on in this case?
2. Identify the main organizational problem in this case.
3. What are three factors contributing to this problem?
4. Provide three possible solutions to the problem you identified.
5. Provide your reflections and personal opinions as well as your recommendations for addressing this problem.

Additional Resources

Buchbinder, S. B., Shanks, N. H., & Kite, B. J. (2021). *Introduction to health care management* (4th ed.). Jones & Bartlett Learning.

Choi, Y. J., & Kim, H. (2019). Effect of pharmacy-led medication reconciliation in emergency departments: A systematic review and meta-analysis. *Journal of Clinical Pharmacy and Therapeutics, 44*(6), 932–945.

Kennedy, D. M. (2017). Creating an excellent patient experience through service education: Content and methods for engaging and motivating front-line staff. *Journal of Patient Experience, 4*(4), 156–161.

Mueller, S. K., Sponsler, K. C., Kripalani, S., & Schnipper, J. L. (2012). Hospital-based medication reconciliation practices: A systematic review. *Archives of Internal Medicine, 172*(14), 1057–1069.

van der Nat, D. J., Taks, M., Huiskes, V. J., van den Bemt, B. J., & van Onzenoort, H. A. (2021). A comparison between medication reconciliation by a pharmacy technician and the use of an online personal health record by patients for identifying medication discrepancies in patients' drug lists prior to elective admissions. *International Journal of Medical Informatics, 147*, 104370.

Half Dead Pancreas: Part II

Bobbie Kite

After several hours of waiting, Dr. Wrong entered the room with a big smile, "Great news! Your aunt does not require surgery!" Dandie, the niece who flew in from out of town to see about her aunt who was taken to the emergency room, was a bit taken a back and asked "Are you sure? After the roller coaster of the last couple of days, that is indeed great news!" The doctor replied, "Yes, this is just an acute episode of pancreatitis, and I believe it will resolve itself over time. I'm headed out of town on vacation now and the residents will be around later this evening for any questions you have." After confirming what she heard, Dandie decided it was time for her to get some rest and book a flight back home. She let her aunt know she would be back a little later and headed out of the room toward the elevators.

"Dandie, Dandie! You're not leaving are you?" echoed down the hallway. The nurse on shift was running toward Dandie.

"Well yes, the doctor told me the great news!" she replied.

The nurse frowned. "Do you mind waiting a minute while I phone Dr. Wrong?"

Dandie headed back into the room, which was now filled with more family members, to let them know that there was more going on. Looks of confusion stared back at her as silence filled the room.

After what felt like an exceedingly long 15 minutes, the nurse reappeared with not so great news. She informed Dandie and the rest of the family that her aunt would be having surgery and was going to be prepped within the hour. Her gallbladder was being removed, today. The nurse explained that the surgical team believed gallbladder stones were the cause of her pain, not acute pancreatitis.

In the midst of the confusion, a caseworker entered the room. Dandie proceeded to provide every detail of what transpired over the last eight hours. She was concerned Dr. Wrong gave them incorrect information, and she did not understand how that could be possible. The caseworker agreed to look into it.

That night, the caseworker returned and claimed that Dandie misinterpreted Dr. Wrong's explanation. Dandie became furious. "I did not misinterpret his explanation." She pulled her phone from her pocket. "I recorded the entire conversation." She pressed play.

Neither Dr. Wrong nor the caseworker returned to her aunt's room again.

Discussion Questions

1.   What is going on in this case?
2.   Identify the main organizational problem in this case.
3.   What are three factors contributing to this problem?
4.   Provide three possible solutions to the problem you identified.
5.   Provide your reflections and personal opinions as well as your recommendations for addressing this problem.

Additional Resources

Buchbinder, S. B., Shanks, N. H., & Kite, B. J. (2021). *Introduction to health care management* (4th ed.). Jones & Bartlett Learning.

Dahm, M. R., Williams, M., & Crock, C. (2021). 'More than words'–Interpersonal communication, cognitive bias and diagnostic errors. *Patient Education and Counseling.* https:/doi.org/10.1016/j .pec.2021.05.012

Pelaccia, T., Messman, A. M., & Kline, J. A. (2020). Misdiagnosis and failure to diagnose in emergency care: Causes and empathy as a solution. *Patient Education and Counseling, 103*(8), 1650–1656.

Pozgar, G. D. (2016). *Legal aspects of health care administration.* Jones & Bartlett Learning.

CASE 42

Half Dead Pancreas: Part III

Bobbie Kite

After Ms. Nannu arrived home from the hospital, home health scheduled a time to follow up with her to develop an extended care plan. Her niece and daughter called once a day to check on her. On day three, Ms. Nannu mentioned to them that she was being taken in for a CT scan of a cyst they found on her pancreas. In the week and a half prior during her emergency room and hospital stays, no one had said anything about a cyst on her pancreas.

After diligently calling the last hospital Ms. Nannu was treated at, the home health workers, the social workers, and her niece and daughter determined that Ms. Nannu misunderstood something and that there was no cyst to be scanned. With cognitive decline due to multiple past traumatic brain injuries, misunderstanding what medical providers said was unfortunately a common occurrence with Ms. Nannu.

Two days later, Ms. Nannu's local hospital called (not the one she was initially treated at) to remind her of her upcoming CT scan appointment. Once again, she mentioned this to her niece and daughter, who eventually were able to track down the local provider. The local provider informed the family that the large hospital in the large urban center, where Ms. Nannu had been treated, *had* completed some imaging. The large hospital in the large urban center had missed diagnosing a cyst on her pancreas.

Discussion Questions

1. What is going on in this case?
2. What responsibility does each health care entity have in this situation?
3. If you were a manager of the home health facility, how would you move forward?
4. Provide three possible solutions to the problem you identified.
5. Provide your reflections and personal opinions as well as your recommendations for addressing this problem.

Additional Resources

Bellon, J. E., Bilderback, A., Ahuja-Yende, N. S., Wilson, C., Altieri Dunn, S. C., Brodine, D., & Boninger, M. L. (2019). University of Pittsburgh Medical Center home transitions multidisciplinary care coordination reduces readmissions for older adults. *Journal of the American Geriatrics Society, 67*(1), 156–163.

Buchbinder, S. B., Shanks, N. H., & Kite, B. J. (2021). *Introduction to health care management* (4th ed.). Jones & Bartlett Learning.

Callister, C., Jones, J., Schroeder, S., Breathett, K., Dollar, B., Sanghvi, U. J., Harnke, B., Lum, H. D., & Jones, C. D. (2020). Caregiver experiences of care coordination for recently discharged patients: a qualitative metasynthesis. *Western Journal of Nursing Research, 42*(8), 649–659.

Pozgar, G. D. (2016). *Legal aspects of health care administration.* Jones & Bartlett Learning.

Siclovan, D. M., Bang, J. T., Yakusheva, O., Hamilton, M., Bobay, K. L., Costa, L. L., Hughes, R. G., Miles, J., Bahr, S. J., & Weiss, M. E. (2021). Effectiveness of home health care in reducing return to hospital: Evidence from a multi-hospital study in the US. *International Journal of Nursing Studies, 119*, 103946.

CASE 43

The Deep Freeze in the Deep South

Bobbie Kite

Mr. and Mrs. Longfoot have been married for 52 years. They both have medical conditions that require either refrigeration of medication or electricity to power medical devices. It has been a while since they visited family down South, so they decided to go on a road trip. Traveling, in general, required much logistical planning. Considering it was winter, they were certain they wouldn't be dealing with any inclement heat-related weather, as they had in the past.

"Turn that up, turn that up," repeated Mr. Longfoot.

Mrs. Longfoot reached for the TV remote to turn up the volume on the local ten o'clock news. *Breaking News* appeared across the screen in bold red letters.

Mr. Longfoot gasped. "Oh no, what now?"

The deep South was headed for a deep freeze. The meteorologist sounded as worried as he would when a heat wave or hurricane was coming. This could complicate things.

Mrs. Longfoot had long suffered from sleep apnea and her CPAP (continuous positive airway pressure) machine required electricity to deliver oxygen to her while sleeping. Mr. Longfoot required insulin for his diabetes. Insulin requires refrigeration, and on top of that, fluctuation in temperatures can cause it to lose effectiveness. The local news was warning citizens that freezing rain could cause power lines to break, leaving folks without power, heat, or water. They had a history with health services support in the South, and it wasn't a good one. Their experience was that when severe weather rolled in, the infrastructure would fail. They knew this was no exception and leaving wasn't an option at this point.

The following night they woke up shivering; the power had gone out. They were staying at their son's house, and he informed them that, not only was the power out, but the pipes were also frozen as well.

"That was quick!" grumbled Mr. Longfoot, "I expected that we would at least make it through the night before this happened."

They looked around at each other, their electric powered medical machines, and the refrigerator they relied on to survive and wondered what they were going to do.

At home, in times like this, they could call their home health service and request back up power and coolers. They had no such plan in the South.

They called every hotel in the large urban city to try and find a place with power, heat, and water, as they learned they were now under a water boil warning on top of everything else. Eventually, they were able to secure a room, but it wasn't for a few more days. Plus, they weren't even sure of the road conditions to get there. Finding food was the next big hurdle. They had some, but nothing they could eat without cooking. By this point, every grocery store in the town was closed for several reasons including road conditions that kept employees from driving, lack of supplies, and loss of power. Most places couldn't even process cash transactions.

Over the next three days, their situation escalated. Mrs. Longfoot slept up-right in a recliner to try and mitigate breathing without her CPAP machine. Mr. Longfoot continued the use of his insulin, but he was now suffering from complications that arise from improper storage. The supply chain had broken down, and gas stations didn't have enough supply to keep up with demand. They still couldn't even try to head home. They were trapped for a week before being able to travel back North, and it took over 30 days for their resulting medical complications to be sorted out.

Discussion Questions

1. What is going on in this case?
2. Identify the main public health concerns in this case.
3. What are three factors contributing to these problems?
4. Provide three possible solutions to two problems you identified.
5. Whose responsibility is it to address these types of issues when an entire large urban city is affected?

Additional Resources

Buchbinder, S. B., Shanks, N. H., & Kite, B. J. (2021). *Introduction to health care management* (4th ed.). Jones & Bartlett Learning.

Vallianou, N. G., Geladari, E. V., Kounatidis, D., Geladari, C. V., Stratigou, T., Dourakis, S. P., Andreadis, E. A., & Dalamaga, M. (2021). Diabetes mellitus in the era of climate change. *Diabetes & Metabolism, 47*(4), 101205.

You Should Have Been Crying

Bobbie Kite

Vanilla Bean woke up one morning and didn't feel quite right. She took her temperature, and not having a fever she decided to go ahead and go on to work. Around 7:30 AM, the general bad feeling progressed, and she was considering going back home. By 10 o'clock she knew that she should head to the emergency room; something was terribly wrong. She called her wife to come and drive her to the emergency room. She was afraid of passing out at the wheel. She was pretty certain she was passing another kidney stone but couldn't be positive. She'd passed about one kidney stone a month for the past three years. She learned not to take pain pills, so she didn't have to rely on them to function.

After arriving at the emergency room around 11 AM, she was seen around 11:30 AM. When the health care provider asked what pain meds she had taken, she responded she hadn't taken any.

The Physician Assistant (PA) decided it wasn't a kidney stone and called for an ultrasound, thinking that it may be an ovarian cyst.

Vanilla mentioned that her kidney stones only showed up on the CT scan with contrast, and she was fairly certain this was a large stone. Vanilla waited patiently for hours while they performed an x-ray, vaginal ultrasound, abdominal ultrasound, and then decided to have Vanilla wait to see if the pain progressed.

Finally, at 7:45 PM, after Vanilla asked again for a CT scan with contrast, they decided to order one. At 9:30 PM, they performed the CT scan with contrast.

The tech immediately asked, "Do you have a history of kidney stones?"

Vanilla replied, "Yes I do, how big is it?"

The tech said, "At least 9 millimeters."

Vanilla was then prepared for transport to a different hospital for emergency surgery, which was performed at 1 AM.

Before being transferred, the PA came to apologize and offered Vanilla some pain medicine. "I'm sorry, you should have been crying."

Discussion Questions

1.   What is going on in this case?
2.   Identify the main organizational problem in this case.
3.   What are three factors contributing to this problem?
4.   Provide three possible solutions to the problem you identified.
5.   Provide your reflections and personal opinions as well as your recommendations for addressing this problem.
6.   Did you make any assumptions while reading this case regarding race, ethnicity, gender or gender identity, sexual orientation, socioeconomic status, culture, or other protected class? Were these assumptions focused at the individual/staff level, clinical/program level, or organizational/ administrative level? How do these assumptions affect cultural awareness, cultural knowledge, behaviors, and/or skill development?

Additional Resources

Buchbinder, S. B., Shanks, N. H., & Kite, B. J. (2021). *Introduction to health care management* (4th ed.). Jones & Bartlett Learning.

Center for Substance Abuse Treatment (US). (2014). *Improving cultural competence.* Substance Abuse and Mental Health Services Administration (US).

Haverfield, M. C., Giannitrapani, K., Timko, C., & Lorenz, K. (2018). Patient-centered pain management communication from the patient perspective. *Journal of General Internal Medicine*, 33(8), 1374–1380.

Wells, N., Pasero, C., & McCaffery, M. (2008). Improving the quality of care through pain and assessment management. In R. G. Hughes (Ed.), *Patient safety and quality: An evidence-based handbook for nurses* (Chapter 17). Agency for Healthcare Research and Quality. https://www .ncbi.nlm.nih.gov/books/NBK2658/

CASE 45

A Gut Feeling

Matthias Ojo

On Wednesday evening at 6:13 PM, a patient was rushed into the emergency room (ER) at Autumn Maranta Medical Center (AMMC), a level II trauma center.

"We have a male GSW (Gun Shot Wound) victim with two bullets lodged in the lower abdomen. No exit wound. He is stabilized," one of the EMTs exclaimed as she handed him off to nurses Amy and Tammy in the ER.

With 20 years of trauma experience under her belt, Nurse Amy took the lead and grabbed the stretcher and muttered, "I was about to leave, and I just worked a double!" As Nurse Amy clutched the stretcher, she told Nurse Tammy, a newly trained nursing school graduate, to retrieve the rest of the patient's belongings from the ambulance.

Dr. Griffith, the 35-year-old chief resident, who had been paged prior to the arrival of the ambulance, raced over to the bleeding but conscious patient. Nurse Amy continued to apply pressure at the site of the wound. The rooms at AMMC had already been filling up due to injuries local citizens had sustained during social protests, some of which had been reported to be violent in nature.

Nurse Tammy ran back to the GSW patient and placed a backpack with an AP Statistics textbook peeking out at the foot of the stretcher. After a brief assessment of the patient and his injuries, Dr. Griffith put his stethoscope back around his neck and growled, "Put him in bay three, hang a bag of Ringer's lactate, and order an abdominal CT." Frowning, fiddling with a pen between his fingers, and muttering, Dr. Griffith walked away to attend to another patient.

Seeking confirmation of the doctor's instruction, Nurse Amy yelled to him, "Shouldn't we add a morphine drip?"

Dr. Griffith turned around, his face twisted with anger. "I know what I am doing! He's stable, his symptoms aren't bad for two bullet wounds, and he looks okay. We'll get the CT and operate. If he wasn't running in the streets and rioting, he wouldn't be here. If he needs morphine, I will order it when I feel like it 'matters'!"

Shocked by the doctor's hostile response and his use of air quotes when saying the word "matters," Nurse Tammy glanced at the bloody abdomen of the patient. It was only then that she noticed his ripped open shirt read "BLACK LIVES MATTER."

Hesitant but compliant, the two nurses did as Dr. Griffith instructed and placed the stable patient in bay three.

Exhausted and running out of steam, Nurse Amy turned to her less experienced colleague, Nurse Tammy. "Monitor him and page the Charge Nurse if he gets worse. Don't allow any visitors to see him. Dr. Griffith should be with him soon. I need a cig. My shift is over!" She closed the curtain and left the patient and Nurse Tammy alone.

Nurse Tammy kept watch over the young patient and did as she was told. The patient started to groan and showed clear signs of discomfort, but refused to talk to her or to provide her with any identifying information. She looked at her watch, noticed it was now 7:36 PM, more than an hour after his initial arrival and assessment. Per protocol, she took the patient's vital signs and noted his pulse was getting weaker. Dr. Griffith had yet to return to see the patient. She didn't like how things were going and paged the Charge Nurse for assistance. The Charge Nurse informed her she was eating her dinner, *finally*, because the shift change had run over. Nurse Tammy held onto the wrist of the young man whose pulse continued to weaken. She had only been a member of the ER nursing staff for five months since graduating from nursing school. She felt terrified and out of her depth. She knew they were understaffed in the ER that evening, but she wanted to reassure him—and herself.

"Don't worry, the doctor will be with you as soon as he can."

Discussion Questions

1.   What are the main facts of the case?
2.   Do you think Dr. Griffith spent sufficient time with this patient? Should Nurse Amy have responded differently?
3.   What ethical dilemmas does this case demonstrate?
4.   Do you think Nurse Tammy handled the situation appropriately? What should she have done differently?
5.   What is the role of the Charge Nurse in this scenario? What actions should she have taken?
6.   As you read and envisioned the case, what race did you consciously or subconsciously give to the patient, the doctor, and the nurses?
7.   What implicit or explicit biases do you see in this case?
8.   Should Dr. Griffith be reported for his behavior? Why or why not?
9.   Did you make any assumptions while reading this case regarding race, ethnicity, gender or gender identity, sexual orientation, socioeconomic status, culture, or other protected class? Were these assumptions focused at the individual/staff level, clinical/program level, or organizational/administrative level? How do these assumptions affect cultural awareness, cultural knowledge, behaviors, and/or skill development?

Additional Resources

Agrawal, S., & Enekwechi, A. (2020, January 15). It's time to address the role of implicit bias within health care delivery. *Health Affairs.* https://www.healthaffairs.org/do/10.1377/forefront.20200108.34515/full/

Buchbinder, S. B., Shanks, N. H., & Kite, B. J. (2021). *Introduction to health care management* (4th ed.). Jones & Bartlett Learning.

Center for Substance Abuse Treatment. (2014). Improving cultural competence. *Substance Abuse and Mental Health Services Administration.* https://www.ncbi.nlm.nih.gov/books/NBK248428/

DeAngelis, T. (2019). How does implicit bias by physicians affect patients' health care? *Monitor on Psychology, 50*(3), 22–31

Dehon, E., Weiss, N., Jones, J., Faulconer, W., Hinton, E., & Sterling, S. (2017). A systematic review of the impact of physician implicit racial bias on clinical decision making. *Academic Emergency Medicine, 24*(8), 895–904.

Donaldson, M. S., Corrigan, J. M., & Kohn, L. T. (Eds.). (2000). *To err is human: Building a safer health system.* The National Academies Press.

Johnson, M., Felton, O., Moore, F. A., Perry, W., & Boatright, D. (2016). Diversity matters: Implicit bias and its role in patient care. *Emergency Medicine News, 38*(12), 12–13.

Zeidan, A. J., Khatri, U. G., Aysola, J., Shofer, F. S., Mamtani, M., Scott, K. R., Conlon, L. W., & Lopez, B. L. (2019). Implicit bias education and emergency medicine training: Step one? *Awareness. AEM Education and Training, 3*(1), 81–85.

Lack of Coordination in the Pediatric Intensive Care Unit

Tolulope Oyewumi

You are the director of the Pediatric Intensive Care Unit (PICU) at Intermountain WellCare Hospital (IWC), the only Level 1 critical care facility among the 10 neighboring states. This status creates a large volume for care at this hospital. Despite the heavy demand, your hospital had prioritized patient safety and evidence-based infection control practices and has been deemed the safest children's hospital in the region for eight years in a row by the Joint Commission. However, last year you missed the mark and your hospital has been working hard to get that award and recognition this year. Everything is well on its way for that to happen. You and the hospital are excited to be celebrated as the safest hospital in the region three months from now. Then, things take a dramatic turn.

A 10-year-old boy comes into your PICU with a contact sport injury and must have emergency surgery on his left leg. He has also been in treatment for a solid tumor cancer for the past three years. The cancer has been in remission for almost seven months; however, two days after the surgery, he spikes a 100-degree fever. The results of the complete blood count (CBC) and differential test show an excess white blood cell count, an indicator of an active infection. The Director of Infectious Disease (ID), Dr. Mullins, evaluates the patient and orders a new antibiotic treatment regimen. Ten days later, the patient is still running a fever, has low blood pressure, and then codes, i.e., has a cardiopulmonary arrest, in the PICU. The child must be intubated to support his vital organs.

Dr. Mullins returns to the PICU and upon review of the patient's chart finds one of the key medications she ordered was never initiated or given. Upon further inquiry, she discovers that two days after her initial conferral, there was a consult to Dr. Tavern of the pediatric hematology-oncology (HemOnc) unit due to concerns that the CBC differential showed signs of cancer. Dr. Tavern stopped two of the antibiotics Dr. Mullins had ordered, stating the "possible re-emergence of cancer cells" caused the patient's unrelenting fever and continuous low blood pressure post-operatively. While Dr. Mullins's unit is investigating why Dr. Tavern stopped the antibiotic without speaking with Dr. Mullins, the patient codes—again. The child is now in renal failure, necessitating an urgent kidney transplant to get him out of the PICU alive.

It is now 15 days after surgery. The patient's condition is declining, and his parents are threatening to sue and call the media. You have *finally* been made aware of what is going on and you call an emergency meeting of the seven departments involved in the care of this 10-year-old patient: the pediatric orthopedic unit, PICU, pediatric infectious disease, social services, HemOnc, pediatric rehabilitation services, and the child transplant program.

During your meeting with these department heads, you are informed that Dr. Mullins placed the patient on the right antibiotic for the right course of time for a pathogen the lab isolated—the very pathogen that has the potential of infecting vital organs like the kidneys. Because Dr. Tavern stopped the antibiotic without talking to Dr. Mullins, the pathogen not only had the opportunity to infect the kidneys but also launched the patient into renal failure. To make matters worse, you also discover that Dr. Tavern did not run additional tests to confirm the patient's fever was due to re-emergence of cancerous cells. In addition, Dr. Tavern placed the patient on unwarranted anti-cancer medications.

You are in the midst of a disaster with a young patient's life at risk and your hospital's reputation on the line. Something drastic needs to be done STAT.

Discussion Questions

1. What are the facts in this case?
2. At what point in this case should the PICU department head have been involved?
3. Where do you think the communication breakdown started?
4. What pro-active measures should the department heads take to mitigate miscommunication in a case like this?
5. Should Dr. Tavern face disciplinary actions? Why or why not?

Additional Resources

Burgener, A. M. (2017). Enhancing communication to improve patient safety and to increase patient satisfaction. *The Health Care Manager, 36*(3), 238–243. https:/doi.org/10.1097/HCM.0000000000000165

Dingley, C., Daugherty, K., Derieg, M. K., & Persing, R. (2008). *Improving patient safety through provider communication strategy enhancement.* Agency for Healthcare Research and Quality. https://www.ahrq.gov/downloads/pub/advances2/vol3/advances-dingley_14.pdf

Medline Plus. (2020, July 31). *Complete blood count.* https://medlineplus.gov/lab-tests/complete-blood-count-cbc/

The Joint Commission (TJC). (n.d.). *Sentinel event.* https://www.jointcommission.org/resources/patient-safety-topics/sentinel-event/

The Joint Commission (TJC). (2020, July). *The national patient safety goals effective July 2020.* https://www.jointcommission.org/-/media/tjc/documents/standards/national-patient-safety-goals/2020/npsg_chapter_hap_jul2020.pdf

PART 4

Finance

CASE 47

To Hold or Not to Hold?

Jenn Block

You are the practice manager of the Feel Good Family Practice Clinic in a factory town outside of Philadelphia, Pennsylvania. You have mixed demographics in your patient population and the majority have commercial insurance through employer-based plans with a minority of patients being seniors in Medicare Advantage plans (Medicare.gov, n.d.). Similar to other patients across the country, your patients are finding it difficult to meet the financial obligations of the deductibles in high cost-sharing plans (HealthCare.gov, n.d.). The good news is, your clinic has a strong leadership team and has been proactive in creating policies to manage the operations and other aspects of the business. The bad news is, the printed policies in the binder in your office have not been routinely updated.

Recently your practice has joined a Clinically Integrated Network to gain access to better value-based contracts (VBC) with the insurers (payors). A VBC is a written contract between payors and providers where payment is tied to achievement of specific clinical goals (Bailey, 2021, para. 1). One of the benefits of belonging to the network is enhanced data for your patient population, including quality outcomes and measures of performance, utilization information, and population health metrics regarding the most common chronic conditions. You recently received data that suggests your patient population has had an increase in emergency department (ED) visits over the last year. You call a meeting with your practice and the payor that provided the data to brainstorm reasons for this spike in utilization. You wonder if these ED visits are the result of an inability for a patient to obtain an appointment with your clinic. After reviewing data regarding appointment schedules and access, you find there are appointments routinely available the same day or next day that a patient calls. Next, you turn your attention to the urgent care centers in the area. Have they closed? After ruling this and other reasons for the increase in ED visits out, you are ultimately left unsure of the cause.

Two weeks after the meeting, you hear an anecdotal story from a case manager who was following up with a patient after a trip the ED. The patient stated they had gone there because they were unable to make an appointment with the practice.

Luckily, the case manager asked additional questions, and the patient shared the clinic had placed them on a financial hold because they still owed their last two office copays. Because of recent hardships within the family, they were unable to make that payment. On a hunch, you decide to explore this further and review the financial hold policy in your policy binder which indicates the clinic places financial holds on patients who have accrued a balance greater than 30 days old, regardless of amount. The policy indicates patients are asked to pay that balance prior to being seen for any scheduled visits. However, in exceptional circumstances managers have the ability to override this policy.

You meet with your scheduling team to inquire whether they are sharing this policy with patients in full, i.e., the potential for managerial overrides. You discover none of the schedulers were aware of this aspect of the policy. Schedulers who have since left the practice on-boarded the current schedulers, and turnover in these positions is high. You decide to look at a sample of the records from the patients who had ED visits. In particular, you want to see if any of these visits were avoidable, or non-emergent visits. You find the practice had placed over half (57%) of these patients on a financial hold. Now that you have a clue about what might be causing the patients' behaviors, the challenge is determining what to do to reduce the inappropriate utilization and promote the idea of the right patient at the right place at the right time.

Discussion Questions

1. What is the definition of a value-based contract?
2. How does the current financial policy encourage patients to seek care at the ED for non-emergent or avoidable visits?
3. Based on the clinic's population and insurance plans, which do you think is the more costly method: not collecting the past due balances, or the costs of ED visits?
4. What recommendations would you make to address the shift in patient behaviors?
5. What barriers might you encounter and how will you overcome them?
6. Did you make any assumptions while reading this case regarding race, ethnicity, gender or gender identity, sexual orientation, socioeconomic status, culture, or other protected class? Were these assumptions focused at the individual/staff level, clinical/program level, or organizational/administrative level? How do these assumptions affect cultural awareness, cultural knowledge, behaviors, and/or skill development?

Additional Resources

Bailey, P. V. (2021, June 2). The why, what, where, and how of value-based contracts. *Bulletin of the American College of Surgeons.* https://bulletin.facs.org/2021/06/the-why-what-where-and-how-of-value-based-contracts/

Butts, D., Strilesky, M., & Fadel, M. (2014, April 17). The 7 components of a clinical integration network. *Becker's Hospital Review.* https://www.beckershospitalreview.com/hospital-physician-relationships/the-7-components-of-a-clinical-integration-network.html

Center for Substance Abuse Treatment. (2014). *Improving cultural competence.* Substance Abuse and Mental Health Services Administration. https://www.ncbi.nlm.nih.gov/books/NBK248428/

Enard, K. R., & Ganelin, D. M. (2013). Reducing preventable emergency department utilization and costs by using community health workers as patient navigators. *Journal of Healthcare Management, 58*(6), 412–428. https://www.ncbi.nlm.nih.gov/pmc/articles/PMC4142498/

Hajjaj, F. M., Salek, M. S., Basra, M. K. A., & Finlay, A. Y. (2010). Non-clinical influences on clinical decision-making: A major challenge to evidence-based practice. *Journal of the Royal Society of Medicine, 103*(5), 178–187. https://www.ncbi.nlm.nih.gov/pmc/articles/PMC2862069/

HealthCare.gov. (n.d.). *High deductible health plan (HDHP)*. https://www.healthcare.gov/glossary/high-deductible-health-plan/

Heiser, S., Conway, P. H., & Rajkumar, R. (2019). Primary care selection: A building block for value-based health care. *JAMA, 322*(16), 1551–1552. https://jamanetwork.com/journals/jama/article-abstract/2751521

Medicare.gov. (n.d.). *Medicare advantage plans*. https://www.medicare.gov/sign-up-change-plans/types-of-medicare-health-plans/medicare-advantage-plans.

CASE 48

A Problem to Be Solved: Meeting Metrics the Right Way, Leading and Lagging Indicators

Robert Casanova

Our tertiary acute care hospital has been successfully meeting corporate measures of performance. However, over the last three quarters of the past fiscal year, one of our measures trended to an unacceptable level. Our denial rate for medicine admissions from the emergency department (ED) went up. The corporate chief financial officer (CFO) made it very clear this was unacceptable and needed to be rectified immediately. It was communicated as "no more denials!" We informed our ED leadership, the administrative emergency room director and the medical director of the ED, of this issue and made it very clear that this needed to improve.

Our director of the ED was well known as an effective manager with many outstanding achievements in performance such as key through-put times for admitted patients. The ED leadership promptly instituted some documentation and referral process changes for medical patients. After that, the denial rate moved from the plateau it had been on, back down to the acceptable range. Subsequently, the denial rate remained steady at this low rate, much to the relief of those reporting to the corporate CFO.

Shortly after this successful improvement and over the next couple of quarters, the hospital CFO noticed that revenues had trended downward. This was attributed to a decrease in ED admissions and an increase in the rate of patients being transferred from the ED to an inpatient unit for observation which, in some cases, lasted for many days. Most of these observation patients were discharged to home or a post-acute facility, with a small percentage admitted as inpatients. It should be noted that revenue for the typical observation patient is significantly below that of an inpatient with the same or similar admission complaint. This reduction in revenue was having a negative impact on the hospital's margin. How can our quality metric team meet this new challenge?

Discussion Questions

1. Is the denial rate for an inpatient admission a leading or lagging indicator?
2. What are the drivers or potential root causes for inpatient denials?
3. What appears to be the solution the ED leadership developed for the denial problem?
4. What were the benefits and disadvantages of the apparent solution to the problem of denials?
5. What should the hospital CFO do to address the issue of reduced revenue?
6. What might be another improvement approach that could solve the denial problem, without the disadvantages of reduced revenue through an increase in observation versus inpatient admissions?

Additional Resources

Joy, I. (2019). *An implementation guide to leading indicators*. Campbell Institute. https://www.thecampbellinstitute.org/wp-content/uploads/2019/08/Campbell-Institute-An-Implementation-Guide-to-Leading-Indicators.pdf

Marr, B. (2020, October 23). What's the difference between lagging and leading indicator? *Forbes*. https://www.forbes.com/sites/bernardmarr/2020/10/23/whats-the-difference-between-lagging-and-leading-indicator/?sh=2f806c295009

McChesney, C., Covey, S., & Huling, J. (2012). *The 4 disciplines of execution*. Free Press.

Tuazon, N. (2019, July). Achieving balance: Re-examining leading and lagging metrics. *Texas Organization for Nursing Leadership (TONL) Monthly*. http://www.naylornetwork.com/tne-nwl/articles/index-v2.asp?aid=567641&issueID=65461

CASE 49

The Eager New Speech Pathologist

Sarah Hess and Kristen Dugan

Rachel was a brand-new speech pathologist. A recent graduate with high honors, she was also the recipient of the highest honor within her discipline, the integrity before self (IBS) award. After researching many positions, she decided to take her first job at a rural hospital in a tiny community where many in her family resided. During the interview process, the conversation turned to cutting costs and increasing profits. The interviewer did not hide any of the previous year's fiscal numbers, both negative and positive. He was eager to report that even though some departments were under re-evaluation, the speech pathology department was reporting a significantly higher profit margin than in years past. He was anxious to make her part of the team. Rachel accepted the position with delight; she desperately wanted to move closer to family. The same day she bought a new home two blocks away from the hospital.

The Speech Pathology Department consisted of five speech pathologists and one intermediate supervisor. Rachel was personable, eager to do a good job and to make friends within her department. One day, during the first week of training, Rachel witnessed a heated discussion between her preceptor and her intermediate supervisor. Rachel saw the supervisor show her preceptor one of the charge sheets Rachel recognized and heard her say, "The reason does not matter, always charge for the full hour." Following the confrontation, Rachel asked her preceptor if she was all right because she looked quite disturbed. Her preceptor told her it would be best not to discuss the situation. She followed this by saying "If you know what's good for you, you should do as you are told if you want to save your job. And you better not ask questions." The preceptor then walked off, leaving Rachel very confused. The last thing Rachel wanted to do was make friction in the department, so she dropped the issue, took her preceptor's advice, and did not ask questions.

The following day right before the department birthday luncheon, Rachel saw another one of her coworkers in what looked to be another uncomfortable heated discussion with the intermediate supervisor. She overheard the supervisor tell her coworker to repeat the evaluation conducted the day before for cognitive deficits on Ms. Landry in room 646, except this time to finish the assessment regardless of the time and to charge the full hour. Rachel could see her coworker was displeased and was looking at the floor mumbling comments as their supervisor walked off. Rachel thought about what room number she had overheard and knew that all the rooms between 640 and 659 were part of the end-of-life hospice care unit, as this was where her grandmother was transferred to just a few short months before. Remembering the warning the day before, Rachel chose not to ask any questions.

Rachel completed her two weeks of orientation and her preceptor approved her to work independently. During her first week, she alone saw 14 different patients. An hour-long speech pathology consult counted as one full unit of charge billed for the department. Of the 14 patients Rachel assessed, two patients were children under 12, one was a 24-year-old patient suffering from almost continual subclinical seizure activity, and the other 11 were patients over 65 years of age. Rachel soon found out the children were more complex, and one of the two could not complete the evaluation because of anxiety issues. The patient who had subclinical seizures was not able to respond appropriately when commands were given, so their evaluation was incomplete. Of the 11 elderly patients, three were on the same floor her grandmother had been on previously. Rachel completed the charts, billed for her 14 patients, and turned in nine full unit charges. It had been busy, but a gratifying, week for Rachel. She was looking forward to her weekend off.

On Monday, when Rachel returned to work, she was approached at lunchtime by her intermediate supervisor and questioned about the week prior. The supervisor wanted to know why only nine unit charges were reported. Rachel explained the complex patient, the one who had a lack of attention and awareness due to her seizure disorder, and the three who were virtually unresponsive in the hospice unit. Rachel was then counselled on how important it was to make sure each patient was to be charged the full amount, and that the three elderly patients had excellent insurance plans. Rachel repeated that the patients were unable to complete the evaluation and the supervisor reminded her she was on a 60-day trial period at the medical center, and everyone needed to be a participant in the overall goal of increasing profits for the hospital.

As the supervisor walked away, Rachel was left wondering what to do. How could she charge for patients who were unable to complete an assessment? How could Rachel charge for patients who were unresponsive? What was she to do if she lost her job? She just bought a new house!

Discussion Questions

1. What are the facts of the case?
2. From Rachel's perspective, what underlying concerns do you think she has?
3. What are the leadership issues in this case?
4. What evidence of bullying do you find?
5. What are the management issues in this case?
6. What are the ethical responsibilities in this case?
7. What legal ramifications does this case present?

Additional Resources

Ali, A., Sidra, T., Shazia, A., & Moniba, N. (2020). The role of high-performance work system on organizational performance: Mediating role of workplace bullying. *Journal of Managerial Sciences, 13*(4), 133–142.

Horner, J., Modayil, M., Chapman, L. R., & Dinh, A. (2016). Consent, refusal, and waivers in patient-centered dysphagia care: Using law, ethics, and evidence to guide clinical practice. *American Journal of Speech-Language Pathology, 25*(4), 453–469.

Jackson, E. (2015). The relationship between medical law and good medical ethics. *Journal of Medical Ethics, 41*(1), 95–98.

Lewis, M. A., & Tamparo, C. D. (2007). *Medical law, ethics, & bioethics for the health professions* (6th ed.). F. A. Davis Company.

Mendlelson, D., Freckelton, I. R., & Abington, O. (2016). *Causation in law and medicine*. Routledge.

Naseem, K., & Ahmed, A. (2020). Presenteeism as a consequence of workplace bullying: Mediating role of emotional exhaustion and moderation of climate for conflict management. *Pakistan Journal of Commerce and Social Sciences, 14*(1), 143–166.

Park, H., Bjorkelo, B., & Blenkinsopp, J. (2020). External whistleblowers' experiences of workplace bullying by superiors and colleagues. *Journal of Business Ethics, 161*(3), 591–601. https://link.springer.com/article/10.1007%2Fs10551-018-3936-9

Pozgar, G. D. (2016). *Legal aspects of health care administration*. Jones & Bartlett Learning.

CASE 50

Do This or You'll Die

Bobbie Kite

Pippi started a new job and as a result had access to solid health insurance for the first time in several years. She had a few chronic conditions, one of them being ulcerative colitis. Pippi struggled with this disease on and off for three decades and sometimes had the financial means to treat it and sometimes didn't. Now that she had health insurance, she excitedly scheduled an appointment with a gastroenterologist to set up a colonoscopy and talk about a long-term treatment plan. At this time, her ulcerative colitis was in remission.

When she arrived for the appointment, she was ushered back by a medical provider and asked a series of questions. She started to feel uncomfortable as she began to realize that the feedback provided to every answer, she gave somehow evolved to showcase how damaged and doomed she was. The provider remarked that her liver was probably permanently damaged due to past medication history and the steroids she was required to take as a teenager. They also mentioned she probably had a severe loss of bone mass, so they urged her to get an immediate bone density test. On top of this, the medical provider informed her, in fact, that if she didn't go on biologics immediately, she would relapse and probably die of ulcerative colitis within a couple of years. Incredibly alarmed, Pippi wanted to get out of there immediately and did.

Pippi completed the follow-up procedures and tests suggested to her, including the colonoscopy, blood work to determine liver damage, and the bone density test. She asked the gastroenterology office staff repeatedly if these procedures and tests would be covered by her insurance plan and had them call the insurance company with her standing there to verify. She had learned many lessons from the past about how these things could go very wrong!

After all was said and done, the colonoscopy was not coded correctly by the doctor's office, resulting in large out-of-pocket costs, and neither test suggested was covered under her insurance plan because of her age. After many phone calls and heated discussions with the insurance company and doctor's office staff, Pippi ended up paying $1,250 out-of-pocket. There were no findings on the colonoscopy, no liver damage, and no bone loss was noted.

After years of taking any care she could get, she was very hesitant to call and ask to be assigned to a different medical provider. It was difficult for her to even consider going back for future yearly colonoscopies that she knew she would need. She forced herself to call and change providers and has since maintained the recommended periodic care. Her ulcerative colitis remained in remission, and she didn't have to take the strongly recommended treatments to avoid dying.

Discussion Questions

1. What is going on in this case?
2. At what point does a practice recommend clinical treatment guidelines versus a personal approach?
3. Is there anything that the gastroenterology office staff could do to help with the insurance billing issues?
4. Provide three possible solutions to the problem you identified.
5. Provide your reflections and personal opinions as well as your recommendations for addressing this problem.

Additional Resources

Buchbinder, S. B., Shanks, N. H., & Kite, B. J. (2021). *Introduction to health care management* (4th ed.). Jones & Bartlett Learning.

Natale, G. L. (2019). *Experiencing invisible chronic illnesses at work and in the clinic: "It's almost like people have to physically see it"* (Publication No. 27534773) [Doctoral dissertation, Kent State University]. ProQuest Dissertations Publishing.

Roberts, C. M., Gamwell, K. L., Baudino, M. N., Grunow, J. E., Jacobs, N. J., Tung, J., Gillaspy, S. R., Hommel, K. A., Mullins, L. L., & Chaney, J. M. (2020). The contributions of illness stigma, health communication difficulties, and thwarted belongingness to depressive symptoms in youth with inflammatory bowel disease. *Journal of Pediatric Psychology, 45*(1), 81–90.

U.S. Department of Health and Human Services. (2017, January 31). *Pre-existing conditions.* https://www.hhs.gov/healthcare/about-the-aca/pre-existing-conditions/index.html

CASE 51

The $4,000 Eye Exam

Bobbie Kite

Mr. Pepper had a busy Saturday planned with a trip to his favorite retail store after lunch. While there, he decided to go ahead and get the eye exam he had been putting off months. After all, he thought, "They make these eye exam centers as convenient as possible, and the cost is covered my health insurance."

As the provider was completing the eye exam, frantically he informed Mr. Pepper, "You need to go directly to the emergency room!"

Quite alarmed, Mr. Pepper asked, "For what?"

Mr. Pepper called for his husband, Mr. Salt, who was in the waiting room. "Go ahead doctor, please explain to us why I need to go directly to the emergency room."

The provider took a deep breath and explained that he noticed Mr. Pepper had swollen optic nerves, which is a symptom of brain tumors, but only an MRI could determine that. "I have seen this many times in my career, you need to head there straight away!"

Mr. Salt inquired if there was a less alarmist path forward. The doctor mentioned there was one other option they could try before heading to the ER, an emergency eye imaging clinic down the road. They drove there immediately.

After an exam and imaging there, the ophthalmologist agreed Mr. Pepper did indeed need to head directly to the emergency room. "One last thing," the doctor said as they were headed out, "here are a couple of phone numbers for some oncologists we regularly refer people to."

Mr. Salt became angry, "How about not assuming things until we have been through the proper tests and diagnosis!!"

After arriving at the ER, they were told an MRI couldn't be done until the next morning, which was 12 hours away. The ER doctor recommended Mr. Pepper get a spinal tap; this would determine the amount of the fluid around the brain, and if elevated, it could turn out to be the culprit of the swollen optic nerves, ruling out a brain tumor. Not wanting to wait until the next day for answers, they decided to go ahead with the spinal tap. After a couple more hours, it was determined that there was actually less fluid around the brain. The MRI was ordered for the next day.

Mr. Pepper was kept overnight for observation. Morning finally came and the MRI was performed. They waited approximately another 12 hours for the results. Nothing significant was found, and they both took a big sigh of relief. Mr. Pepper was released shortly after the results were given and told to follow up with a neuro-ophthalmologist.

Later that evening Mr. Pepper developed an excruciating headache. Crying, he asked his husband to please call the doctor, "Something is terribly wrong."

Mr. Salt spoke with the nurse, who told them to head back to the emergency room. Within eight hours of leaving the hospital, they were headed back for a different reason. It was determined that Mr. Pepper needed something called a "blood patch" to stop the cerebral fluid from continually leaking out of the spinal column after the spinal tap. The ER doctor had to page the on-call anesthesiologist to perform the procedure, which caused another several hour delay in treatment. During all the communication, neither Mr. Pepper nor Mr. Salt verified this anesthesiologist was a part of their insurance network of providers.

Finally, the anesthesiologist arrived and asked the nurse to begin withdrawing blood from Mr. Pepper's arm to insert into the lower back. Four vials were needed. This procedure can be complicated as the blood needs to be injected into the spine directly after being taken from the body.

"What is taking so long?" the doctor yelled.

"Sir, the blood just won't drain," the nurse replied.

The doctor, leaving the spinal tap in, walked around to the other side of the bed and began squeezing Mr. Pepper's arm.

"Are you sure that is helpful and necessary? It hurts!" cried Mr. Pepper.

Mr. Salt didn't have any medical experience, but he knew squeezing an arm wouldn't lead to more blood coming out of a vein. "It's not a tube of toothpaste," he said under his breath.

The emergency room attending physician then stepped in and asked the anesthesiologist to stop, immediately.

Eventually the nurse was able to get enough blood to complete the blood patch, and Mr. Pepper was asked to rest for the next hour.

The total cost was just over $4,000, and the diagnosis? Drusen under the retina: yellow-colored spots seen under the retina of the eye made up of proteins and lipids.

Discussion Questions

1.   What is going on in this case?
2.   What are some of the ethical issues raised in this case?
3.   What does this case reveal about the continuity of treatment in the health care delivery system?
4.   Provide your reflections and personal opinions as well as your recommendations for addressing this problem.

Additional Resources

Brennan, D. (2021, June 21). *What are retinal drusen?* WebMD. https://www.webmd.com/eye-health /what-are-retinal-drusen

Buchbinder, S. B., Shanks, N. H., & Kite, B. J. (2021). *Introduction to health care management* (4th ed.). Jones & Bartlett Learning.

Cooper, Z., Nguyen, H., Shekita, N., & Morton, F. S. (2020). Out-of-network billing and negotiated payments for hospital-based physicians: The cost impact of specialists who bill patients at out-of-network rates even though the patients do not choose and cannot avoid these specialists, such as anesthesiologists. *Health Affairs, 39*(1), 24–32.

Mukamal, R. (2020, January 16). *20 surprising health problems an eye exam can catch.* American Academy of Ophthalmology. https://www.aao.org/eye-health/tips-prevention /surprising-health-conditions-eye-exam-detects

CASE 52

Lean Methodology

Nichole Marksbury

A Midwest regional hospital has recently implemented a new electronic health record (EHR) in their acute care facility and specialty clinics. The hospital leadership incorporated this project into its strategic initiatives and vision of delivering evidence-based, high-quality, cost-efficient, patient-centered care. The infrastructure supported a robust safety culture, and every decision and activity focused on supporting and implementing these initiatives. The leadership team incorporated project management methodologies and principles, workflow analysis, change management, and Lean methodologies to remove redundancy and non-value processes. They focused on streamlining processes using Lean Six Sigma techniques that added evidence-based practices, accountability, compliance, and quality workflow processes.

The workflow analysis completed in the cardiovascular procedure labs identified several bottlenecks that stemmed from non-value processes. The clinical staff were entering itemized procedure charges in three disparate systems for each case. The charge systems didn't communicate with each other, and the documentation burden fell on the clinical staff. The burdensome process added one to three hours of extra work each day.

The informatics nurse lead (INL) and the health information technologies teams incorporated Lean methodologies and delivered an EHR solution. The procedural and supply items were scanned into the EHR via a handheld scanner throughout the case. This electronic system attached to the inventory management system and automatically removed the items from the inventory system and auto-reordered when a certain level of inventory was reached. The scanned charges uploaded to the master charge index for claim preparation and billing. The automation helped the billing staff submit more accurate and timely claims. The staff was delighted, and this colossal win solidified their buy-in for consistent scanner usage.

The chief executive officer (CEO) requested a 90-day quality look back meeting with the cardiology director, the information technology director, and the INL. The 90-day post-live meeting discussed variations or deviations in practice that detracted from best practices established and implemented in the new EHR. The CEO reported the department was losing approximately $15,000 per month. The staff was not documenting stop times for intravenous (IV) fluids and antibiotic administrations. Without stop times recorded, the facility couldn't obtain reimbursement for the IV fluid and antibiotics.

The CEO now has an upcoming budget meeting with the hospital board of directors. To meet their projected budgets, they need to eliminate the waste and implement a Lean solution to recover lost revenues. The team has three months to identify, optimize, and provide supporting data. The CEO knows the staff has worked diligently for the past three months learning to use the EHR. However, the CEO must press further to eliminate the waste and recapture the lost revenues. Every dollar captured aligns with the Lean methodology infrastructure and supports high-quality, low cost, patient-centered care. The cardiology director and INL will work together to address and solve the issue.

Discussion Questions

1. What are the elements of Lean Methodology, Lean Six Sigma, and PDSA (Plan, Do, Study, Act)?
2. What are the elements of a high-reliability organization?
3. What are the elements of workflow analysis?
4. What change management models can be used to support Lean methodologies? How can you use change management models to help the clinical staff prepare for more change improvements?
5. Given the staff have worked diligently to use the newly implemented EHR, is this an appropriate time to ask for more documentation compliance?
6. What is the Triple Aim in health care? To meet the Triple Aim, how can the organization leaders improve documentation to lower costs? What would you propose to solve the issue? Can this issue be resolved in three months? Is your solution a sustainable automatic process?
7. How can the leaders connect with their staff and emphasize relationships over tasks, yet recapture lost revenues?
8. What method would you use to improve leadership, teamwork, and clinical best practices to address the problem?
9. What type of communication or support needs to happen to support the solution?

Role-Based Questions

CEO Role:

1. Given that the employees have worked long hours through a newly implemented EHR, is this an appropriate time to ask for more?
2. As a CEO, what would be a leadership approach to this situation?
3. What are the elements of a high-reliability organization?

Cardiology Director Role:

1. What communication styles can the cardiology role use to collaborate with the staff, the INL, and the CEO?
2. What leadership approach would you use?
3. What change theory or model would you use?
4. Will the re-design support an automated, sustainable process?

Informatics Nurse Lead Role:

1. What are the elements of a workflow analysis?
2. What is Lean methodology, Lean Six Sigma, PDSA (Plan, Do, Study, Act)?
3. How can change management models be used to support Lean methodologies?
4. How can you use change management models to support the clinical staff to prepare for more change?
5. Would the CUSP method (comprehensive unit-based safety program) from the Agency for Healthcare Research and Quality (AHRQ) help to incorporate a sustainable Lean methodology solution? Is this an iterative approach to improve the unit's teamwork? Is there another approach or solution to this issue?
6. Will champions be needed to implement this solution? If so, where would they be required during the planning and execution phases?

Additional Resources

Agency for Healthcare Research and Quality (AHRQ). (2019, August 20). *The CUSP method.* https://www.ahrq.gov/hai/cusp/index.html

Buchbinder, S. B., Shanks, N. H., & Kite, B. J. (2021). *Introduction to health care management* (4th ed.). Jones & Bartlett Learning.

Guise, J.-M., Savitz, L. A., & Friedman, C. P. (2018). Mind the gap: putting evidence into practice in the era of learning health systems. *Journal of General Internal Medicine, 12,* 2237–2239. https://doi.org/10.1007s11606-018-4633-1

McBride, S., & Tietze, M. (2019). *Nursing informatics for the advanced practice nurse* (2nd ed.). Springer Publishing Company.

McGonigle, D., & Mastrian, K. G. (2018). *Nursing informatics and the foundation of knowledge* (4th ed.). Jones & Bartlett Learning.

Melnyk, B. M., & Fineout-Overholt, E. (2019). *Evidence-based practice in nursing and health care* (4th ed.). Wolters Kluwer.

Melnyk, B. M., & Raderstorf, T. (2021). *Evidence-based leadership, innovation, and entrepreneurship in nursing and healthcare.* Springer Publishing Company.

Weberg, D., & Davidson, S. (2021). *Leadership for evidence-based innovation in nursing and health professions* (2nd ed.). Jones & Bartlett Learning.

White, K. M., Dudley-Brown, S., & Terhaar, M. F. (2016). *Translation of evidence into nursing and health care* (2nd ed.). Springer Publishing Company.

CASE 53

Helping Patients Keep the Lights On: Issues in Bariatric Care, Part I

Jane H. Schulze

As the clinic manager of six outpatient facilities, you frequently conduct audits to examine both patient satisfaction and clinic finance continuity. Of the six sites, one is a clinic that specializes in bariatric care. The majority of care provided is not deemed medically necessary, which requires out-of-pocket payments from patients. Additionally, patients seen in this ambulatory department are often referred by providers to advanced imaging and require surgical procedures for treatment. Depending on the patient's insurance coverage, or lack thereof, and diagnosis code attached to the visit, these medical costs must be billed as self-pay (i.e., the patient is responsible for full payment). The clinic does not currently require pre-service payment.

During the most recent audit, you discovered that treating uninsured and underinsured patients is becoming a financial liability. Upon investigation, you found the clinicians have neither been refusing to deny or limit treatment to any patients due to finances, nor been requiring set payments. As a previously practicing medical doctor, you understand the clinicians' desire to focus on patients, but as a manager responsible for the success of this clinic, you must ensure the clinic reaches a financial solution for stability. Based on the audit, payments are going to need to be collected from patients for clinic visits, pre-surgical services, and imaging completed within the clinic. To accomplish this, a policy must be developed for both the clinic staff and patients while still allowing for patient care and patient satisfaction to be maintained.

You have been tasked to identify or create a prior authorization approval policy and billing process for the uninsured to utilize in the clinic that will meet clinic financial needs as well as patient care goals. This process must incorporate clear financial guidelines for uninsured and underinsured patients who do not meet medical necessity based on payors' requirements. This policy must also follow the Health Insurance Portability and Accountability Act (HIPAA) guidelines, offer options for patients to continue treatment with no delays, and meet the state and or federal guidelines for medical necessity. Secondarily, based on a previous audit, it has been discovered that patients with active medical coverage require prior authorization from their payor to be seen in the bariatric clinic regardless of the reason for their visit. However, if it proves the patient has insufficient ability to cover medical care, it becomes the clinic's responsibility to authorize treatment and collect payments, which is not currently being done.

The audit also showed some very impressive organizational strengths outside of the financial strain, which explain why the clinic is so successful when it comes to patient care and patient satisfaction. Some of the strengths that have been mentioned are a very cohesive atmosphere where providers feel supported to do what is best for patients. This clinic also has some of the highest Press Ganey scores within the organization for high-quality patient-provider relationships. There have been requests from providers to expand the clinic to a second location. However, based on the audit, without clear next steps on an internal prior authorization process, this will not be possible.

Opinions differ on next steps to a financial solution. Your immediate superior, who is the director of utilization review and care management, sees an opportunity to limit patients without coverage, while you see an opportunity for growth with a new financial plan to help all patients who need elective bariatric care. Without a long-term solution, the current suggestion is to limit self-pay patients who are uninsured and underinsured to meet the growth goals. You want to make sure everyone is working to find a solution that will incorporate clinic expansion, focus on exceptional patient care, and also encourage a lasting internal prior authorization process despite patient billing status.

Discussion Questions

1. What do you think should be considered as a top priority for identifying a solution to this situation? Should the team focus on patient satisfaction or financial stability?
2. Do you think it is possible to achieve the clinic's financial goals while still making sure the clinic is accessible to all patients?
3. How do you think the clinic can utilize a prior authorization structure similar to a commercial payor for financial stability?
4. Given the desire for growth of the specialty, what would the clinic's next steps be to make this a reality?
5. How does the clinic make it clear to patients who have been given a commercial payor authorization, but have insufficient coverage for treatment, that they will be required to make out-of-pocket payments?
6. Is there a way for the clinic manager to approach this situation that will make both the providers and the supervisors feel comfortable with next steps?

Additional Resources

Buchbinder, S. B., Shanks, N. H., & Kite, B. J. (2021). *Introduction to health care management* (4th ed.). Jones & Bartlett Learning.

Gold, J. (2009). *The 'underinsurance' problem explained*. Kaiser Health Newtork. https://khn.org /news/underinsured-explainer/

Healthcare.gov. (n.d.). *Out-of-pocket costs*. https://www.healthcare.gov/glossary/out-of-pocket-costs/

CASE 54

Ethical Medical Necessity Billing Practices: Issues in Bariatric Care, Part II

Jane H. Schulze

In addition to needed front-end policy updates identified in Part I of this case, the clinic has also identified a billing process concern with potential ethical implications. Unlike the front-end collections, which are causing significant financial strain, the billing process concern is impacting their patient satisfaction once patients have completed treatments or are no longer covered by a commercial payor.

The majority of bariatric care within this clinic is billed out-of-pocket. However, because of the diagnostic aspects of treatment, patients cannot always use a commercial payor for the initial visit and, at times, some additional treatments. It is ultimately up to the commercial payor to decide on claim processing and repayment based on medical necessity and diagnosis after patient treatment. As the billing manager, you have had a number of patient calls escalated to you of late. Upon further review, it seems these claims are being denied for non-covered services. The majority of these denials are because the treatment is not deemed medically necessary and is thus not eligible for reimbursement. Additionally, after further internal investigation, it seems the front office staff have told patients at the time of scheduling their care will be covered as a diagnostic billing code and paid through insurance. As this is not always the case throughout the course of treatment, the clinic manager has been receiving a number of negative reviews. Patient satisfaction scores have declined in relation to quality of communication outside of medical care.

In recent phone calls to the billing team, patients have also been reporting that providers are offering inaccurate information regarding their treatment being medically necessary and covered by commercial payors. This is a concerning, and potentially unethical, claim to make to a patient as their treatment may eventually become an out-of-pocket expense depending on services rendered. For example, patients may be referred to this facility for treatment of morbid obesity and request surgery. If the payor deems diet and exercise should be the first course of treatment, additional treatments could be deemed not medically necessary and denied payment by the payor. Similarly, if the patient agrees to try diet and exercise and then moves to a medically necessary surgery, anything after that surgery could be deemed no longer medically necessary and denied payment by the payor.

Once commercial coverage has been exhausted, or denied, patients have been calling the billing office to dispute claims and explanation of benefit documents received from their payors. Based on information received from the front office at the time of scheduling, or at times from providers, patients have been attempting to dispute claims denied for non-payment. These disputes are ongoing, despite the medical data and provider entry during patient care. In addition, many patients have requested that their visits be re-coded and resubmitted for claim processing to their payor based on what they deem to be medically necessary care. While claims staff continue to seek assistance from providers, often these claims are deemed to be correct, and a patient's claim is ultimately denied even if resubmitted. After consistent provider review, the clinic has found it is getting close to breaching contracts with payors in allowing providers to re-code visits. For this reason, strict guidelines have been put in place unless a genuine medical code entry error was made. Changes must be cleared with the billing team prior to being re-coded.

After setting these strict re-coding rules and receiving consistent complaints from staff and patients, the clinic manager has agreed to review disputed claims with providers. The goal is not to re-code claims but to provide education to clinical staff on medical necessity and how to discuss covered care versus potentially not medically necessary services with patients. You have also been asked to provide standard education and scripting for both front-end staff and clinical staff when discussing commercial coverage with patients. You are not sure where to start for these requests or who to work with to meet the requests of clinical staff, ancillary staff, billing staff, and patients. Moving forward, you want to make sure patients feel like both the front-end staff and clinical staff are knowledgeable and accurate when describing potential out-of-pocket costs to patients. You also must ensure that clinic providers are presenting ethical practices when it comes to billing and coding for patient care. Where do you to start?

Discussion Questions

1. One suggestion from upper management was to prohibit providers from discussing billing with patients. Do you think this will improve patient satisfaction surrounding billing?
2. Do you think it is truly unethical for a provider to guarantee payment from a commercial coverage for treatment?
3. When discussing provider education, what is the best way to educate providers on the true severity of this problem?
4. When identifying a script or policy for ancillary staff, what needs to be considered for continued patient satisfaction when it comes to billing?
5. Is there a way that the clinic could utilize aspects of the electronic health record or patient information to explain diagnostic services versus elective?

Additional Resources

Buchbinder, S. B., Shanks, N. H., & Kite, B. J. (2021). *Introduction to health care management* (4th ed.). Jones & Bartlett Learning.

Gold, J. (2009). *The 'underinsurance' problem explained.* Kaiser Health Network. https://khn.org/news/underinsured-explainer/

Healthcare.gov. (n.d.). *Out-of-pocket costs.* https://www.healthcare.gov/glossary/out-of-pocket-costs/

CASE 55

Risks in Detecting Fraudulent Financial Statements

Charisse F. Wernecke

You are a manager for an independent auditing firm. Your client, Reclamation and Renewal, Inc. (R&R), is a company that performs in- and outpatient rehabilitation services. Started in 2009 by entrepreneur Johnny Cleaver, the company grew from one location to 235 throughout the continental United States. Four years ago, the company became publicly traded on the New York Stock Exchange (NYSE). At that time, Johnny recruited an impressive group of highly visible board members: General Lewis Jefferson, former head of Homeland Security; Martha Bluford, retail businessperson and television personality; Senator Jeffery Morrill of Kentucky; Pulitzer-prize winning author Michelle Preston; and Olympic athlete and tennis star, Scott Stevens.

As a leader, Johnny is a firm believer in written goals and objectives with a keen emphasis on surpassing Wall Street annual growth expectations, which R&R has surpassed 12 percent a year since the company went public. Competition in this industry has become fierce, as large hospital systems build new modern centers for rehabilitation services. An avid skydiver and skier, Johnny creates large-scale events for his top executives and clients, featuring his favorite sports.

Recently, there has been turnover in the finance accounting office, which you were told is due to personal family issues. The senior auditor on this engagement was recently recruited to be the company's vice president for finance. You've been informed the controller of this company works evenings and weekends and never takes a vacation.

You are conducting a risk analysis in preparation for the annual audit. The interim (six-month financial statements) compared to the past three years are provided here. Your job is to review the statement and to identify potential areas that could materially misstate the financial statements (See **Figure 55.1**).

Balance Sheet	Jun. 30, 2020	Dec. 31, 2019	Dec. 31, 2018	Dec. 31, 2017
Assets				
Current Assets				
Cash and cash equivalents	$ 170,789,992	$ 262,753,834	$ 236,478,451	$ 243,572,804
Short term investments	$ 34,554,178	$ 86,385,445	$ 82,930,027	$ 84,588,628
Patient accounts receivable	$ 334,284,294	$ 208,927,684	$ 197,499,254	$ 158,249,478
Allowance for Uncollectible Accounts	$ 9,000,000	$ 25,080,000	$ 22,000,000	$ 20,000,000
Supplies Inventory	$ 20,265,985	$ 20,892,768	$ 17,758,853	$ 15,095,025
Other current assets	$ 16,338,145	$ 19,221,347	$ 15,377,078	$ 13,070,516
Current assets	$ 567,232,594	$ 573,101,078	$ 528,043,663	$ 494,576,451
Property, plant, and equipment	$ 876,082,289	$ 871,185,651	$ 805,455,882	$ 733,194,581
Accumulated depreciation	$ 196,194,464	$ 184,438,021	$ 127,871,031	$ 76,960,740
Fixed assets, net	$ 679,887,825	$ 686,747,630	$ 677,584,851	$ 656,233,841
Other assets	$ 17,710,985	$ 15,327,873	$ 9,466,496	$ 4,667,678
Total Assets	$ 1,264,831,404	$ 1,275,176,581	$ 1,215,095,010	$ 1,155,477,970
Liabilities and Equity				
Current Liabilities				
Accounts payable	$ 240,702,453	$ 171,930,323	$ 143,254,007	$ 114,603,206
Accrued expenses	$ 206,253,031	$ 185,965,162	$ 160,858,744	$ 136,729,932
Current portion long-term debt	$ 80,555,813	$ 71,930,323	$ 60,404,022	$ 50,777,645
Total current liabilities	$ 527,511,297	$ 429,825,809	$ 364,516,773	$ 302,110,783
Pension liability	$ 102,554,728	$ 157,776,505	$ 134,110,029	$ 113,993,525
Long-term debt	$ 195,010,570	$ 275,566,383	$ 346,080,706	$ 406,484,728
Total Liabilities	$ 825,076,595	$ 863,168,697	$ 844,707,508	$ 822,589,036
Equity				
Common stock $10 par value	$ 20,000,000	$ 20,000,000	$ 20,000,000	$ 20,000,000
Additional paid-in capital	$ 52,134,037	$ 52,134,037	$ 52,134,037	$ 52,134,037
Retained earnings	$ 367,620,772	$ 339,873,848	$ 298,253,465	$ 260,754,897
Total equity	$ 439,754,809	$ 412,007,885	$ 370,387,502	$ 332,888,934
Total Liabilities and Equity	$ 1,264,831,404	$ 1,275,176,582	$ 1,215,095,010	$ 1,155,477,970
Reclamation and Renewal, Inc.				
Statement of Retained Earnings				
Beginning balance	$ 339,873,849	$ 298,253,465	$ 260,754,897	$ 224,010,644
Net income	$ 27,746,923	$ 55,493,846	$ 49,998,090	$ 48,992,338
Dividends paid		$ 13,873,462	$ 12,499,522	$ 12,248,084
Ending Balance	$ 367,620,772	$ 339,873,849	$ 298,253,465	$ 260,754,897

Balance Sheet	Jun. 30, 2020	Dec. 31, 2019	Dec. 31, 2018	Dec. 31, 2017
Reclamation and Renewal, Inc.				
Income Statement	2020	2019	2018	2017
Operating Revenues				
Inpatient revenue	$ 131,791,738	$ 387,622,758	$ 337,231,799	$ 293,391,666
Outpatient revenue	$ 57,140,662	$ 178,564,569	$ 151,779,884	$ 129,012,901
Total patient revenue	$ 188,932,400	$ 566,187,327	$ 489,011,683	$ 422,404,567
Contractual allowance	$ 34,892,951	$ 150,285,793	$ 127,742,924	$ 106,026,627
Net Patient Revenues	$ 154,039,449	$ 415,901,534	$ 361,268,759	$ 316,377,940
Operating Expenses				
Salaries and benefits	$ 43,690,822	$ 109,227,054	$ 92,842,996	$ 77,988,117
Professional services	$ 18,616,241	$ 53,189,260	$ 44,678,978	$ 37,083,552
Supplies	$ 21,670,847	$ 72,236,155	$ 63,784,525	$ 54,854,691
Depreciation	$ 11,756,443	$ 59,544,200	$ 56,566,990	$ 50,910,291
Bad debt expense	$ 5,699,901	$ 28,499,503	$ 22,799,602	$ 18,239,682
Other	$ 14,861,911	$ 37,154,777	$ 31,547,775	$ 25,238,220
Total operating expenses	$ 165,675,723	$ 331,351,446	$ 289,421,264	$ 246,074,871
Operating income	$ 42,275,044	$ 84,550,088	$ 71,847,495	$ 70,303,069
Interest expense	$ 246,613	$ 493,226	$ 443,903	$ 332,928
Income from investments	$ 4,945	$ 24,723	$ 22,251	$ 18,913
Income before taxes	$ 42,040,793	$ 84,081,585	$ 71,425,842	$ 69,989,054
Income tax expense	$ 14,293,869	$ 28,587,739	$ 21,427,753	$ 20,996,716
Net Income (Loss)	$ 27,746,923	$ 55,493,846	$ 49,998,090	$ 48,992,338

Figure 55.1 Reclamation and Renewal, Inc., Financial Data

Discussion Questions

1. Identify all qualitative potential issues for the current year audit.
2. Identify the types of accounts and circumstances that raise concern for misstatement of financial statements.
3. Which financial statement do most users review? Why is the balance sheet critical for effective financial statement analysis?
4. Review the three years of financial statements and the interim statements. Perform ratio and other analysis to identify accounts and balances that should be examined during the course of the year-end substantive audit work.
5. Compare and contrast the net income amounts to cash increases or decreases. Does this make sense? What does a disparity between income and cash flows suggest?

Additional Resources

Buchbinder, S. B., Shanks, N. H., & Kite, B. J. (2021). *Introduction to health care management* (4th ed.). Jones & Bartlett Learning.

McCann, D. (2017, March 27). *Two CFOs tell a tale of fraud at HealthSouth.* https://www.cfo.com/fraud/2017/03/two-cfos-tell-tale-fraud-healthsouth/

Solomon, D., Carrns, A., & Terhune, C. (2003, March 20). SEC alleges HealthSouth faked $1.4 billion in profits. *Wall Street Journal.* https://www.wsj.com/articles/SB1048061083485665080

PART 5

Health Care Professtionals/Human Resources

CASE 56

Give Us Scope!

Jenn Block

You are a clinical operations leader overseeing acquired physician practices. Due to reimbursement changes, acquisitions of physician practices topped 80,000 in 2018 (Rosenberg, 2018). It is critical to establish a shared understanding of important areas that can create risk for the organizations involved, including such items as the scope of practice for medical assistants (MAs). Having this type of discussion prior to an acquisition is important because of the potential impact it could have on work distribution and organizational policies after acquisitions. As the formation of unit-based teams and role optimization have become commonplace, this has become even more essential. As a clinical operations leader, you have individual cultures to address within these newly acquired physician practices. However, you have some physicians in the practices who have maintained autonomy for decades who are resistant to limiting, or even expanding, the scope of practice for MAs.

Leadership has asked for your help with this challenge. You must instill both a sense of corporate culture and duty to the greater good, while maintaining physician autonomy. To ensure a smooth acquisition, your bosses have asked you to have discussions in advance with all the physicians regarding expectations. This includes a conversation concerning not only corporate culture but also physician autonomy and expectations to conform to corporate policies and standards.

Finding a scope of practice for MAs has been elusive—like chasing a rainbow, it is always out of reach. However, some states like California explicitly outline what is and isn't acceptable to delegate to an MA. Most states, however, subscribe to the notion that it is the physician's responsibility to determine what they feel comfortable delegating, and provide only guidelines preventing them from doing anything that would be considered "practice of medicine" or any task that requires the exercise of medical judgment. There are two foreseeable issues with this vague guideline. First, if you were to ask 10 different people to define what that means, you would likely get at least a handful of answers. Secondly, because private practices are acquired with their own unique cultures and practices, it is safe to assume that they also have different beliefs when it comes to what they delegate to their MAs.

One reason this is important to leadership is the shift in risk from the individual practice to the organization as a whole, not to mention the matter of patient safety. One benefit of joining a larger organization is the economies of scale that come from shared resources. Sharing resources can include sharing clinical staff to respond to the need for coverage of increasing or decreasing patient volumes. Moving staff means changing cultures from one independent office to another. Because offices will often have different workflows, this opens the possibility for safety occurrences and a variation in practices such as the scope of practice for MAs if a corporate policy has not been established. One example of potential variation is medication administration. In one practice, a physician who orders a medication will verify that it is not on the patient's allergy list. In another, the physician might expect the MA to do this verification. In the absence of established protocols, a traveling MA could create a potential sentinel event by administering the medication without verifying the patient is not allergic to it.

With all these things in mind, how should you proceed?

Discussion Questions

1. What are the current applicable laws and regulations within the U.S. as they pertain to scope of practice for Medical Assistants?
2. What is the importance of identifying clear roles for clinical support staff, especially when it comes to safety?
3. How can organizations who have acquired physician practices engage providers to work toward common definitions such as an acceptable scope of practice for medical assistants?
4. What are some barriers that may occur during this process, and what would be the plan to overcome them?

Additional Resources

American Association of Medical Assistants. (2020). *State scope of practice laws*. https://www.aama
    -ntl.org/employers/state-scope-of-practice-laws#COscope
Becker's Hospital Review. (2012, March 1). 5 considerations for successful physician acquisitions.
    https://www.beckershospitalreview.com/hospital-physician-relationships/5-considerations-for
    -successful-physician-acquisitions.html
Medical Board of California. (2020). *Frequently asked questions: Medical assistants*. https://www.mbc
    .ca.gov/Licensees/Physicians_and_Surgeons/Medical_Assistants/Medical_Assistants_FAQ.aspx
Rosenberg, J. (2018, March 21). Hospital acquisition of independent physician practices
    continues to increase. *American Journal of Managed Care*. https://www.ajmc.com/view
    /hospital-acquisition-of-independent-physician-practices-continues-to-increase

CASE 57

Is Ignorance an Excuse?

Jenn Block

River recently started working at a community health clinic as the Director of Quality. River was hired because of a vast amount of experience in the field. Considered an expert, River continued to serve as faculty in the graduate health care administration program at the local university. River was a disabled veteran and had also done a lot of work bringing awareness to hidden disabilities, particularly in veterans, due a diagnosis of post-traumatic stress disorder (PTSD) and Systemic Lupus Erythematosus (SLE). When River started with the organization, the protected class of disabled veteran was disclosed, but River did not ask for any accommodations. This organization had been known for and took pride in hiring veterans into their workforce. Shortly after starting, River's boss, Mx. Ohno started as the new Executive Director, responsible for all aspects of the business. Mx. Ohno had previously been a consultant and therefore had experience working in teams but had never directly managed employees. During the first year, the team worked well despite their offices being spread across multiple buildings across the city. However, going into the second year, the team was finally able to work in the same location. This change brought new challenges.

Almost immediately after the transition in August, Mx. Ohno accidentally startled River by quietly coming up behind River while working. The offices had positioned all desks with the monitor along the side wall. This arrangement required employees working at their computers to have their backs to the open door. River laughed the interaction off the first time but decided to notify the facilities staff with a request to reconfigure the office layout in hopes of mitigating any future occurrences. Facilities stated the offices were to be kept the same as all of the others unless a doctor's note was produced. One of the facilities employees was a veteran, too and offered to move the monitors closer to the front of the desk to provide more warning of an approaching visitor. Thinking this would resolve the situation, River was surprised when Mx. Ohno made it a point to drop in without warning again. At this point, River requested that the behavior cease as it was "triggering PTSD."

Over the next four weeks, River became withdrawn and tried to work outside of the office to avoid Mx. Ohno. River was experiencing increased anxiety when in the office and didn't want any more negative encounters. It was September, and River was scheduled for a two-week vacation in the middle of November that would hopefully reset the current progression of anxiety. However, the anxiety continued to escalate, and River was forced to seek treatment through the mental health department at the Veteran's Affairs (VA) Medical Center.

By the end of September, Mx. Ohno had purposely startled River again and laughed about how funny it was. Laughing, Mx. Ohno added that this would "eventually desensitize the [PTSD]." This further escalated River's anxiety, which in turn exacerbated the SLE. Shortly after this, River consulted another Marine Corps veteran in the office about a hypothetical situation. River asked for input about any potential consequences for sharing the experiences with human resources. The Marine Corps veteran urged River not to do it for fear of being "labeled" by the organization. This feedback confirmed River's existing concerns.

In early October, Mx. Ohno scheduled their first ever one-on-one meeting with River, at which time Mx. Ohno asked if they were "ok." Unsure of what was really being asked and afraid to confront the issue, River responded they were and continued to cover the agenda. After walking out of the office, and after considering the conversation, River decided it was unfair not to provide honest feedback to Mx. Ohno. River returned to Mx. Ohno's office and explained that typically a situation like this would just "roll off the back," citing "thick skin," but shared that Mx. Ohno's actions over the past two months had been a cause of great anxiety. Mx. Ohno's behaviors had resulted in River trying to minimize their already rare interactions. Mx. Ohno seemed quite taken aback and provided what River perceived to be an empty apology. The conversation was ended abruptly. River resumed work and reflected on a recent session with a new psychiatrist who offered that it was not River's fault that Mx. Ohno was ignorant.

Time flew by the next month, and River went on the highly anticipated overseas vacation, returning before Thanksgiving. The day after returning to work, Mx. Ohno scheduled their second one-on-one meeting and updated River on what had occurred while out of the office. At the end of the meeting, Mx. Ohno's voice quieted and she opened a folder and presented a Performance Improvement Plan (PIP). River was horrified. This had never happened during River's entire career. River asked for specific feedback because the paperwork was vague. Mx. Ohno cited feedback received from "other" colleagues while River was on vacation. River listened and decided to go home and think about the action plan prior to responding. The next day River scheduled time with Mx. Ohno again, asking for clarification on why there had not been any verbal warnings prior to the PIP. Mx. Ohno stated that it was an uncomfortable thing to do, and that they didn't have that type of working relationship with one another and offered hope it could change in the future.

Although River decided to do the assigned leadership courses as a method of self-improvement, River also scheduled time to meet with the Director of Human Resources (HR). During that meeting, River shared concerns, confidentially, that the PIP was in retaliation for bringing forth the issues of Mx. Ohno's behaviors, and further explained that while there had not been any recent issues with PTSD, it felt very personal and she didn't want to be "that veteran" who complained about such things. The HR Director seemed surprised to hear this information. The director assured River that PIPs were designed for employees the organization had "confidence" in, to allow them to correct any adverse behaviors, and it was separate from the corrective action process. River left the meeting feeling very discouraged about being able to turn the situation around.

Discussion Questions

1. What organizational issues can you identify?
2. What potential legal risk is there to Mx. Ohno's actions?
3. Should it be left to the employee, River, to take action in this situation?
4. What steps would you suggest to arrive at some resolution in this situation?
5. Did you make any assumptions while reading this case regarding race, ethnicity, gender or gender identity, sexual orientation, socioeconomic status, culture, or other protected class? Were these assumptions focused at the individual/staff level, clinical/program level, or organizational/ administrative level? How do these assumptions affect cultural awareness, cultural knowledge, behaviors, and/or skill development?

Additional Resources

Center for Substance Abuse Treatment. (2014). *Improving cultural competence.* Substance Abuse and Mental Health Services Administration. https://www.ncbi.nlm.nih.gov/books/NBK248428/

Christensen, B. (2019, November 11). 5 easy ways to be more veteran-friendly in the workplace. *Inc.* https://www.inc.com/ben-christensen/5-easy-ways-to-be-more-veteran-friendly-in-workplace .html

Eurich, T. (2018). Working with people who aren't self-aware. *Harvard Business Review.* https://hbr .org/2018/10/working-with-people-who-arent-self-aware

CASE 58

To Standardize or Not to Standardize?

Jenn Block

Apple is the Vice President of Quality for the ambulatory division of a not-for-profit hospital-based health care system outside of Denver, Colorado. The organization has acquired over 250 primary care practices over the last three years, and the practices have continued operating under their original policies and procedures, as well as their unique independent cultures. As the practices have been acquired, there has been a standardized process to assess financials, patient volumes, and other metrics. However, there has been no formal process to onboard the new providers or guidance provided on set expectations, policies, or procedures. The one area of conformity has been the transition to a single electronic medical record (EMR), which each practice is mandated to implement within a year after being acquired. Included in this process is the movement of pertinent patient medical records into the new EMR. While the new practices have transitioned to the same EMR, different workflows are being used. Each practice is determining its own preferences and shortcuts, as well as the roles that each of the support staff provide to their physicians.

Due to staffing shortages across the system, Apple has been looking at implementing a shared pool of medical assistants (MAs). This arrangement would provide a shared pool of staff for practices to fill vacancies as they occur or when patient volumes fluctuate. It is determined that a shared collection of policies and procedures is needed, and specific workflows must be standardized to have consistency as staff move around to the various practices. Apple has already been forced to conduct a root cause analysis (RCA) on a medication error because a medical assistant became confused with the differences in workflows between two practices. Luckily, the patient was safe, but the incident highlighted the risks of inconsistency. Apple is not eager to have another incident of this nature. As such, it has been identified that not only does the medication administration process need standardization, but others such as MA scope of practice, medication reconciliation, documentation guidelines, common protocols to delegate to MAs, and verbal orders, among others, do as well.

Apple approaches the Chief Medical Officer (CMO) and shares a plan to streamline the practices so the MA pool can be created. Apple cites the various efficiencies that would be gained, in addition to the improved patient safety, quality outcomes, and patient satisfaction. The CMO understands the need to leverage resources but shares concern with what is perceived as infringement on the autonomy of the physicians and their individual practices. Even though Apple has made a great business case, the CMO is not willing to make this transition mandatory. The CMO suggests that Apple work with the providers and convince them to agree to it voluntarily. Frustrated and overwhelmed by the sheer number of providers in 250 practices, as well as the CMO's lack of support, Apple is unsure of next steps and has little hope that the physicians will voluntarily change their practices.

Discussion Questions

1. What are the benefits of standardizing some workflows, policies, and procedures for multi-practice medical groups?
2. What are the major risks of having clinical support staff frequently transitioning to various clinics with different workflows, policies, and procedures?
3. What are some of the barriers to creating standardization among so many different practices, especially after an acquisition is completed?
4. What recommendations would you make as to next steps so that Apple has a high chance of success in gaining physician buy-in to creating the standardization?
5. Should Apple be updating her resume and looking for another job?

Additional Resources

Curoe, A., Kralewski, J., & Kaissi, A. (2003). Assessing the cultures of medical group practices. *Journal of the American Board of Family Practice, 16*(5), 394–398. https://pdfs.semanticscholar.org/fcd6/c16456026e72534d7c58db8755f0b91f8f6f.pdf

Hansom, R. (2018, February 15). Variation in healthcare delivery: The need for standardization. *Becker's Hospital Review.* https://www.beckershospitalreview.com/healthcare-information-technology/variation-in-healthcare-delivery-the-need-for-standardization.html

Intermountain Healthcare. (2014, January 13). *Medical assistant-float pool* [Video]. YouTube. https://youtu.be/M9nlXVEdtk8

Monica, K. (2017, December 5). Standardization biggest barrier to healthcare interoperability. *EHR Intelligence.* https://ehrintelligence.com/news/standardization-biggest-barrier-to-healthcare-interoperability

SRH Is the Place to Be!

Susan Casciani

Nunya loved the holiday season. Something in the air just made everything more exciting, and he could not understand why his wife, Molly, didn't feel the same way. They were attending Some Random Hospital's (SRH's) annual holiday party, and Nunya thought his employer had done a great job once again of making sure all employees were having a wonderful time. There was a lively band playing, plenty of refreshments available, raffles, and door prizes. How could you not have fun? Nunya's boss, John, the Director of Nursing, was talking with a few of the custodial staff, probably telling them what a good job they had been doing. John was like that, always quick to give staff a compliment.

Nunya stopped to chat with Naomi and Mason, two of the emergency department (ED) registrars. Naomi was commiserating with Mason about the latest HCAHPS (Hospital Consumer Assessment of Healthcare Providers and Systems) survey. SRH had earned high marks for clinical care, but low marks for the percentage of patients who would recommend the hospital. Nunya realized that this was a trend for SRH, and he wondered how they could be doing such a great job and yet patients weren't recommending the hospital. He decided to go ask Armando, the hospital's Chief Executive Officer (CEO), who he could see was at the refreshment table.

As he walked toward Armando, he noticed Molly sitting at a table looking incredibly bored, and he knew that meant it was time to leave. Molly never seemed to have fun at these functions. Nunya figured he would stop by Armando's office tomorrow instead.

The next day, Nunya was caring for a patient who had a central line IV placed the day before. As Nunya checked the port, the patient asked what he was doing. Nunya told the patient he wanted to make sure she didn't get a CLABSI (central line-associated bloodstream infection) and then opened the window curtain. It was a beautiful day, the sun was shining, and Nunya thought the patient might like to see the sun coming through the trees. This made Nunya think about the patient in the next room who had just been admitted; he should probably open that patient's curtain as well. As Nunya left the room, he didn't notice that the sun was shining in the patient's eyes.

Nunya went to the next room and opened the window curtain, letting in the sunshine. The patient had been resting and was surrounded by family members. Nunya chatted with the patient's parents as he changed the dressing on the patient's wound and learned the patient's brother was coming into town today to visit. Just then, Nunya received a call on his pager and had to leave. It seemed there was always something else to attend to, and Nunya loved how every day was different in his job.

As Nunya headed to the nursing desk to respond to the page, he ran into Maria, the head of the IT (information technology) department. Maria had helped Nunya with a computer problem the other day and asked Nunya if he was still having problems. Nunya had not had any more issues, but told Maria that Naomi mentioned she was having some trouble with the ED registration system, and Maria said she would be happy to follow up with Naomi.

As it turned out, Naomi was indeed having trouble with the registration system and was becoming increasingly frustrated. As she struggled to input data, she reminded herself how the director of facilities made sure that every staff member had an ergonomically correct workstation. At home, she always had to sit on the couch to use her laptop and it always made her neck hurt; at least here she was always comfortable. Thinking about this, she made another attempt and managed to get the system to accept the data and then called for the next patient to come to registration. As the patient entered Naomi's cubicle, Naomi saw the patient's husband and two children were with her. They seemed quite concerned about the patient, so Naomi did not ask them to leave, even though there wasn't room for everyone in the cubicle. Naomi wondered if it wouldn't have made more sense for the husband to stay home with the children than for all of them to come here. After all, EDs are notorious for long wait times.

Later that day, Naomi ran into Nunya at the pickup volleyball game on the hospital's back field. Naomi loved these weekly games and never missed one. When Nunya saw Naomi, he asked if Maria was able to fix the registration system, and Naomi shared that Maria had been incredibly helpful, as always. Naomi then thought about the HCAHPS survey again and wondered aloud why patients don't recommend this hospital. Nunya said he was confused as well, since SRH had such excellent clinical outcomes, and then remembered he had meant to stop by Armando's office. As Nunya looked around at the mix of employees on the court, he couldn't help but wonder why everyone didn't love SRH as much as he did.

Discussion Questions

1. What is going on in this case?
2. Identify the main organizational problem in this case.
3. What are three factors contributing to this problem?
4. Provide three possible solutions to the problem you identified.
5. Provide your reflections and personal opinions as well as your recommendations for addressing this problem.

Additional Resources

Agency for Healthcare Research and Quality (AHRQ). (2020). *Section 5: Determining where to focus efforts to improve patient experience.* https://www.ahrq.gov/cahps/quality-improvement/improvement-guide/5-determining-focus/index.html

Davidson, K. W., Shaffer, J., Ye, S., Falzon, L., Emeruwa, I. O., Sundquist, K., Inneh, I. A., Mascitelli, S. L., Manzano, W. M., Vawdrey, D. K., & Ting, H. H. (2017). Interventions to improve hospital patient satisfaction with healthcare providers and systems: A systematic review. *BMJ Quality & Safety, 26*(7), 596–606. https://doi.org/10.1136/bmjqs-2015-004758

CASE 60

Simone's First Assignment

Laura M. Fricker

Recently, Simone joined the Human Resources (HR) department at ABC University Hospital. She was excited to begin her new position helping managers with workforce planning. Her first assignment seemed easy: the director of finance requested her help to evaluate an opening in his staff created by a recent termination. The finance department was plagued with near constant turnover, and the annual engagement survey taken by employees ranked the director among the lowest leaders in the organization. Further, the director often complained to the leaders of HR that his office was the busiest in the organization, but he would not hire a manager to assist in everyday tasks.

Simone pulled together the job description and the salary range, and called the director to discuss the details of the job. The director stated the open position was a challenging one, so he would only accept the most qualified applicants to review. He had no interest in "training up" anyone and expected the new person would "hit the ground running." The job description included language surrounding degree and experience requirements, with the best consideration candidate possessing a Master's degree plus five years' work history with similar responsibilities. Experience could be exchanged for education, with two years' experience substituting for every one year of education.

After working with the director, Simone met with her partnered recruiter to discuss options. "I don't think I can present just anyone to him. The candidate has to be really experienced!" The recruiter posted the position, and one week later presented three candidates to Simone. Simone reviewed the resumes, and felt that all of the applicants had a background that fit the job description.

Candidate A was relocating to the area after 11 years working in a similar position. She had her Associate's degree, interviewed well on the phone, and her experience was excellent.

Candidate B was an internal candidate, with a newly earned Master's degree with nearly five years, similar experience, and a long work history. He had worked his way up through the housekeeping service. He put himself through school and landed a position working in the president's office.

Candidate C presented with 20 years' experience in a similar role. She was looking for a new position after the department where she was working was dissolved during a hospital merger. She had excellent references, but did not have a degree.

Simone was pleased with her choices, and sent the resumes and contact information to the director. The director responded by email over the next week with "not a good fit" and "not sure would work out here" and "not a good match." Confused, she called the director to a meeting to further discuss the job description.

"What did I miss," she thought as she waited for the director to respond to her meeting invite. "I hope I haven't failed my first assignment!" Before he could respond to her invite, she decided to visit him in person, as the office was only a couple of buildings away, across the hospital campus.

After finding the building and office address, Simone nervously rode the elevator up to the fifth floor. As she stepped off the elevator, Simone approached the receptionist, a pretty blonde.

"Hello. My name is Simone, and I work in HR. I am wondering if the director would have a few minutes to speak to me regarding his job opening?"

Just as she finished her sentence, the director walked through the reception area surrounded by four of his account managers. All were dressed in white shirts and dark ties. Simone looked further into the office, and she spied several cubicles, all occupied by younger versions of the director. Every cubicle was occupied by clean cut, light skinned men who wore white shirts and dark ties.

Simone frowned. "This is going to be tougher assignment that I thought. There is a lot more going on here than a job opening!"

Discussion Questions

1. What major issue did Simone uncover during her visit to the finance department? Was it a different issue than she originally thought she would encounter?
2. Do you envision a quick fix for the issue identified?
3. What would be Simone's first steps to address the issue she identified? Would she need some help? From whom?
4. What are the disadvantages to a workplace experiencing these types of issue? What are the advantages that could be gained by fixing the identified issues?
5. Did Simone do enough homework before jumping in and creating the job description? Would it have made more sense for her to have investigated the finance department before proceeding with the job description?
6. Should the HR director have provided more guidance and direction to Simone at the outset?
7. Did you make any assumptions while reading this case regarding race, ethnicity, gender or gender identity, sexual orientation, socioeconomic status, culture, or other protected class? Were these assumptions focused at the individual/staff level, clinical/program level, or organizational/administrative level? How do these assumptions affect cultural awareness, cultural knowledge, behaviors, and/or skill development?

Additional Resources

American College of Healthcare Executives (ACHE). (2020). *Increasing and sustaining racial/ethnic diversity in healthcare leadership.* https://www.ache.org/about-ache/our-story/our-commitments/policy-statements/increasing-and-sustaining-racial-diversity-in-healthcare-management

Center for Substance Abuse Treatment. (2014). *Improving cultural competence.* Substance Abuse and Mental Health Services Administration. https://www.ncbi.nlm.nih.gov/books/NBK248428/

Wilbur, K., Snyder, C., Essary, A. C., Reddy, S., Will, K. K., & Saxon, M. (2020). Developing workforce diversity in the health professions: A social justice perspective. *Health Professions Education,* 6(2), 222–229.

CASE 61

Adding Mental Health Benefits?

Nancy H. Shanks

The ramifications of the coronavirus pandemic have been widespread for all types of organizations, from health care providers to tech companies to retailers. The changes in the way we work and where we work have resulted in positive and negative outcomes for both employers and employees. A specific area of concern, according to Kearney et al. (2021), is that "the coronavirus pandemic in the U.S. and the changes in the daily lives of Americans that ensued have taken a toll on people's mental health and created new barriers for those seeking mental health care" (para. 1). The stress created by these changes is real, making it difficult for employees to balance their work tasks and their homelife. This is particularly true if there are children in the home. And, if employees are stressed, this will have an impact on their motivation and performance, as well as on retention.

The problem with recruiting employees has intensified as many employers are having a difficult problem hiring new staff. The U.S. Bureau of Labor Statistics (2021) estimated that 10.9 million jobs were unfilled as of July 31, 2021. With so many unfilled jobs, there is an incentive for employers to work harder at retaining their existing workforce.

You are completing your health care management internship with the director of human resources at a large chain of for-profit nursing homes. The director has just been tasked by the board of trustees with assessing this situation in long-term care, coming up with a white paper that discusses the issues, and proposing a plan to address them. The director has decided this will be one area of your internship.

The chain has never provided many mental health benefits for its employees. The director thinks this should be a primary emphasis of the assessment. It has come to the attention of HR that many employees are stressed and seeking mental health care. You are asked to focus on this.

Discussion Questions

1. What are the specific problems raised by the coronavirus pandemic for employees in long-term care? Who has been mainly impacted by these problems? Is it women, low-wage earners, or others?

2. What are some strategies to retain employees in long-term care facilities?
3. What are some strategies to recruit new employees to long-term care?
4. What are the barriers to getting access to mental health care for many people?
5. Should mental health benefits be added as part of the chain's plan?
6. Which benefits make the most sense? Provide the rationale for your recommendations.

Additional Resources

Banerjee, K. (2021, January 9). *Why companies are adding mental health benefits for employees.* https://www.zenefits.com/workest/why-companies-are-adding-mental-health-benefits-for -their-employees/

Buchbinder, S. B., Shanks, N. H., & Kite, B. J. (2021). *Introduction to health care management* (4th ed.). Jones & Bartlett Learning.

Cahill, K. (2020, December 28). Why it's vital for employers to add mental health benefits. *Forbes.* https://www.forbes.com/sites/forbestechcouncil/2021/12/28/why-its-vital-for-employers-to -add-mental-health-benefits/?sh=1668826d78e7

Kearney, A., Hamel, L., & Brodie, M. (2021, April 14). *Mental health impact of the Covid-19 pandemic: An update.* https://www.kff.org/coronavirus-covid-19/poll-finding/mental-health -impact-of-the-covid-19-pandemic/

Preston, P. A. J. (2018). Addressing employee burnout through mitigation of workplace stressors. *Business Forum, 27*(1), 17–23.

U.S. Bureau of Labor Statistics. (2021). *Job openings and labor turnover – July 2021.* https://www.bls .gov/news.release/jolts.nr0.htm

Impacts of Requiring Staff Vaccination

Nancy H. Shanks

The coronavirus pandemic has had a crippling impact on all aspects of our lives and our country, to say nothing of the rest of the world. Just as many folks thought the country might be getting a handle on and controlling the coronavirus spread, the disease mutated, with new variants of COVID-19 being found everywhere. This has become a vexing public health problem for health care facilities.

For many years, health care providers have required their employees to get vaccinated for many different diseases. The Centers for Disease Control and Prevention (CDC) (2016) discussed the intent of this as an effort to protect health care workers, patients, family members, and other visitors from spreading "vaccine-preventable diseases" and included the following in its list of recommendations: hepatitis B; influenza; measles, mumps and rubella; chickenpox; tetanus, diphtheria, pertussis; and meningococcal disease. The specific types of health care workers the CDC recommended covering included "physicians, nurses, emergency medical personnel, dental professionals and students, medical and nursing students, laboratory technicians, pharmacists, hospital volunteers, and administrative staff" (CDC, 2016, para. 2). The issue of whether the COVID-19 vaccination should be added to this list will eventually be considered by the CDC, while many hospitals, health care systems, nursing homes, and other types of health care providers have already made this decision and are requiring their employees to get the COVID-19 vaccination.

Vaccine hesitancy has, however, become a major problem across the country and, despite urging by the CDC and from the federal government, there has been opposition to vaccine mandates. This resistance has been found among certain groups of people and in certain areas of the country. This has not only been an issue for the general public but also for health care workers. Vaccine hesitancy has become a particular concern in health care facilities, thereby confounding efforts on the part of these facilities to get their employees vaccinated. The rationale underlying vaccine hesitancy has been summarized by Eniola and Sykes (2021) and includes the following explanations:

- Safety and efficacy concerns;
- Preference for physiological immunity (becoming immune by getting infected);
- Distrust in government and health organizations; and,
- Autonomy and personal freedom.

Hesitancy in the general population and in health care workers is not uniform across areas of the country (e.g., rural versus urban areas, and the North versus the South, the Midwest versus either coast). Hesitancy has also varied across different racial, ethnic, and age groups.

Based on the significant evidence of the safety and efficacy of the COVID-19 vaccinations, many health care organizations established specific deadlines for their employees to get vaccinated (Spolar, 2021). As a result, health care workers who have not complied with these mandates "have been fired for noncompliance and some have resigned or quit" (Gooch, 2021, para. 1). In its review and compilation of data reported by many institutions, *Becker's Hospital Review* found that between June and October 12, 2021, 27 health care organizations had lost employees. Though the *Becker's* list is not comprehensive, these departures represent large numbers of employees for some providers. For example, 400 of the 33,000 employees (approximately 1%) quit the Henry Ford Health System in Detroit, and 1,400 (<2%) left by either resigning or being terminated at Northwell Health in New Hyde Park, NY (Gooch, 2021).

You are the vice president of human resources at a hospital that has lost several hundred employees recently. Your board of directors is concerned about the impact of this on quality and patient care. They need to understand what is going on and how the hospital is going to address the impact of this. The CEO has asked you to prepare a position paper for the board.

Discussion Questions

1. Explore the issue of vaccine hesitancy in more depth. What does the data show about vaccine hesitancy across the country?
2. Are the unvaccinated health care workers typical anti-vaxxers or is there something different about the COVID-19 vaccination resistance movement?
3. What are the reasons for their reluctance? What are the differences in reasoning in certain areas of the country, such as in the South and/or rural areas? What are the differences for various groups of people?
4. What are the potential risk management and legal liabilities of employees not being vaccinated?
5. Have some providers taken steps to prevent the exodus of staff? What are the strategies they have used in this regard?
6. How are hospitals and other providers that have seen a sizable exodus of employees dealing with this problem? What specific strategies are being used?
7. What are the human and monetary cost associated with these types of turnover?

Additional Resources

Altman, D. (2021, January 12). *The challenge of vaccine hesitancy in rural America.* https://www
.kff.org/coronavirus-covid-19/perspective/the-challenge-of-vaccine-hesitancy-in-rural-america/
Buchbinder, S. B., Shanks, N. H., & Kite, B. J. (2021). *Introduction to health care management*
(4th ed). Jones & Bartlett Learning.
Centers for Disease Control and Prevention (CDC). (2016, May 2). *Recommended vaccines for
healthcare workers.* https://www.cdc.gov/vaccines/adults/rec-vac/hcw.html

Centers for Disease Control and Prevention (CDC). (2021, June 25). *Keep variants at bay. Get vaccinated today.* https://www.cdc.gov/coronavirus/2019-ncov/covid-data/covidview/index .html

Eniola, K., & Sykes, J. (2021, April 27). Four reasons for COVID-19 vaccine hesitancy among health care workers, and ways to counter them. *FPR Journal blog.* https://www.aafp.org/journals /fpm/blogs/inpractice/entry/countering_vaccine_hesitancy.html

Gooch, K. (2021, October 12). Vaccination-related employee departures at 27 hospitals, health systems. *Becker's Hospital Review.* https://www.beckershospitalreview.com/workforce /vaccination-requirements-spur-employee-terminations-resignations-numbers-from-6-health -systems.html

Mayo Clinic. (2021, June 26). *Covid-19 vaccines: Get the facts.* https://www.mayoclinic.org /diseases-conditions/coronavirus/in-depth/coronavirus-vaccine/art-20484859

Ortaliza, J., Orgera, K., Amin, K., & Cox, C. (2021, October 13). *COVID-19 continues to be a leading cause of death in the U.S. in September 2021.* https://www.healthsystemtracker.org/brief /covid19-and-other-leading-causes-of-death-in-the-us/

Spolar, C. (2021, June 18). The hard realities of a 'no jab, no job' mandate for health care workers. *Kaiser Health News.* https://khn.org/news/article/covid-vaccination -employer-mandate-health-care-workers-no-jab-no-job

Vines, B. (2021, February 8). Addressing Covid-19 vaccine hesitancy among black Americans. *Consumer Reports.* https://www.consumerreports.org/vaccination/addressing-covid-19 -vaccine-hesitancy-among-black-americans/

Health Disparities/ Cultural Competence

Collection of RELP Data in Ambulatory Clinics

Jenn Block

You are the practice manager at the Sunnyside Family Practice Clinic in a major urban city with a diverse clinic population that includes patients who are insured and uninsured. You have eight providers, over 20 support staff, and manage over 18,000 patients annually, many of whom have chronic conditions. Since the implementation of the Affordable Care Act in 2010, more patients complete preventative screening, but there is still room for improvement. You know from the literature that the completion of preventative screening is affected by health disparities, and you are curious how your practice population is impacted (Mullins et al., 2005). Healthy People 2020 defines a health disparity as

> a particular type of health difference that is linked with social, economic, and/or environmental disadvantage. Health disparities adversely affect groups of people who have systematically experienced greater obstacles to health based on their racial or ethnic group; religion; socioeconomic status; gender; age; mental health; cognitive, sensory, or physical disability; sexual orientation or gender identity; geographic location; or other characteristics historically linked to discrimination or exclusion. (U.S. Department of Health and Human Services, 2008, para. 10)

Recently, you attended a conference that outlined health disparities in specific populations and have brought the information back to discuss with your practice in relation to increasing preventative screening rates.

Your providers understand there are specific medical conditions that have a higher prevalence within the populations you serve, as well as the strong association between race, ethnicity, and socioeconomic status with many health care outcomes (Perez-Stable & Rodriguez, 2020). However, the providers are currently overburdened by the sheer volume of patients and have expressed concerns about taking on a new project.

You decide to do some data analysis to determine where your opportunities are. You realize that while you can pull preventative screening gap information for some conditions and populations, you are unable to correlate that data with your specific practice population. To complicate matters, the discrete fields that capture race and ethnicity in your electronic medical record (EMR) software are not typically filled out when registering patients or upon checking them in for their appointments. Knowing this would require a change in process and education for the staff, you decide to meet with one of the providers who is especially interested in health outcomes within specific groups (Kindig & Stoddart, 2003).

This provider, Dr. Lake, shares your passion for wanting to address the specific needs of your patient population, but wants to see the data to support such an endeavor. You research community demographics in the areas served by your clinic and discover that the racial and ethnic breakdown are as follows:

- White, alone: 41%
- Hispanic or Latino: 24%
- White alone, not Hispanic or Latino: 17%
- Black African American alone: 28%
- Asian alone: 14%
- Two or more races: 4%
- American Indian or Alaska Native alone: 0.6%
- Other: 8%

Based on these demographics, you decide to make the case to begin consistently collecting race, ethnicity, and language preference (RELP) data as a first step to increasing preventative screening rates. Dr. Lake agrees that if the patient population mirrors the diversity of the community, specific preventative screening programs could be developed. The doctor agrees to be the provider champion if you are able to develop the business case to present to the staff.

Discussion Questions

1. What is the importance of collecting race, ethnicity, and language preference information (RELP)?
2. Which stakeholders would you need to include in the discussion of implementing this data collection?
3. What barriers might you experience and how might you overcome them?
4. What other data should you explore to build the business case?

Additional Resources

Artiga, S., Orgera, K., & Pham, O. (March 4, 2020). *Disparities in health and health care: Five key questions and answers.* Kaiser Family Foundation. https://www.kff.org/racial-equity-and-health-policy /issue-brief/disparities-in-health-and-health-care-five-key-questions-and-answers

Kindig, D., & Stoddart, G. (2003). What is population health? *American Journal of Public Health*, 93(3), 380–383.

Mullins, C. D., Blatt, L., Gbarayor, C. M., Yang, H. W. K., & Baquet, C. (2005). Health disparities: A barrier to high-quality care. *American Journal of Health-System Pharmacy*, 62(18), 1873–1882.

Perez-Stable, E. J., & Rodriguez, E. J. (2020). Social determinants and differences in mortality by race/ethnicity. *JAMA Network Open*, 3(2), e1921392. https://jamanetwork.com/journals /jamanetworkopen/fullarticle/2761540

U.S. Department of Health and Human Services. (2008). *The Secretary's Advisory Committee on National Health Promotion and Disease Prevention Objectives for 2020. Phase I report: recommendations for the framework and format of Healthy People. Section IV: Advisory Committee findings and recommendations.* https://www.healthypeople.gov/2020/about/foundation-health-measures/Disparities

CASE 64

Cultural Competence in Telehealth

Jenn Block

Moon is a practice manager at the White Plains Family Practice clinic just outside of Boston, Massachusetts. There are 10 providers in the clinic, including six physicians and four advanced practice nurses. The practice also has approximately 24 support staff, including four schedulers/front desk staff, two billers and coders/back-office staff, one registered nurse, two licensed practical nurses, and 15 medical assistants. The practice is extremely busy and provides care for almost 40,000 patients. Many are Medicare/Medicaid patients, although the commercial population has been growing as large new corporations have moved into the area. The demographics are varied and include the following:

- Male: 48%; Female: 52%
- 65 & older: 32.2%; and under 18: 21.7%
- White: 42.2%; White, not Hispanic or Latino: 18.1%
- Hispanic or Latino: 29.3%
- Black or African-American: 33.2%
- Asian or Pacific Islander: 2.4%
- Other: 1.1%
- Two or more races: 4.8%

The clinic transitioned approximately two years ago to a cloud-based electronic medical record (EMR). This new system allowed them to connect and share data with pharmacies, hospitals, and insurance companies (payors). It also has a robust patient portal module; however that and the telehealth module have yet to be implemented. Productivity after the EMR implementation suffered for more than six months, and the clinic lost two providers because of the additional stress it caused them. However, with the Medical Director's support, they finally succeeded in creating the integrated team-based care that they had dreamed of by leveraging the accessibility to the patient records by all members of the care team—simultaneously.

Now, the Medical Director approaches Moon and asks to explore a new telehealth program for patient visits as a way to leverage the technology within the practice. The Medical Director indicates that many of the large medical groups in the area have started using telehealth for these purposes. Moon has had no experience in implementing telehealth. In fact, there was a struggle transitioning to the EMR with other staff. Moon is concerned that implementing a new technology innovation project might cause the practice to lose further productivity, cause more turnover, and have a negative impact on patient experience. Specifically, Moon is concerned their patient population might not have the ability or desire to use telehealth services. The clinic staff are educated in cultural competence; however, this education has been more about race and ethnic health disparities as it pertains to chronic diseases—not technology gaps. Moon isn't aware of what, if anything, exists for the use of telehealth in the patient population and is not sure of where to start.

Discussion Questions

1. Did you make any assumptions while reading this case regarding race, ethnicity, gender or gender identity, sexual orientation, socioeconomic status, culture, or other protected class? Were these assumptions focused at the individual/staff level, clinical/program level, or organizational/administrative level? How do these assumptions affect cultural awareness, cultural knowledge, behaviors, and/or skill development?
2. What challenges might Moon encounter implementing telehealth within this population?
3. What specific interventions would you implement to reduce the potential of creating additional health disparities in this patient population?

Additional Resources

American Medical Association. (2020). *Telehealth implementation playbook.* https://www.ama-assn .org/system/files/2020-04/ama-telehealth-playbook.pdf

Bailey, M. (2020, May 12). *Culturally competent healthcare: Lessons from a safety-net hospital in the COVID era.* Boston Medical Center, Health City. https://www.bmc.org/healthcity /population-health/culturally-competent-healthcare-lessons-covid-19

California Telehealth Resource Center. (2020, November 30). *The CTRC telehealth program developer kit: A roadmap for successful telehealth program development.* https://telehealthresourcecenter.org /resources/toolkits/ctrc-telehealth-program-developer-kit/

Center for Substance Abuse Treatment. (2014). *Improving cultural competence.* Substance Abuse and Mental Health Services Administration. https://www.ncbi.nlm.nih.gov/books/NBK248428/

Hidden Disabilities and Patient Terminations Within Ambulatory Clinics

Jenn Block

Wind recently moved to Firestone, Colorado and decided to change primary care providers to one closer to home. Previously, Wind had been seen by another primary care provider (PCP), but the PCP retired around the same time Wind moved across town. Prior to the first scheduled appointment, Wind requested all medical records be sent to the new PCP; however, they did not arrive prior to the initial appointment with her new PCP, Dr. Rain. The practice was one of 50 primary care practices that had been acquired by a large hospital-based health care system in the area, and Dr. Rain was one of five providers within the practice.

Wind walked into the Bloomie's Internal Medicine clinic to check in for the appointment, accompanied by a small service dog. The front desk associate provided a clipboard and a pen, and asked Wind to take a seat in the waiting room and to fill out a packet of information. Wind was having problems filling out the paperwork and had set the clipboard down in frustration when the front desk associate noticed the service dog. The front desk associate made a noise to get its attention but was quickly met with Wind's raised voice.

"Don't call my dog! It is a service dog, and you cannot look at my dog!"

Confused, the front desk associate sat down and resumed work. There had only been a couple of service dogs in the clinic in the past, and no one had ever gotten angry for giving the dogs attention.

Dr. Rain's medical assistant (MA) came out to the waiting room and called Wind to the exam room. The assistant escorted Wind back, took vital signs, and asked for the completed paperwork. Wind handed over mostly blank pages, which confused the MA because Wind had not asked for assistance while filling out the paperwork. The MA reached to close the door while exiting the room; however, Wind immediately opened it and yelled that the door must stay open. The MA tried to explain that it needed to stay closed to maintain patient privacy and proceeded to shut the door again. Wind jumped up and grabbed the handle of the door to hold it open, which surprised the MA, who decided to quickly walk away in an effort to not attract any additional attention to the disruption. After having been briefed on Wind's behaviors since checking in for the appointment, Dr. Rain entered the room about 15 minutes later.

Like most providers, Dr. Rain was protective of staff members and was not pleased to hear what had been shared. After entering the room Dr. Rain sat down at the computer only to notice that Wind had positioned the chair right next to the open door. Dr. Rain began reviewing the almost empty paperwork Wind had provided. The lack of records from the previous practice was going to require the tedious task of taking a detailed patient history. This would put Dr. Rain further behind. Dr. Rain rushed through introductions and quickly moved on to asking the detailed patient history questions.

This abruptness overwhelmed Wind, who was slow to respond under normal circumstances. Wind tried to explain that the medical history was in the missing records and requested a prescription refill for a medication that was running low. When pressed further, Wind disclosed a past fall from a horse caused post-traumatic stress disorder (PTSD) but could not provide any specifics beyond that. Dr. Rain decided to end the visit, explaining that the medical records were necessary in order to provide care or refill prescriptions. However, Dr. Rain decided to place a consult for mental health and one for neurology.

Wind became very upset by this turn of events but decided to leave out of sheer exhaustion. The barrage of questions was mentally straining, and the information was difficult to process. Wind made, and ultimately cancelled, a follow-up appointment for a week later, hoping the records would be in by then, but still they had not arrived. In the first week after the initial appointment, Wind called the office nearly every day for updates on the medical records request and the requested consults. During the phone calls, Wind became increasingly irritated and yelled at the office staff when they were unable to provide updates or were unpleasant.

About a week after the initial visit, the practice manager notified the risk manager that Wind had been sent a termination letter. The patient termination policy required the risk manager to be notified *prior* to the letter being sent out. It was the risk manager's job to review these types of communications to ensure appropriate steps had been followed. The copy of the letter in the chart stated the patient was being dismissed from the practice for being "too complex," which was not approved language. This phrase concerned the risk manager. Upon looking into the patient's visits, it was revealed the date on the letter was the day after Wind's cancelled follow-up visit, but there was a pending appointment for the following week. Knowing the patient might not receive the letter before the next scheduled appointment, the risk manager consulted the new VP of Quality. Although the risk manager had already spoken to the practice manager to gather more information about why the patient was being terminated and to reiterate the appropriate process according to the patient termination policy, the VP of Quality decided to further investigate the case.

Through the process of the investigation, the VP of Quality consulted with an Americans with Disabilities Act (ADA) expert and discovered the organization had not appointed anyone as required by Section 1557 of the Affordable Care Act. The wording in the termination letter could be seen as violation of the ADA if the patient's behaviors were being caused by an underlying medical condition, and if those behaviors were the reason the patient was being terminated. Furthermore, the investigation revealed other required steps outlined in the termination policy had not been followed. There was no documentation of any warning to Wind about being terminated if the behaviors continued, nor had they notified the health plan the patient was going to be terminated so the plan could reassign Wind to another provider. Most concerning was the fact the patient had immediate unmet health care needs and was scheduled for an upcoming appointment. If Wind came in for the rescheduled appointment only to be told about the termination policy, the situation could escalate. A solution was needed, quickly.

Discussion Questions

1. What are the major issues presented in this scenario?
2. What are the specific points of failure in the patient termination process and what should be done to address them?
3. What steps would you immediately take to mitigate the risk to the organization and to meet the needs of the patient?
4. Is there specific training that you would recommend for the employees at this practice?
5. Did you make any assumptions while reading this case regarding race, ethnicity, gender or gender identity, sexual orientation, socioeconomic status, culture, or other protected class? Were these assumptions focused at the individual/staff level, clinical/program level, or organizational/administrative level? How do these assumptions affect cultural awareness, cultural knowledge, behaviors, and/or skill development?

Additional Resources

Brightwell, J., & Cahill, R. (2019, June). *Terminating patient relationships.* https://www.thedoctors.com/articles/terminating-patient-relationships/

Center for Substance Abuse Treatment. (2014). *Improving cultural competence.* Substance Abuse and Mental Health Services Administration. https://www.ncbi.nlm.nih.gov/books/NBK248428/

U.S. Department of Health & Human Services. (2020). *Section 1557 of the Patient Protection and Affordable Care Act.* https://www.hhs.gov/civil-rights/for-individuals/

U.S. Department of Labor. (2020). *Section 504, Rehabilitation Act of 1973.* https://www.dol.gov/agencies/oasam/centers-offices/civil-rights-center/statutes/section-504-rehabilitation-act-of-1973

Mosquito Bitten: Part I

Sharon B. Buchbinder

Lakeisha Johnson just obtained her first job in Happy Hollow Health Care's (HHHC) Patient Accounts Department as an Accounts Representative I, an entry level position. The Human Resources Director noted that she would have opportunities for advancement, should she perform well in the job. Lakeisha graduated with honors from an HBCU, a Historically Black College or University, with a double major in health care management and accounting. Due to the COVID-19 pandemic, she and many other students had been forced to complete required internships either on campus or as remote assignments. She was a little anxious about going into the workplace, as there had been COVID clusters in nearby towns. However, she had been reassured by her physician at her pre-employment health assessment that HHHC was a reputable hospital and would have proper precautions in place for their employees. Sure enough, when she arrived at Human Resources (HR), in addition to her identification (ID) badge, she received a care package: an HHHC branded mask, a face shield, hand sanitizer, and a squeeze ball emblazoned with the hospital logo.

When Lakeisha arrived on her first day at work, she was excited, nervous, and happy. Her new supervisor, Janet Overlord, a peppy woman with bright red hair wearing an HHHC mask, introduced her to the Patient Accounts team and took her on a tour of the facilities, including a sizable break room for the large department to decrease possible cross-contamination from the clinical side. With a refrigerator, a high-end coffee pot with free pods in multiple brands, two microwaves, a sink, and water cooler, the room was a welcoming space for coffee and lunch breaks. It also served as a place to go to decompress from an angry patient or frustrating insurance company interaction.

Janet invited Lakeisha to put her lunch in the refrigerator and led her to her cubicle. Posted on the walls were the mission, vision, and values of HHHC, affirming its commitment to respect for all stakeholders. In addition, there were scripts for interacting with patients and insurance companies. Janet pointed around the cube. "The gray walls are pretty drab so you're welcome to post photos of family, friends, and pets. We want you to feel good when you come to work, not like you're going into a cube farm." Janet's bright blue eyes widened. "Now, let's get you to your training session, shall we?"

Lakeisha eased into her new role, each day getting a bit easier for her. She brought in photos from her virtual graduation and posted them on the walls of her cube. In her favorite, her family and friends all stood six feet away from each other in front of the HBCU campus entry with the name of the university and the year of her graduation in the center. She smiled every time she looked at it. In spite of COVID and her grandmother's premature death due to the virus, she had made it.

One day, one of her co-workers, Brenda Bradshaw, stuck her head into her cube. "Hey, it's Janet's birthday," she said through her mask. "We're going to have a virtual birthday party for her at noon. Everyone in the department will be there. I'm sending out a link now. You should login."

Lakeisha nodded, "Thanks for letting me know. I'll be there."

Brenda's gaze landed on Lakeisha's prized photo. "One of my neighbors graduated from there, same year as you. Maybe you know her? Charmaine White?"

Lakeisha thought a moment. "No, sorry, she must have been in a different major."

"I thought you guys all knew each other." Brenda shrugged. "See you in a bit."

Shaking her head and laughing at Brenda's cluelessness, Lakeisha went back to work.

Online in the virtual party, a jovial crowd popped up in the gallery to celebrate Janet's birthday. She was a well-liked boss, and the employees belted out the birthday song to her. Janet thanked the group and made a point of welcoming Lakeisha to the team.

Everyone smiled and waved. Jennifer, a middle-aged blonde, cocked her head, smiled at Lakeisha, and asked, "I like your hair. Is it real?"

Heart hammering in her throat, Lakeisha was too stunned to respond. The chatter continued all around her, but Lakeisha barely heard it.

At last, Janet thanked the group for her birthday aria, and said, "You made my day."

Lakeisha logged off and thought to herself. *Yeah, mine, too.*

Discussion Questions

1. What is going on in this case?
2. Identify the main organizational problem in this case.
3. What are three factors contributing to this problem?
4. Provide three possible solutions to the problem you identified.
5. Provide your reflections and personal opinions as well as your recommendations for addressing this problem.

Additional Resources

Ballinson, P., Decherd, W., & Guttman, M. (2020, June 23). *Understanding organizational barriers to a more inclusive workplace.* McKinsey. https://www.mckinsey.com/business-functions/organization /our-insights/understanding-organizational-barriers-to-a-more-inclusive-workplace

Buchbinder, S. B., Shanks, N. H., & Kite, B. J. (2021). *Introduction to health care management* (4th ed.). Jones & Bartlett Learning.

DiAngelo, R., & Dyson, M.E. (2018). *White fragility: Why it's so hard for White people to talk about race.* Beacon Press.

Fusion Comedy. (2016). *How microaggressions are like mosquito bites. Same difference* [Video]. YouTube. https://youtu.be/hDd3bzA7450

Holm, A. L., Gorosh, M. R., Brady, M., & White-Perkins, D. (2017). Recognizing privilege and bias: An interactive exercise to expand health care providers' personal awareness. *Academic Medicine, 92*(3), 360–364.

Kendi, I. X. (2019). *How to be an anti-racist.* One World.

McIntosh, P. (1989). *White privilege: Unpacking the invisible knapsack.* https://www.racialequitytools.org/resourcefiles/mcintosh.pdf

Office of Minority Health. (2020). *Think cultural health. What is CLAS?* https://thinkculturalhealth.hhs.gov/clas/what-is-clas

Sue, D. W., Capodilupo, C. M., Torino, G. C., Bucceri, J. M., Holder, A. M. B., Nadal, K. L., & Esquilin, M. (2007). Racial microaggressions in everyday life: Implications for clinical practice. *American Psychologist, 62*(4), 271–286.

U.S. Equal Employment Opportunity Commission. (2020). *Harassment.* https://www.eeoc.gov/harassment

Mosquito Bitten: Part II

Sharon B. Buchbinder

Six months later, Janet Overlord recommended Lakeisha for promotion to Accounts Representative II. In her request to HR, she cited several reasons for the promotion, including Lakeisha's double degree in health care management and accounting and her uncanny problem-solving abilities that made both patients and insurance companies satisfied. Janet worried that Lakeisha would go to work for their competitor in the city, Health Integrated Systems, Inc. (HISI). They had already poached two of her star employees, and she feared Lakeisha would be next.

When HR approved Janet's recommendation to advance Lakeisha to the next level, she called her employee into her office to share the good news. She had not mentioned the possible promotion to Lakeisha. Janet had worried HR would not approve and did not want to disappoint her.

Lakeisha took a seat. "Is there a problem?"

Surprised, Janet said, "No, on the contrary. I have great news for you. You're getting a promotion to Accounts Rep II."

Sitting back in her chair, Lakeisha blew out a long breath and shook her head. "Wow."

"You don't sound excited," Janet said. "What's wrong?"

"I've been offered a position with HISI, as an Accounts Rep II. I was just about to give you my two weeks' notice."

"I didn't know you were looking for another job. Is it a higher rate of pay?"

Lakeisha shook her head. "No, it's the same pay as HHHC for the same job title and the same benefits."

"You're one of our star employees, that's why I recommended this promotion for you. Why are you leaving?"

Lakeisha placed her hands on the arms of her chair. "Do you want an honest answer?"

"Yes, please."

"I'm the only Black employee in this department. At least once a week, a co-worker says something that upsets me, like today: 'Are your parents from this country?'"

Janet put her hand on her heart. "I'm so sorry. I wish I had known."

"You've seen it happen and you've said nothing."

"I don't understand." Janet's stomach roiled. *What did I do wrong?*

"Your birthday party, remember that?"

Janet nodded.

"Jennifer asked me if my hair was real."

"I don't understand."

"Has anyone ever asked you if *your* hair is real?"

"No." The light was beginning to dawn. "What else?"

"When I walk into the break room, a group of women stops talking and just stares at me. All I want to do is eat my lunch, but they make me uncomfortable. Most days I eat at my desk."

Janet shook her head. This was terrible. "That's like high school."

Lakeisha agreed. "The worst thing is when people ignore me like I'm invisible. Except when someone wants something. Then they give me backhanded compliments, like 'Can you handle this patient? You're so articulate.'"

Janet was near tears. Lakeisha was the third Black employee she might lose to HISI. "I'm so sorry. What can we do to keep you here?"

Discussion Questions

1. What is going on in Part II of this case?
2. Identify the main organizational problem in Part II of this case.
3. What are three factors contributing to this problem?
4. Provide three possible solutions to the problem you identified.
5. Provide your reflections and personal opinions as well as your recommendations for addressing this problem.

Additional Resources

Ballinson, P., Decherd, W., & Guttman, M. (2020, June 23). *Understanding organizational barriers to a more inclusive workplace.* McKinsey. https://www.mckinsey.com/business-functions/organization/our-insights/understanding-organizational-barriers-to-a-more-inclusive-workplace

Buchbinder, S. B., Shanks, N. H., & Kite, B. J. (2021). *Introduction to health care management* (4th ed.). Jones & Bartlett Learning.

DiAngelo, R., & Dyson, M.E. (2018). *White fragility: Why it's so hard for White people to talk about race.* Beacon Press.

Fusion Comedy. (2016). *How microaggressions are like mosquito bites. Same difference* [Video]. YouTube. https://youtu.be/hDd3bzA7450

Holm, A. L., Gorosh, M. R., Brady, M., & White-Perkins, D. (2017). Recognizing privilege and bias: An interactive exercise to expand health care providers' personal awareness. *Academic Medicine, 92*(3), 360–364.

Kendi, I. X. (2019). *How to be an anti-racist.* One World.

McIntosh, P. (1989). *White privilege: Unpacking the invisible knapsack.* https://www.racialequitytools.org/resourcefiles/mcintosh.pdf

Office of Minority Health. (2020). *Think cultural health. What is CLAS?* https://thinkculturalhealth.hhs.gov/clas/what-is-clas

Sue, D. W., Capodilupo, C. M., Torino, G. C., Bucceri, J. M., Holder, A. M. B., Nadal, K. L., & Esquilin, M. (2007). Racial microaggressions in everyday life: Implications for clinical practice. *American Psychologist, 62*(4), 271–286.

U.S. Equal Employment Opportunity Commission. (2020). *Harassment.* https://www.eeoc.gov/harassment

CASE 68

Where's My Baby?

Sharon B. Buchbinder

Enola Nez arrives at the Women's Medical Center in Albuquerque, New Mexico, in active labor. The admissions desk screens her temperature, which is normal, then asks if she's been in contact with anyone with COVID-19. She says no. In fact, Mrs. Nez has taken extensive precautions to protect her entire family and has not allowed anyone other than her immediate family into her house for the last three months.

The clerk asks for her address and zip code. "Ah. You must be tested for COVID."

Mrs. Nez consents to the test and is sent to the delivery room. This is her third baby, and she delivers quickly, much to her and her husband's relief. The delivery room nurse shows them their healthy baby boy and tells the happy parents she is going to get the baby cleaned up and will be back with him soon.

The nurse does not return with the child. Instead, another nurse takes Mrs. Nez to a private room and tells her she is being separated from her newborn until her results for COVID-19 are returned.

Mr. Nez frowns, and Mrs. Nez says, "When will we get the results?"

"All COVID-19 tests are sent out to a lab. It could take up to three days to get the tests back. You'll know as soon as we do."

Mrs. Nez says, "I want to see my baby *now*. It's important for me to have skin to skin contact and to nurse him."

"Sorry," the nurse holds her hands up. "Hospital policy."

Discussion Questions

1. What is going on in this case?
2. Identify the main organizational problem in this case.
3. What are three factors contributing to this problem?
4. Provide three possible solutions to the problem you identified.
5. Provide your reflections and personal opinions as well as your recommendations for addressing this problem.

Additional Resources

Buchbinder, S. B., & Kite, B. J. (2019). Addressing health disparities: Cultural proficiency. In S. B. Buchbinder, N. H. Shanks, & B. J. Kite (Eds.), *Introduction to health care management* (4th ed.) (pp. 351–370). Jones & Bartlett Learning.

Furlow, B. (2020, June 13). A hospital's secret coronavirus policy separated Native American mothers from their newborns. *Propublica*. https://www.propublica.org/article/a-hospitals-secret-coronavirus-policy-separated-native-american-mothers-from-their-newborns

Furlow, B. (2020, June 14). State investigating hospital with coronavirus policy that profiled pregnant Native American mothers and separated them from newborns. *Propublica*. https://www.propublica.org/article/state-investigating-hospital-with-coronavirus-policy-that-profiled-pregnant-native-american-mothers-and-separated-them-from-newborns

Furlow, B. (2020, August 22). Federal investigation finds hospital violated patients' rights by profiling, separating Native mothers and newborns. *Propublica*. https://www.propublica.org/article/federal-investigation-finds-hospital-violated-patients-rights-by-profiling-separating-native-mothers-and-newborns

Office of Minority Health. (2020). *Think cultural health. What is CLAS?* https://thinkculturalhealth.hhs.gov/clas/what-is-clas

Satcher, D., & Dawes, D. E. (2021). Race and the patient-physician relationship in 2021. *JAMA, 326*(7), 595–596. https//doi.org/10.1001/jama.2021.12454

Addressing Racial Disparities in Infant Mortality

Christina Cottrell

Two years ago, Nurse Practitioner Rowan Lee, who hails from New York City, began her job in the OB-GYN department at Cheddar Memorial Hospital (CMH), a 1,300-bed teaching hospital in Milwaukee. While not as diverse as the patient population she served in New York, her current patients vary primarily by socioeconomic status. A majority of the women are White and nearly 15% are African American. A personable and empathic health care provider, Rowan tends to form bonds and close relationships with many of the moms-to-be within the practice. She knows them by first name, remembers their hobbies, and can even tell you some of their most embarrassing moments.

One of Rowan's favorite patients is Jan, a bubbly 20-year-old African American, pregnant with her second child. Single and supporting herself with a waitressing job, she lost her first child over a year ago from sudden infant death syndrome (SIDS). Another is Kelly, a good-natured 32-year-old married law professor. She and her husband recently lost their baby girl due to complications of premature birth. Kelly is also African American. A third patient, Madison, 24, is unemployed, living with an ex-boyfriend, and pregnant with her third child. She is White. Rowan begins to notice a trend—the African American babies are dying at a much higher rate at the hospital than White babies. The experiences of Jan and Kelly are not singular.

When Rowan mentions this trend to the 68-year-old department chair, Dr. Mark Reagan, his response is nonchalant. "It's just the nature of the beast," he says. "These babies are dying because they have moms that are druggies and not taking care of themselves. That's how *they* are. It is what it is."

Rowan is shocked, bites her tongue, and pushes for more information. "How is the hospital tracking these deaths? There has to be some type of reporting mechanism, right? I can't be imagining these patterns."

"Not really," shrugs Dr. Reagan. "I think we share some information with the health department, but that's about it. It's not my job to worry about it."

Rowan remembered reading an article in the *New York Times Magazine* that discussed the issues surrounding the experiences of Black mothers and babies. She thinks maybe she should share this article with Dr. Reagan and others on the

OB-GYN team. In addition, Rowan wonders what other research and information exists about this alarming trend.

Discussion Questions

1. What is going on in this case?
2. Identify the main organizational problem in this case.
3. What are three factors contributing to this problem?
4. Provide three possible solutions to the problem you identified.
5. Provide your reflections and personal opinions as well as your recommendations for addressing this problem.
6. Did you make any assumptions while reading this case regarding race, ethnicity, gender or gender identity, sexual orientation, socioeconomic status, culture, or other protected class? Were these assumptions focused at the individual/staff level, clinical/program level, or organizational/administrative level? How do these assumptions affect cultural awareness, cultural knowledge, behaviors, and/or skill development?

Additional Resources

Center for Substance Abuse Treatment. (2014). *Improving cultural competence*. Substance Abuse and Mental Health Services Administration. https://www.ncbi.nlm.nih.gov/books/NBK248428/

Hardeman, R. R., Karbeah, J. M., & Kozhimannil, K. B. (2020). Applying a critical race lens to relationship-centered care in pregnancy and childbirth: An antidote to structural racism. *Birth*, 47(1), 3–7.

Villarosa, L. (2018, April 11). Why America's black mothers and babies are in a life-or-death crisis. *New York Times Magazine*. https://www.nytimes.com/2018/04/11/magazine/black-mothers -babies-death-maternal-mortality.html

Sinus Infection or Chest Exam?

Bobbie Kite

Quinn opened her eyes to feeling badly for the fourth day in a row, her face sore to the touch. She had no medical insurance and was terrified of going to the doctor both because of cost as well as how she might be treated. Unfortunately, the sinus infection she was fighting was out of control, and she was sure she needed antibiotics. So, she scraped up the $75 for an office visit and headed down to the first-come-first-serve local safety net clinic.

Dr. Trout came into the room and began his examination. He immediately focused in on listening to her chest and said, "Would you please remove your clothes from the waist up and put on this gown to where it opens in the front? Leave the door cracked when you are done changing."

"Sure, I can do that, doctor. Quick question, are you concerned I have bronchitis or something? I came in today for a sinus infection."

Dr. Trout gave a non-answer and left the room. Quinn was slightly uncomfortable but went with it, she really needed some antibiotics. Upon re-entering the room, he began to examine her chest once more. While examining her for several minutes, he asked repetitive questions, "Are you on any hormone treatments? Do you have a history of hormone dysfunction in your family? When did you start experiencing swelling?"

Quinn, now extremely uncomfortable, asked, "Why are you so preoccupied with examining my chest? Are there swollen lymph nodes?" Quinn tries to redirect the exam. "How do my ears look? Do they have fluid in them?"

He then said, "I have never seen such large mammary glands on a male."

Quinn responded, "I am a female, and would you please treat me for the sinus infection that I came in for?" She was afraid to say much more because she knew she needed the antibiotics and didn't have the money to pay for another visit somewhere else.

Dr. Trout then asked, "But are you a biological female? Born a female? A real female?"

The temperature in the room felt like it dropped 30 degrees. Quinn was mortified. She simply replied, "Yes, I am, and have always been."

There was no apology, and the doctor left the room. Quinn quickly got dressed. A nurse entered the room a little while later, handed her a prescription for some medicine, and pointed her to the exit.

Discussion Questions

1. What is going on in this case?
2. Why do you think the provider felt like it was okay to move forward with this line of questioning?
3. What role do you think the clinic being for the less fortunate part of the community played, if any, in the patient not saying anything to anyone?
4. If you were running a clinic such as this one, what would you do to prevent this type of thing from happening, considering these things might not be reported?
5. Did you make any assumptions while reading this case regarding race, ethnicity, gender or gender identity, sexual orientation, socioeconomic status, culture, or other protected class? Were these assumptions focused at the individual/staff level, clinical/program level, or organizational/administrative level? How do these assumptions affect cultural awareness, cultural knowledge, behaviors, and/or skill development?

Additional Resources

Buchbinder, S. B., Shanks, N. H., & Kite, B. J. (2021). *Introduction to health care management* (4th ed.). Jones & Bartlett Learning.

Center for Substance Abuse Treatment. (2014). *Improving cultural competence*. Substance Abuse and Mental Health Services Administration.https://www.ncbi.nlm.nih.gov/books/NBK248428/

Kcomt, L., Gorey, K. M., Barrett, B. J., & McCabe, S. E. (2020). Healthcare avoidance due to anticipated discrimination among transgender people: A call to create trans-affirmative environments. *SSM-Population Health, 11*, 100608.

Mounsithiraj, A. K., Hubley, B., McClendon, M. A., & Abraham, S. P. (2020). Healthcare experiences of transgender patients. *International Journal of Science and Research Methodology, 14*(3), 99–110.

Nowaskie, D. Z. (2020). *Evaluation of the four national lesbian, gay, bisexual, transgender, and queer (LGBTQ)-competent provider directories in the United States*. Semantics Scholar. https://10.21203/rs.3.rs-19669/v1

Pozgar, G. D. (2016). *Legal aspects of health care administration*. Jones & Bartlett Learning.

Conflict of Interest with LGBTQ Patient

Allison O'Grady

Javier, a 37-year-old patient who lives in Denver, Colorado, just switched to a new organization and decided to schedule an annual check-up with his new physician. Javier is a relatively healthy individual but wanted to talk to his health care provider about strategies to manage his low blood pressure. Javier identifies as a Latino man and has been in a same-sex relationship for 11 years. The practice assigned Javier to Dr. Jackson for primary care. Dr. Jackson is a 68-year-old male physician who has been practicing medicine for 38 years. He identifies as White and is in a heterosexual marriage.

Javier filled out pre-screening paperwork for his first visit with Dr. Jackson. Once the vitals were taken, the physician came into the room to visit with Javier. Dr. Jackson welcomed Javier to the practice and read over the intake screening. Relationship status was not on the original paperwork as the forms were outdated.

Dr. Jackson asked if he was married. Javier said yes, he was recently married, and the doctor asked what his wife does for a living. Javier hesitated for a moment; this was a common experience for him. After a brief moment of silence, he informed Dr. Jackson that he was married to his same-sex partner of 11 years.

Dr. Jackson turned his chair around, made a note, and said, "I see." Then Dr. Jackson took off his glasses and said, "Well, I am sorry to have to do this, but I am going to have to recuse myself from being your doctor. I hold religious beliefs that conflict with your lifestyle."

Javier didn't know what to say. He stared in silence and felt so embarrassed and judged. Javier said, "Okay, well this isn't fair, but can I get into another doctor today? I really want to talk about my low blood pressure."

Dr. Jackson said that, unfortunately, Javier would have to come back another time and would receive a call from the care team to assign him to another doctor.

After the appointment, Dr. Jackson did not mention this encounter to his clinical care manager (CCM) or the lead physician.

On the drive home, Javier became upset. After talking with his partner, he decided to call and report his negative experience the next morning.

Discussion Questions

1. What are the main concerns of this case?
2. What are the ethical responsibilities of a physician as related to treating a patient?
3. What obligations does a physician have to report this encounter?
4. Should lesbian, gay, bisexual, transgender, and queer (LGBTQ) training be a specific requirement for health care providers?
5. How does the intersection of race and sexual orientation impact this case?
6. What are the first three steps the CCM should take upon receiving the call from the patient?

Additional Resources

Aleshire, M. E., Ashford, K., Fallin-Bennett, A., & Hatcher, J. (2019). Primary care providers' attitudes related to LGBTQ people: A narrative literature review. *Health Promotion Practice*, 20(2), 173–187.

Goldhammer, H., Maston, E. D., Kissock, L. A., Davis, J. A., & Keuroghlian, A. S. (2018). National findings from an LGBT healthcare organizational needs assessment. *LGBT Health*, 5(8), 461–468. http://doi.org/10.1089/lgbt.2018.0118

Klein, E. W., & Nakhai, M. (2016). Caring for LGBTQ patients: Methods for improving physician cultural competence. *The International Journal of Psychiatry in Medicine*, 51(4), 315–324.

Mirza, S. A., & Rooney, C. (2018). Discrimination prevents LGBTQ people from accessing health care. *Center for American Progress*, 18.

Morris, M., Cooper, R. L., Ramesh, A., Tabatabai, M., Arcury, T. A., Shinn, M., & Matthews-Juarez, P. (2019). Training to reduce LGBTQ-related bias among medical, nursing, and dental students and providers: A systematic review. *BMC Medical Education*, 19(1), 325.

Powell, A. (2018). The problems with LGBTQ health care. *Harvard News Gazette*. https://news.harvard.edu/gazette/story/2018/03/health-care-providers-need-better-understanding-of-lgbtq-patients-harvard-forum-says/

Rossman, K., Salamanca, P., & Macapagal, K. (2017). "The doctor said I didn't look gay": Young adults' experiences of disclosure and non-disclosure of LGBTQ identity to healthcare providers. *Journal of Homosexuality*, 64(10), 1390.

Wahlen, R., Bize, R., Wang, J., Merglen, A., & Ambresin, A. E. (2020). Medical students' knowledge of and attitudes towards LGBT people and their health care needs: Impact of a lecture on LGBT health. *PloS One*, 15(7), e0234743.

It's Not Just the Music

Monika Piccardi

Chris was in her cubicle working on grant reviews when she heard music playing from the next cubicle. Her co-worker, Jill, was playing her religious music—again. Chris did not think anything of it at first, but then she overheard Jill on the phone speaking to a friend. Part of the conversation entailed a discussion about the most recent sermon at their church and how gay people were an abomination to God. The phone conversation disturbed Chris, but she figured that if Jill kept this to herself, it was none of her business.

Chris and Jill had been co-workers for a brief time. Jill had started three months ago, whereas Chris had been with the large multinational health care company for several years. When she was hired, Jill appeared to be a team player, and Chris was looking forward to working with her. Chris was in a more senior position and tried to include Jill in all office activities to make her feel welcome.

Chris, while private about her personal life at work, was open to co-workers who had known her for some time and would speak up about lesbian, gay, bisexual, transgender, queer (LGBTQ) issues as they arose. Over time, Jill became aware of Chris's sexual orientation and would often try to force her into a discussion about religion. Chris would engage in general conversations with Jill but declined to discuss religion, as they had differing views.

In addition to her usual spiritual music, Jill began to play religious sermons loud enough for Chris to hear. Chris asked her to turn it down. Jill would lower the volume, but over time it crept up to the previous level. Chris also noticed that Jill became short with her during conversations and was slow to respond to her emails. Over the next month, Jill began to exclude Chris from general office discussion and became even more vocal about her religious beliefs. In the hope of working things out, Chris asked Jill if she had issues collaborating with her. Jill declined to answer.

Chris's next step was to speak to their department director. The situation with Jill was affecting her work and the office morale. The director stated she did not notice any problems with Jill's behaviors. Her religious music and anti-gay sermons were not that important—as long as she performed effectively. Chris tried to point out that being slow to respond to emails, being short with her during discussions and meetings, and being left out of office discussions were, in fact, affecting both of their work and the office morale. The director did not see how Jill's behaviors were more than just an issue of two coworkers not getting along.

After getting no support from her director, Chris pondered what she should do next.

Discussion Questions

1. What is happening in this case?
2. Is Chris being bullied? Explain your answer.
3. If you were Chris, what would your next step be?
4. If you were the director, how would you manage the situation between Chris and Jill?
5. What is the office director's responsibility in this situation?
6. You are in Human Resources and this situation was brought to your attention, how would you respond?
7. What organizational issues does this case represent, and how would you effect change?

Additional Resources

Buchbinder, S. B., Shanks, N. H., & Kite, B. J. (2021). *Introduction to health care management* (4th ed.). Jones & Bartlett Learning.

Darden, Q. (2020, July 23). 8 steps to stamp out LGBT discrimination. *Business Management Daily.* https://www.businessmanagementdaily.com/61620/8-steps-to-stamp-out-lgbt-discrimination/

Gleeson, B. (2017, October 31). Strategies for making organizational change stick and building a bright future. *Forbes.* https://www.forbes.com/sites/brentgleeson/2017/10/31/strategies-for -making-organizational-change-stick-and-building-a-bright-future/?sh=2dff5dfd6f7a

Nielsen, M. B., & Einarsen, S. (2018). What we know, what we do not know, and what we should and could have known about workplace bullying: An overview of the literature and agenda for future research. *Aggression and Violent Behavior, 42,* 71–83.

Webber, A. (2019, Mary 17). Seven in 10 LGBT staff sexually harassed at work. *Personnel Today.* https://www.personneltoday.com/hr/seven-in-10-lgbt-staff-sexually-harassed-at-work/

Witeck, B. (2014). Cultural change in acceptance of LGBT people: Lessons from social marketing. *The American Journal of Orthopsychiatry, 84*(1), 19–22. https://doi.apa.org/doiLanding?doi=10 .1037%2Fh0098945

CASE 73

These Boots Were Not Made for Running

Madison Price

Alejandro Sanchez was a hard-working 45-year-old construction worker at Mesa Valley Construction in Houston, Texas. He had been working for the company for over two years since moving from Mexico where he was born and raised. Although he had been living in the United States for a few years, he could not speak or understand English. Additionally, while his verbal Spanish-speaking skills were well developed, he had limited proficiency when it came to reading Spanish.

One day while at work, Alejandro started to experience sharp chest pain and shortness of breath as he carried heavy machinery up a hill. He stopped walking and his symptoms resolved about a minute later. Figuring the pain must have been heartburn or muscle spasms, he continued his work for the rest of the day. Later that night when he was telling his wife about his day, he mentioned the unusual symptoms he had experienced. She grew concerned that Alejandro's symptoms might be related to his heart, as she had lost her father to a heart attack after he experienced similar symptoms. She begged him to schedule an appointment with a cardiologist to undergo an evaluation.

With his wife's help, Alejandro was able to find a cardiologist near them who spoke Spanish. Unfortunately, when he called the office, the only times Dr. Romero had available for an appointment were on the days when his wife would be out of town. Therefore, Alejandro knew he was going to have to go to the appointment alone. Luckily, Alejandro's wife helped him fill out all the new patient paperwork online prior to his appointment. This helped tremendously, as he could not comprehend what the forms were asking. When he arrived for his appointment the following week, he handed the forms to the receptionist, told them his name, and took a seat in the waiting room until he was called back for his appointment.

After conducting his physical evaluation, Dr. Romero told Alejandro he thought it would be wise for him to undergo a stress test in their office to assess for any blockages in his heart. As he was starting to explain the test to Alejandro, his pager went off and he was called away to an emergency. As Dr. Romero was leaving the clinic, he asked one of the medical assistants (MAs) to print out the stress test guidelines for

Alejandro in Spanish. He would have asked the case manager in the clinic to go over these with him, but she was at lunch. Unable to wait for her to return, Dr. Romero told Alejandro to come back the next day at 10 a.m. for the test and then rushed out of the room before Alejandro had a chance to ask him any follow-up questions. An MA came into his room a short time later with the protocols in hand. Embarrassed to admit he could not read Spanish, he quietly took the forms and left the clinic. When he got home, he threw the protocols in the trash.

The next day when he arrived back at the clinic, he was greeted by an MA who had a surprised look on her face as she looked him over head to toe. When she led him back to a room, it was his turn to be surprised. There sitting in the middle of the room was a huge treadmill machine. As the MA turned around to face him, he could tell she was trying to figure out how to communicate with him. She gestured for him to wait and then walked out of the room with a smirk on her face.

The MA approached Dr. Romero, who was talking to other coworkers at the time. The MA stifled a laugh and rolled her eyes as she told Dr. Romero, "I have seen people show up to do treadmill stress tests in jeans before, but I have never seen them show up in jeans and cowboy boots. I think you need to go talk to Alejandro because clearly he did not take the time to read the test protocols we gave him."

As the other coworkers laughed, Dr. Romero excused himself. When Dr. Romero walked into the treadmill room, he asked Alejandro where his tennis shoes were. "¿Dónde están tus zapatos de tenis?"

Alejandro responded they were at his house. "Mi casa."

Dr. Romero nodded and then explained to him they would not be able to complete the test because it required Alejandro to run on the treadmill machine. Clearly something he would not be able to do in the cowboy boots he was currently wearing. Sensing his confusion, Dr. Romero sat down and explained to Alejandro what all the stress test involved. He asked Alejandro if he had received the protocols he had asked the MAs to give him. Alejandro was forced to admit he could not read Spanish, which made him feel even more embarrassed than he already did. Dr. Romero told him not to worry. They would get him rescheduled the following week for the test. He told Alejandro to come dressed in tennis shoes and athletic wear for the appointment. Despite Dr. Romero's reassurances, Alejandro left the clinic upset that he would have to miss another day of work.

Discussion Questions

1. What cultural and health biases and disparities are evident in this case? How do these biases and disparities impact the care Alejandro received from the clinic?

2. According to the Agency for Healthcare Research and Quality (AHRQ), health care organizations can take a number of approaches to improve cultural competence among their workforces. Suggestions include language assistance, cultural brokers, cultural competence training, and a TeamSTEPPS Limited English Proficiency Module (AHRQ, 2019). Review the suggestions found in the resources provided below. Which suggestion do you believe could be most successfully implemented in this case study to help improve the clinic's cultural competency? Explain your rationale.

3. Although Dr. Romero got paged away on an emergency, do you believe he is partially to blame for the breakdown of communication in this case? How could he have handled the situation differently to ensure Alejandro received all of the proper information prior to his stress test?
4. What ethical principles did the MA violate in this case? Do you believe a lack of cultural awareness contributed to her actions? Provide evidence from the case or other resources to back up your answer.
5. Have you ever been embarrassed or ashamed to admit a lack of proficiency in a certain area to a health care provider? How did you handle that situation or how would you if you found yourself in that situation in the future? Do you feel such a situation could impact the care you receive?

Additional Resources

Agency for Healthcare Research and Quality. (2019, December 19). *Cultural competence and patient safety.* https://psnet.ahrq.gov/perspective/cultural-competence-and-patient-safety

Hostetter, M., & Klein, S. (2018, September 27). *In focus: Reducing racial disparities in health care by confronting racism.* Commonwealth Fund. https://www.commonwealthfund.org/publications/2018/sep/focus-reducing-racial-disparities-health-care-confronting-racism

Egede, L. E. (2006). Race, ethnicity, culture, and disparities in health care. *Journal of General Internal Medicine, 21*(6), 667–669. https://link.springer.com/article/10.1111%2Fj.1525-1497.2006.0512.x

Shepherd, S. M., Willis-Esqueda, C., Newton, D., Sivasubramaniam, D., & Paradies, Y. (2019). The challenge of cultural competence in the workplace: Perspectives of healthcare providers. *BMC Health Services Research, 19*(135). https://bmchealthservres.biomedcentral.com/articles/10.1186/s12913-019-3959-7

CASE 74

How Cute, Are They Adopted?

Rachel Rogers

Mrs. Road hadn't been feeling good for a couple of days but was trying to push through. With her husband and two children in tow, they headed off to the recital. By the time it ended, and they were back at the car, it was clear they were headed to the emergency room (ER).

Mr. Road and the children were nervous but happy to be so close to a reputable hospital. After what seemed like hours, Mrs. Road was diagnosed with acute appendicitis and rushed off for an emergency appendectomy. Since they had no options for childcare, Mr. Road and the children waited patiently in the waiting room.

While waiting, a couple sitting across from them inquired where Mr. Road's daughters were from, he replied, "Here." Then they inquired further, "Yes, but where are they really from?" Mr. Road was used to this question and answered politely, "Here."

Later, Mr. Road checked in at the nurse's station to ask how things were going, the nurse asked him to wait a moment and promised to return as soon as possible with an update. When the nurse returned, the last comment stung Mr. Road a second time, "Where are your daughters from? They are so cute and have beautiful skin. So good of you to adopt them, we need more people like you and your wife!"

Mr. Road took a deep breath and replied, "We are all from here, the United States. Thank you for the update."

Once the surgery was completed and Mrs. Road was in recovery, a certified nursing assistant (CNA) was sent to invite the family to see Mrs. Road. As the children excitedly gather their items to see their mother, the CNA asked, "I'm sorry, but are those Mrs. Road's real children? If not, are they adopted?"

That's when Mr. Road could take no more. "They are our children. Yes, she is their mother. By the way, you are going to need to call a patient advocate to the room."

Discussion Questions

1. What lack of cultural competency is being displayed here?
2. How might an organization demonstrate their cultural competence in rectifying this situation?
3. Even though none of these people meant to offend, are their microaggressive actions acceptable? Defend your stance.
4. What consequences might the hospital face if they do not address microaggressions and issues of cultural competence?
5. What tools could be used to support the staff in an effort to acknowledge microaggressions and address the cultural competence needs of patients?
6. Do microaggressions also occur from patients to health care providers and staff? How do these impact patient care?

Additional Resources

Ehie, O., Muse, I., Hill, L., & Bastien, A. (2021). Professionalism: Microaggression in the healthcare setting. *Current Opinion in Anesthesiology, 34*(2), 131–136. https://doi.org/10.1097/ACO.0000000000000966

Feaster, B., McKinley-Grant, L., & McMichael, A. J. (2021). Microaggressions in medicine. *Cutis, 107*, 235–237.

Miller, L. R., & Peck, B. M. (2020). A prospective examination of racial microaggressions in the medical encounter. *Journal of Racial and Ethnic Health Disparities, 7*(3), 519–527.

Overland, M. K., Zumsteg, J. M., Lindo, E. G., Sholas, M. G., Montenegro, R. E., Campelia, G. D., & Mukherjee, D. (2019). Microaggressions in clinical training and practice. *PM&R, 11*(9), 1004–1012.

CASE 75

No Animal Products in My Medicine Please

Rachel Rogers

An independent primary care practice in a mid-sized city on the east coast of the United States has been providing care in a racially and ethnically diverse neighborhood for the last five years. This practice hasn't yet been bought up by a larger, integrated health system, and the practice prides itself on that fact. This small, independent clinic employs four full-time family medicine physicians, one part-time nurse practitioner, two registered nurses, four medical assistants, three front office specialists, and a clinic manager. The clinic uses a certified electronic health record (EHR) for clinical documentation and e-prescribing. Lab, radiology, and other ancillary services are outsourced to third-party vendors.

Amandeep Kaur has recently moved into the neighborhood near the clinic and is scheduled for an appointment to establish care with Dr. Ulmer. Mr. Kaur moved from a large urban area with a close-knit Sikh community that included a family friend who was an internal medicine physician in a large, integrated health system close to Amandeep's previous home. Mr. Kaur has been relatively healthy but hasn't been feeling particularly well over the last month since he moved to this new city.

At the first appointment, Mr. Kaur answers all of the usual "new patient" questions including the demographic question about religion. Dr. Ulmer and Amandeep discuss his recent fatigue and decide to order a few lab tests including a test for hypothyroidism. Dr. Ulmer, in an attempt to make Mr. Kaur's life a little easier, suggests that if the thyroid testing comes back indicating diminished thyroid function, they will call in a prescription for a thyroid medication.

Amandeep states, "I can't take that brand of thyroid medication."

Dr. Ulmer asks Amandeep to explain.

"My wife has a thyroid condition and our family friend and physician at our previous practice prescribed a different medication that doesn't contain animal products," Amandeep replied. "As Sikhs, we do not consume any meat or products derived from animals. You may not find all Sikhs follow this practice, but we do. I'd like to find an alternative, please."

Dr. Ulmer finds a suitable replacement for Mr. Kaur, documents the information in a narrative note in the EHR and informs the clinical team. Dr. Ulmer wraps up the day at the clinic and begins to think of other patients in the practice who might have dietary needs related to their religion or lifestyle. The realization hits that the clinic has never considered this before and wouldn't even know where to reliably access this information in the patient record.

Dr. Ulmer heads off to see the clinic manager for a conversation. They start looking through patient records and find no pattern of documentation other than in demographics and some mention of pork allergy in a number of patients who identified their religion as either Jewish or Muslim. The two decide to head home for the night and tackle the problem in the morning.

Discussion Questions

1. Is religious preference part of cultural competence? Defend your stance.
2. How might an organization demonstrate that they acknowledge and accept religious preferences?
3. Dr. Ulmer was fortunate that Mr. Kaur took the time to explain religious needs during the visit. What other reactions might the clinical staff see from patients as the result of not addressing religious preferences?
4. What consequences might a clinical practice face if they do not address issues of religious aspects of care?
5. What tools could be used to support the clinic team in an effort to acknowledge and address the religious needs of patients?

Role-Based Questions

Clinic Manager Role:

1. You are the clinic manager. Dr. Ulmer tells you about the interaction with Mr. Kaur. What are your next steps?
2. As the clinic manager, what would be a leadership approach to this situation?
3. What is your responsibility in this case?

Physician/Clinician Role:

1. What is the responsibility of the clinician in this situation?
2. What is the role of the clinician in the development and maintenance of cultural competence in the clinic setting?

Additional Resources

Eriksson, A., Burcharth, J., & Rosenberg, J. (2013). Animal derived products may conflict with religious patients' beliefs. *BMC Medical Ethics, 14,* 48. https://bmcmedethics.biomedcentral.com/articles/10.1186/1472-6939-14-48

Cunha J. P. (n.d.). *Synthroid vs. armour thyroid.* RxList. https://www.rxlist.com/synthroid_vs_armour_thyroid/drugs-condition.htm

Isaac, K. S., Hay, J. L., & Lubetkin, E. I. (2016). Incorporating spirituality in primary care. *Journal of Religion and Health, 55*(3), 1065–1077. https://link.springer.com/article/10.1007%2Fs10943-016-0190-2

Sattar, S. P., Ahmed, M. S., Madison, J., Olsen, D. R., Bhatia, S. C., Ellahi, S., Majeed, F., Ramaswamy, S., Petty, F., & Wilson, D. R. (2004). Patient and physician attitudes to using medications with religiously forbidden ingredients. *The Annals of Pharmacotherapy, 38*(11), 1830–1835. https://journals.sagepub.com/doi/10.1345/aph.1E001

Swihart, D. L., & Martin, R. L. (2021, November 17). *Cultural religious competence in clinical practice.* StatPearls. https://www.ncbi.nlm.nih.gov/books/NBK493216/

CASE 76

Celebration Gone Wrong?

Nancy H. Shanks

It was a perfect time to celebrate the long-term employment of one of our own—30 years with the Connecticut Health Care System (CHCS). Josephine had started in janitorial services way back when, became enamored with computers, worked her way up in various areas of IT, and was now a leader in that department. She now makes a six-figure salary—and has broken a lot of barriers along the way.

Josephine is a middle-aged Black woman who has earned her promotions and progress at CHCS. She is proud of her African American heritage. Today is a big day for her, offering an opportunity to be recognized for her time at CHCS. She is excited about celebrating with her current and former colleagues, as well as with friends and most importantly with her family, particularly her children.

The party is underway and seems to be going quite well. And then, the White female chief executive officer (CEO) of CHCS, Ms. Clules, makes her grand entry into the celebration. Always wanting to be the center of attention, Ms. Clules comes in dressed to look like Josephine and wears a braided wig. There are gasps coming from many attendees, but Ms. Clules thinks she is being very clever and funny.

Discussion Questions

1. Putting yourself in Josephine's shoes, what are you thinking?
2. What are microaggressions? Does this situation fit the definition? Explain why or why not?
3. Do you think that Josephine should address this with Ms. Clules? When might she do this—right away or at a later point in time? Why? Justify your position.
4. Given what you've learned about microaggressions, please advise Josephine about this and recommend how she might deal with it.
5. Would you recommend that human resources (HR) do some type of training session to educate all employees about microaggression issues? Again, right away? At another time? Focusing on this or another scenario?

Additional Resources

Holm, A. L., Gorosh, M. R., Brady, M., & White-Perkins, D. (2017). Recognizing privilege and bias: An interactive exercise to expand health care providers' personal awareness. *Academic Medicine, 92*(3), 360–364.

Kendi, I. X. (2019). *How to be an anti-racist.* One World.

Knight, R. (2020, July 27). You've been called out for a microaggression. What do you do? *Harvard Business Review.* https://hbr.org/2020/07/youve-been-called-out-for-a-microaggression-what-do-you-do

McIntosh, P. (1989). *White privilege: Unpacking the invisible knapsack.* https://www.racialequitytools.org/resourcefiles/mcintosh.pdf

Office of Minority Health. (2020). *Think cultural health. What is CLAS?* https://thinkculturalhealth.hhs.gov/clas/what-is-clas

Raypole, C. (2021, July 14). *Why microaggressions are a (very) big deal.* Healthline. https://www.healthline.com/health/microaggressions

Sue, D. W., Capodilupo, C. M., Torino, G. C., Bucceri, J. M., Holder, A. M. B., Nadal, K. L., & Esquilin, M. (2007). Racial microaggressions in everyday life: Implications for clinical practice. *American Psychologist, 62*(4), 271–286.

Washington, E. F., Birch, A. H., & Roberts, L. M. (2020, July 03). When and how to respond to microaggressions. *Harvard Business Review.* https://hbr.org/2020/07/when-and-how-to-respond-to-microaggressions

Wilkerson, I. (2020). *Caste: The origins of our discontents.* Random House.

CASE 77

Diversity Disaster for a New Employee

Nancy H. Shanks

City Memorial Hospital (CMH) is a large public institution that serves a diverse clientele in a large metropolitan area in the southwest. As part of its strategic planning process and much like many other large hospitals in the aftermath of the Black Lives Matter (BLM) protests, CMH has been charged with increasing its efforts to focus on diversity and to increase the number of minorities and women that it employs. The bar for recruitment of these candidates, particularly for senior management positions, is extremely high.

The Chief Executive Officer (CEO), Billy Joe, and Vice President of Human Resources (VPHR), Christie Brickel, both of whom are White, are patting themselves on the back and feeling great about their ability to attract a new member of the management team. Serena Smith is a well-educated, well-credentialed African American woman who has held numerous increasingly responsible positions in the health care financial management field. She has recently been recruited and hired as CMH's chief financial officer (CFO). (See Accounting Tools [2021] for a job description.)

Serena is excited about joining the management team, but this new position is a big step up for her. She knows that initially she'll need to concentrate her efforts on getting up-to-speed on the financial systems, getting to know her managers and other members of the finance division, learning to work with the other senior management team and the board of directors, and providing leadership over all department functions.

No sooner has Serena started her employment at CMH than she starts getting bombarded with calls and emails from chairs requesting that she join their committees. These inquiries focus on needing "a diverse representative" on the ethics, patient satisfaction, operations, internal complaints, and various search committees for other departments. Most of the requests come from White managers.

Serena is overwhelmed by this attention. She also knows it will be critical for her to be a key member/leader of the budget/finance and audit committees, as well as representing her department on the CEO's executive leadership committee. There are also many other duties on her job description, such as attending board of director meetings, working with the treasurer of the board and its finance and investment committees, interacting with various contractors who are working with her department, and the list goes on. She wonders what all these committee chairs are thinking. She is the CFO, not the chief diversity officer (CDO). "Instead they seemed to have assigned me some specific role: official interpreter of minority concerns for the organization" (Caver & Livers, 2002, p. 78).

Serena is thinking she is in way over her head and is feeling torn in many different directions. She doesn't want to be *the* diversity representative on every hospital committee, but she knows that she has an important job to perform as well as wanting to be a good team player. Despite this, she is thinking she has made a huge career blunder and may even need to resign. Before doing this, however, she turns to you, her health care finance mentor, for assistance on the next steps.

Discussion Questions

1.   What has changed for many hospitals and businesses in general with respect to diversity concerns, particularly for females and minorities in the last several years?
2.   Explain why diversity issues have become increasingly important to all types of health care providers.
3.   Do White employees understand the pressure put on employees of color, particularly females of color? (Hint: you might want to read the Brown and Caver & Livers articles.)
4.   What has gone wrong in this scenario? Is it appropriate for these committee chairs to be making these requests?
5.   Do you think that Serena and employees like her are set up to fail?
6.   How costly could this problem become for CMH? In what way?
7.   What do you, her mentor, recommend that she do?

Additional Resources

Accounting Tools. (2021, June 15). *Chief financial officer (CFO) job description.* https://www.accountingtools.com/articles/2017/5/14/chief-financial-officer-cfo-job-description

Brosnan, A. (2018, March). *Women in business: Beyond policy to progress.* https://www.grantthornton.global/globalassets/1.-member-firms/global/insights/women-in-business/grant-thornton-women-in-business-2018-report.pdf

Brown, K. (2021, April 30). The fear black employees carry. *Harvard Business Review.* https://hbr.org/2021/04/the-fear-black-employees-carry

Buchbinder, S. B., Shanks, N. H., & Kite, B. J. (2021). *Introduction to health care management* (4th ed.). Jones & Bartlett Learning.

Caver, K. A., & Livers, A. B. (2002, November). "Dear white boss . . ." *Harvard Business Review,* 80(11), 76–81.

Caver, K. A., & Livers, A. B. (2020, September 15). What has – and hasn't – changed since "Dear white boss..." *Harvard Business Review.* https://hbr.org/2020/09/what-has-and-hasnt-changed-since-dear-white-boss

Davis, M. W. (2018). Absence of diversity at the leadership level. *Journal of Practical Consulting,* 6(1), 148–154.

Ely, R. J., & Thomas, D. A. (2020, November/December). Getting serious about diversity. Enough already with the business case. *Harvard Business Review,* 98(6), 114–122.

Fifer, J. J. (2020, October 14). *Promoting a more diverse and inclusive healthcare workforce is everyone's job.* Healthcare Financial Management Association. https://www.hfma.org/topics/leadership/article/promoting-a-more-diverse-and-inclusive-healthcare-workforce-is-e.html

Wilkerson, I. (2020). *Caste: The origins of our discontents.* Random House.

PART 7

Ethics/Law/Conflict of Interest

CASE 78

Should I Ignore What I Have Seen?

Jenn Block

You are a physician at the Sumner Primary Care clinic in Denver, Colorado, part of a larger hospital-based system. Your clinic manager has recently started a telehealth program to enhance the services for your patients. Other clinics in the area have been leveraging this technology, and your patients are pleased when you announce this is now available. Over the first couple of weeks, this option has become popular, and your schedule has been filled with more patients wanting telehealth. Luckily, your clinic manager has created training sessions, so you have been educated about the legal and ethical aspects of telehealth, including Health Insurance Portability and Accountability Act (HIPAA) laws, personal liability, and the importance of informed consent. You have had a wonderful experience so far and have been able to effectively use this technology to better meet the demands of your patients. An added bonus is patients have reported increased satisfaction.

Your scheduled 9:00 a.m. appointment is with North, a 34-year-old patient with diabetes. You have known North and her family for five years, including her husband, South, and their two small children, East and West. When she comes online for the telehealth visit, you notice she has bruising around her right eye, although it looks like there may be makeup covering it. North immediately starts discussing the new medication she is on and how well she is feeling overall. You notice she is sitting at what must be her kitchen table and mentally note her home looks incredibly well-kept for having two small children. As North is discussing the 10 pounds she has lost recently, you notice her two children run by, followed by her husband.

He yells, "[expletive] North, I thought I told you to get control of these kids, you can't do anything right! You're going to pay for this." He suddenly realizes that she is on a video appointment with you and apologizes. "It's been such a long week, you know how it is."

Although you have not seen South as a patient, you are taken aback. You have met him at previous appointments with North, and he was nice, although not overly talkative. After the incident, you see a notable difference in North's non-verbal communication, and you are concerned. She raises her shoulders up, slinks down in her chair, puts her chin down, and avoids further eye contact with you. Abruptly, she ends the call stating she has to make breakfast and thanks you for seeing her.

While North has never mentioned any issues with her husband, in hindsight, you realize he has accompanied her at every visit. You look back through your previous notes and discover you had noted abnormal bruising on her lower back approximately six months ago at her annual physical, and a broken wrist from when she "fell over a chair" two months ago. You look in the children's charts and don't see anything that would indicate similar concerns. When you are done reviewing the records, you sit at your desk, pondering what you should do.

Discussion Questions

1.   What are the applicable laws for this case?
2.   What are the ethical issues that exist in this case?
3.   What do you recommend as potential solutions?
4.   What are some resources available for victims of domestic violence?
5.   What are some resources available for perpetrators of domestic violence?
6.   Did you make any assumptions while reading this case regarding race, ethnicity, gender or gender identity, sexual orientation, socioeconomic status, culture, or other protected class? Were these assumptions focused at the individual/staff level, clinical/program level, or organizational /administrative level? How do these assumptions affect cultural awareness, cultural knowledge, behaviors, and/or skill development?

Additional Resources

Center for Substance Abuse Treatment. (2014). *Improving cultural competence.* Substance Abuse and Mental Health Services Administration. https://www.ncbi.nlm.nih.gov/books/NBK248428/

Durborow, N., Lizdas, K. C., O'Flaherty, A., & Marjavi, A. (2010). *Compendium of state statutes and policies on domestic violence and health care.* https://www.futureswithoutviolence.org /userfiles/file/HealthCare/Compendium%20Final.pdf

Renault, M. (2020, August 6). What a doctor learns from watching you on video chat. *The Atlantic.* https://www.theatlantic.com/health/archive/2020/08/telemedicine-has-resurrected-house-call /614992/

Simon, M. A. (2021). Responding to intimate partner violence during telehealth clinical encounters. *JAMA, 325*(22), 2307–2308. doi:10.1001/jama.2021.1071

A Missed Cancer Diagnosis

Dale Buchbinder

A 72-year-old male physician with a history of lumbosacral back pain and high cholesterol has been seeing his regular primary care physician (PCP) for several years for annual physical exams. The patient noticed his Prostate-Specific Antigen (PSA) test numbers increased from 1.2 to 2.6. While these numbers were within normal limits, the patient was concerned and discussed the possibility of prostate cancer with his PCP. In addition, the PCP had not done a rectal exam on this patient in several years. After the patient confronted the PCP, he was referred to a specialist in urology.

The urologist examined the patient and found a very hard lesion in the prostate that was suspicious for prostate cancer. Magnetic resonance imaging (MRI) documented a lesion outside of the capsule that was probably prostate cancer. The patient experienced multiple prostate biopsies which demonstrated a high grade, poorly differentiated prostate cancer. The cancer had penetrated the prostate capsule; there was no evidence of metastatic disease with the MRI.

The patient underwent a robotic total prostatectomy that showed the cancer was removed. However, the margins on one side were inadequate. The patient had a course of radiation therapy to where the prostate had been. After several weeks of prostate exercises the patient regained most of his urinary continence.

Discussion Questions

1. What is going on in this case?
2. Identify the main organizational problem in this case.
3. What methods should have been employed to prevent this misdiagnosis?
4. What role might cognitive biases play in this case?
5. What are the options for the patient and family in the future including further treatment and personal plans for dealing with end-of-life disease?
6. Should the patient and his family pursue legal action in this case? If so, for what reasons. What would be the legal basis for such action?
7. Provide your reflections and personal opinions as well as your recommendations for addressing this problem.

Additional Resources

Buchbinder, S. B., Shanks, N. H., & Kite, B. J. (2021). *Introduction to health care management* (4th ed.). Jones & Bartlett Learning.

Desjardins, J. (2021). *Visualizing every single cognitive bias.* World Economic Forum. https://www.weforum.org/agenda/2021/08/cognitive-bias-infographic/

Doherty, T. S., & Carroll, A. E. (2020). Believing in overcoming cognitive biases. *American Medical Association Journal of Ethics, 22*(9), E773–778. doi: 10.1001/amajethics.2020.773.

Kennedy, D. M. (2017). Creating an excellent patient experience through service education: Content and methods for engaging and motivating front-line staff. *Journal of Patient Experience, 4*(4), 156–161.

Lee, C. S., Nagy, P. G., Weaver, S. J., & Toker, D. E. N. (2013). Cognitive and system factors contributing to diagnostic errors in radiology. *American Journal of Roentgenology, 201,* 611–617. doi: 10.2214/AJR.12.10375

Lyratzopoulos, G., Vedsted, P., & Singh, H. (2015). Understanding missed opportunities for more timely diagnosis of cancer in symptomatic patients after presentation. *British Journal of Cancer, 112*(Suppl 1), S84–S91. https://doi.org/10.1038/bjc.2015.47

CASE 80

It's a Private Group Chat

Kevin M. Bush, Jr.

You are the vice president of perioperative services at Amish Country Medical Center (ACMC), a large academic medical center located in rural Pennsylvania. The organization is known for its close knit community and Christian values. ACMC provides health services to all faiths, nationalities, and ethnicities. You received an e-mail from an operating room nurse (ORN) regarding a private group chat between several operating room nurses and clinical nurse leaders. The e-mail reveals that there are photographs of procedures, body parts, and embryos that are now floating around on a social media platform. The ORN mentions in the e-mail that some pictures were particularly unsettling, especially a few that were of an aborted embryo. Many of the nurses often expressed their displeasure with the dilation and curettage (D & C) procedure being performed at the hospital. ACMC has taken the position that this procedure will not be performed unless there are life threatening circumstances or a miscarriage.

You are concerned about this e-mail and schedule a meeting with the ORN. During the meeting you ask to review the private group chat. You find several clinical nurse managers in the group chat, along with about 30 bedside nurses, as well as a few surgeons. There are pictures that do not expose patient identities or medical records; however, there are derogatory remarks regarding patients and procedures. Nurses used surgical slang to refer to D & C procedures as "Dustings and Cleanings" of the uterus. At this point, you have seen enough and return the cellphone. You assure the ORN that the concerns will remain anonymous—however, you are responsible for being ethical.

Discussion Questions

1. What are the facts in this case?
2. What are the legal and ethical ramifications?
3. How should the issues in the case be addressed by management?
4. Is it reasonable to terminate all the parties involved?
5. How could this incident impact the reputation of the organization?
6. Are there any clinical and financial implications?

Additional Resources

Agris, J. L., & Spandorfer, J. M. (2016). HIPAA Compliance and training: A perfect storm for professionalism education? *Journal of Law, Medicine & Ethics*, *44*(4), 652–656.

Johnson, L. J., & Weinstock, F. J. (2012). Correct patient privacy and confidentiality violations. *Medical Economics*, *89*(8), 37–38.

Moses, R. E., Chaitt, M. M., & Jones, D. S. (2014). Social media in health care: Lessons from the field. *Journal of Health Care Compliance*, *16*(5), 17–24.

Social Media Use and Abuse in Health Care

Katherine Corchary

During the COVID-19 pandemic, visitors were not allowed to visit friends and family members in medical facilities to limit contact with COVID-19 positive patients. At this time, Clearview Nursing Facility (CNF) only allowed patients and staff members to enter. With the restriction of visitors, nurses and other medical staff became the patients' only human contacts for days, weeks, and more; patients often developed relationships with the staff.

A nurse, Ford, had been caring for patients who were seriously ill since the beginning of the pandemic. Over the past few months, Ford had become close with several patients. In particular, Ford became close with an elderly man named Mr. Reed who had been sick since testing positive for COVID-19 in May. Mr. Reed initially improved, and he and Ford were able to play cards and trivia games, as well as to share stories from when he fought in World War II. In mid-August Mr. Reed's health began to decline again, and he passed away at the end of August.

Since Ford had a close connection with and had cared for Mr. Reed daily, Ford was deeply affected, and wanted to post a remembrance in his honor on social media. Ford decided to post a picture of them together during the time he was cared for. The post included Mr. Reed's full name, a picture showing his face, and a brief description of their time together.

CNF received notice that a social media post with information about their patient, Mr. Reed, had appeared on Ford's social media account. This post included private information about the patient and had been placed online without the patient's or family's consent. Ford's manager and the human resource (HR) director at CNF have asked to meet with Ford to discuss the social media post.

Discussion Questions

1. What do we know about this case so far?
2. What law has Ford violated?
3. What legal or regulatory entity investigates and resolves this type of concern?

4.   Why do you think the facility staff want to meet with Ford? If you were Ford's manager, what actions would you take?
5.   What legal liabilities might CNF have to deal with, and what might the fallout be from this incident?
6.   What steps should CNF take to prevent this situation from reoccurring?

Additional Resources

Alder, S. (2015, June). What are the penalties for HIPAA violations? *HIPAA Journal.* https://www
     .hipaajournal.com/what-are-the-penalties-for-hipaa-violations-7096/
American College of Surgeons. (2019, May). *Statement on guidelines for the ethical use of social media
     by surgeons.* https://www.facs.org/about-acs/statements/116-social-media
American Medical Association. (n.d.). *HIPAA violations & enforcement.* https://www.facs.org
     /About-ACS/Statements/116-social-media
Desai, D., Ndukwu, J., & Mitchell, J. (2015). Social media in health care. How close is too close?
     The Health Care Manager, 34(3), 225–233. https://journals.lww.com/healthcaremanagerjournal
     /Abstract/2015/07000/Social_Media_in_Health_Care__How_Close_Is_Too.9.aspx
Green, J. (2017). Nurses' online behaviour: Lessons for the nursing profession. *Contemporary Nurse,
     53*(3), 355–367. https://www.tandfonline.com/doi/full/10.1080/10376178.2017.1281749
Jackson, J., Fraser, R., & Ash, P. (2014). Social media and nurses: Insights for promoting health
     for individual and professional use. *The Online Journal of Issues in Nursing, 19*(3). http://
     ojin.nursingworld.org/MainMenuCategories/ANAMarketplace/ANAPeriodicals/OJIN
     /TableofContents/Vol-19-2014/No3-Sept-2014/Insights-for-Promoting-Health.html
Lee Ventola, C. (2014). Social media and health care professionals: Benefits, risks, and best
     practices. *P & T, 39*(7), 491–520. https://www.ncbi.nlm.nih.gov/pmc/articles/PMC4103576/

CASE 82

Surprise MRI

Bobbie Kite

Ms. Shiny was so excited to get her COVID vaccine, as she had waited patiently and was eager to do her part. She was taking what was rumored to be the rougher of the two vaccines in terms of side effects, but she held a positive attitude and knew that none of these possible side effects were deadly. She had had anaphylactic shock before, so after her shot she was asked to stay an extra 15 minutes. No side effects materialized afterward, and she went in for her second shot when it was time. After the second shot, Ms. Shiny experienced what most others did; it wasn't pleasant, but was to be expected.

Four days later, Ms. Shiny developed incredible back pain in the shoulder blade, severe enough to warrant a visit to the nearest urgent care facility. The medical provider identified some possible rotator cuff issues, and recommended magnetic resonance imaging (MRI) and some basic exercises. A couple of days later Ms. Shiny got the MRI, with the most notable finding being intense swelling of the lymph nodes.

She thought to herself, "Could this be a really bad reaction to the second dose?" She asked the provider. They said it was not likely and recommended that she follow up in 30 days to make sure that the swelling resolved.

About five days after this episode, Ms. Shiny went from feeling fine to complete loss of the use of her left arm with excruciating pain within a matter of hours. This prompted another trip to the urgent care. This time, a provider from the same health organization told her that many people had this problem with their shoulder and it was common.

Ms. Shiny asked again, "Could this be a reaction to my second dose of the vaccine?"

The physician said no, it was not, and proceeded to press on Ms. Shiny's arm repeatedly to prove it was a rotator cuff issue, stating, "Many people live with this injury and it isn't a big deal." The physician said, "You need to take this steroid shot, anti-inflammatory shot, and these muscle relaxers now."

Ms. Shiny said, "I have been told not to take either of those, are there alternatives?"

At this question, the physician became incredibly angry and mocked her saying, "You can sit there in pain—or you can do what I am suggesting."

Feeling pressured, Ms. Shiny said okay to the anti-inflammatory shot and the muscle relaxers. The physician stayed in the room until Ms. Shiny took the medicine.

After being made to wait for another hour, the physician returned and Ms. Shiny asked, "Am I free to go now?"

The physician responded with, "I don't know, do you feel relaxed yet?"

To clarify what feeling relaxed meant, Ms. Shiny asked, "Are these pills and shot to actually relax the muscles in my arm, since it still hurts the same amount?"

The physician responded, "They are more for the patient's mental state than treating the actual physical pain."

Feeling insulted and belittled, Ms. Shiny packed up her stuff to leave. She decided to ask one more medical provider, "Do you think the swollen lymph nodes they found on my MRI could be what's causing this pain? Could this all be a reaction to the second vaccination shot?"

She received the similar response, "No, that is highly unlikely." Ms. Shiny suffered in pain for about another two weeks waiting for the lymph nodes to return to normal and then never experienced the shoulder pain again.

Discussion Questions

1.   What is going on in this case?
2.   Identify the main organizational problem in this case.
3.   What are three factors contributing to this problem?
4.   Provide three possible solutions to the problem you identified.
5.   Provide your reflections and personal opinions as well as your recommendations for addressing this problem.

Additional Resources

Buchbinder, S. B., Shanks, N. H., & Kite, B. J. (2021). *Introduction to health care management* (4th ed.). Jones & Bartlett Learning.

Gautham, K. S. (2020). Addressing disruptive and unprofessional physician behavior. *Joint Commission Journal on Quality and Patient Safety*, 46(2), 61–63.

Hanneman, K., Iwanochko, R. M., & Thavendiranathan, P. (2021). Evolution of lymphadenopathy at PET/MRI after COVID-19 vaccination. *Radiology*, 299(3). https://pubs.rsna.org/doi/10.1148/radiol.2021210386

Shapiro, D. E., Duquette, C., Abbott, L. M., Babineau, T., Pearl, A., & Haidet, P. (2019). Beyond burnout: A physician wellness hierarchy designed to prioritize interventions at the systems level. *The American Journal of Medicine*, 132(5), 556–563.

Telehealth Trouble: Follow the Law? Or Do What's Best for the Patient?

Boyd Loehr

You are the clinic manager of a large primary care clinic in the San Diego metro area. Your health center serves many patients who reside in both Baja California, Mexico, and the United States. Often, these patients schedule trips across the border around their medical appointments. Over the past several years, your clinic has invested in innovative care modalities such as synchronous telehealth. The staff have been enthusiastic about buy-in and adoption of this technology. One barrier to implementation of this new technology is that, per law, telehealth services cannot be conducted across state lines or international borders. This law impacts a portion of your clinic's patient population. Many in the clinic believe that offering telehealth services to your multinational patients will further improve their quality of care but have respected the clinic policy and legal limitations in place.

Recently you have learned that one of your providers, Dr. Doright, has been violating your clinic's policy, along with state and federal law, by providing telehealth services to a patient residing in Rosarito, Mexico. You must meet with Dr. Doright to discuss the situation and decide on next steps. In preparing for the meeting, you review applicable state and federal law, as well as relevant clinic policy. You also audit the patient's medical record. During the chart review you see Dr. Doright verified and documented the patient's location but omitted a physical address. Documentation of a patient's physical location during a telehealth visit is standard practice, clinic policy, and a key component of patient safety. Importantly, there has been no negative patient outcome because of these telephone and synchronous video visits.

When you meet with Dr. Doright, you recognize how important the care of this patient is to the doctor. Dr. Doright explains to you that the patient has several medical issues including diabetes and hypertension. Dr. Doright has managed the patient for eight years, and they have an excellent rapport. The patient often said to the doctor, "You're the only one I trust doc, you really understand me." The diabetes and hypertension are well controlled. Dr. Doright worries that if the patient's care is transferred to another physician, or if there is an interruption in routine six-month follow-ups, the patient's health might suffer. Dr. Doright describes the recent transportation problems in coming to San Diego for the patient.

You commend Dr. Doright for their commitment to quality patient care, but must determine if the violations warrant further action. Using an inquiry model and taking a coaching approach, you ask the following questions:

- Do you believe that your actions are in the best interest of the patient?
- If there had been a medical emergency during the visit, what would you have done?
- Are you aware of what the law and our clinic's policy say about conducting telehealth across international borders?

Dr. Doright seems open to your questions, and states, "I was acting in the patient's best interest." The doctor has a general awareness that there is policy against the type of telehealth visit conducted but cannot point to any specific language. It's also noted that Dr. Doright hadn't considered the possibility of an emergency occurring during the visit.

Pushing back with the argument, "For years I've spoken to this patient by phone while living in Mexico. What difference does it make if we're talking by video?"

Later you have an additional conversation and are mindful to respect autonomy. The two of you come to an understanding that, despite the potential benefits to the patient, this type of telehealth encounter across international boundaries can no longer be conducted.

After your conversation you consult with the clinic's risk manager and legal counsel, reviewing with them your conversation with the physician. They determine that, while Dr. Doright did violate clinic policy and state/federal law, the doctor acted with beneficence. As there was no harm to the patient, and anticipating that the licensing board would be unlikely to do any more than provide a warning, the decision is made not to report the incident externally. The incident will be documented only in the human resources file, and the doctor will be provided with additional resources on care delivery via telehealth modalities.

Discussion Questions

1. What are the major issues presented in the case?
2. Was the physician justified in the decision to conduct the visit?
3. What additional actions might the clinic manager have taken?
4. Did the clinic manager, risk manager, and legal team make the correct choice by not reporting the incident to the professional licensing board?
5. In this situation, what other unique circumstances could arise due to the use of telehealth?
6. The physician stated that in the past the patient was contacted by phone while in Mexico. Why is synchronous video different? At what point does a "conversation" become "care"?

Additional Resources

Buchbinder, S. B., Shanks, N. H., & Kite, B. J. (2021). *Introduction to health care management* (4th ed.). Jones & Bartlett Learning.

Kaiser Health News. (2021, September 2). Telehealth's limits: Battle over state lines and licensing threatens patients' options. *U.S. News and World Report*. https://www.usnews.com/news/health-news/articles/2021-09-02/telehealths-limits-battle-over-state-lines-and-licensing-threatens-patients-options

Lee, N. T., Karsten, J., & Roberts, J. (2020, May). *Removing regulatory barriers to telehealth before and after COVID-19*. Brookings Institution Governance Studies and John Locke Foundation. https://www.brookings.edu/research/removing-regulatory-barriers-to-telehealth-before-and-after-covid-19/

Pozgar, G. D. (2016). *Legal aspects of health care administration*. Jones & Bartlett Learning.

Interprofessional Disconnection at a Mental Health Facility

Jihan Mahmoud

Sally is a 37-year-old client with a history of major depressive disorder. She was brought into the mental health care facility by Selina, a neighbor and a close friend. Selina indicated she found Sally wandering around the neighborhood, disoriented, and in poor hygiene. Selina also reported noticeable changes in Sally's behavior over the past few weeks including insomnia, diminished interest in almost all activities they used to do together, and a 10-pound weight loss in four weeks.

Upon arrival to the mental health care facility, Vera, the psychiatric emergency nurse, triaged Sally. Vera noted the client to be verbally and emotionally unresponsive, withdrawn, and apathetic. Dr. Amber, Sally's psychiatrist, ordered intravenous fluids and 30 milligrams of intramuscular imipramine to be given immediately. Vera administered the fluids and medications as prescribed. One hour later, while Vera was preparing to transfer the client to the in-patient unit, Sally was found with a bedsheet tied around her neck, in cardiac arrest. Vera called for a code, and the cardiac arrest code team began resuscitation. Despite the code team's efforts, Sally started having uncontrollable seizures and died. The initial police investigation indicated the client may have attempted suicide. An autopsy detected that the cause of death was lack of oxygen to the brain, anoxic encephalopathy, due to a mixed alcohol and imipramine toxicity.

The mental health facility administrator appointed a safety committee to conduct an incident investigation. The patient's record indicated a recent history of medication nonadherence and missed psychotherapy sessions due to financial challenges and lack of transportation. The mental health nurse who conducted a home visit with the patient two weeks before Sally's emergency admission had made a note in the chart recommending a social worker follow-up visit. However, the social worker follow-up on this recommendation was not evident. During her interview with the safety committee, the social worker informed the safety committee that she attempted to visit Sally, but no one was home.

When Vera was interviewed, she mentioned the client's blood alcohol level was 0.25 during the triage. This level of blood alcohol concentration (BAC) is associated with "severe impairment of mental, physical, sensory function, risk of serious injury" (Lane County Public Health Department, 2021, para. 8). She further indicated that she entered the breathalyzer test result in the client's electronic records and assumed Dr. Amber had reviewed it. However, the documentation of this test or its finding was nowhere to be found in the system. Vera further added that she suspected that the client was suicidal and called Dr. Luis, Sally's psychotherapist, but he was unavailable. When Dr. Amber was questioned by the safety committee, she denied receiving any notification regarding Sally's blood alcohol level or the risk of suicide.

Dr. Luis informed the committee that he ran into Dr. Amber multiple times over the past few weeks and told her Sally was missing the scheduled psychotherapy sessions. However, Dr. Amber denied receiving any information regarding Sally's nonadherence.

The committee concluded that Dr. Amber was responsible for the alcohol-drug toxicity that led to Sally's death. Dr. Amber consulted with an attorney and argued that the client may have died from self-suffocation and demanded an independent autopsy.

Discussion Questions

1. What are the staff- and management-related barriers that interfered with the safety culture at this mental health facility? Provide the rationale for your comments and propose management strategies to overcome these barriers.

2. Outline the gaps in the interdisciplinary team communication and collaboration that led to Sally's death.

3. Reshape the interdisciplinary team collaboration dynamic(s) in this case, demonstrating strategies and a process that bridges the gaps and could have prevented Sally's death.

4. Do you agree with the safety committee conclusion regarding the team member who was responsible for Sally's death? Provide a rationale for your response.

5. Conduct a root-cause analysis (RCA) to examine the causes and the team members who were directly involved in Sally's death.

6. From your RCA, if the independent autopsy revealed that the cause of Sally's death was self-suffocation, would that change the safety committee's conclusion regarding Dr. Amber's responsibility for Sally's death? How might a hypothetical finding impact the RCA outcomes and recommendations?

7. Did you make any assumptions while reading this case regarding race, ethnicity, gender or gender identity, sexual orientation, socioeconomic status, culture, or other protected class? Were these assumptions focused at the individual/staff level, clinical/program level, or organizational/administrative level? How do these assumptions affect cultural awareness, cultural knowledge, behaviors, and/or skill development?

Additional Resources

Center for Substance Abuse Treatment. (2014). *Improving cultural competence*. Substance Abuse and Mental Health Services Administration. https://www.ncbi.nlm.nih.gov/books/NBK248428/

Lane County Public Health Department. (2021). *Alcohol and young adults. What is BAC?* https://preventionlane.org/young-adults-alcohol-bac

Pinals, D. A. (2019). Liability and patient suicide. *Focus (American Psychiatric Publishing)*, 17(4), 349–354. https://doi.org/10.1176/appi.focus.20190023

Pozgar, G. D. (2016). *Legal aspects of health care administration*. Jones & Bartlett Learning.

Sabe, M., Kaiser, S., & Niveau, G. (2021). Suicide in psychiatry and medical liability: A case series. *International Journal of Law and Psychiatry*, 74, 101671.

CASE 85

Medical Equipment and Adverse Drug Events

Marguerite McDowell

You are a surgeon who operated on Anderson to repair a broken leg. The location and type of fracture indicated the recovery period would involve significant pain for the patient. You ordered the use of an intravenous (IV) pain pump. Pain pumps allow the patient to administer their own pain medication, subject to restrictions ordered by the physician. The restrictions limit the amount and timing of the doses. The doses are identical, and the patient can administer a dose by pressing a hand-held button that activates the pump, which then releases the prescribed amount of pain medication into the patient's IV tubing. The medication is available periodically, in this case every two hours. If the patient were to press the button before the two hours have elapsed, nothing would happen.

Prior to each use, the nurse calibrates the pump. The manufacturer supplies the calibration process. Calibration involves the use of harmless saline solution that allows the nurse to observe the amount of fluid flowing through the pain medicine chamber. After calibration, the process requires the nurse who set up the pump to remain at the bedside to supervise the patient during the administration of the first dose.

The nurse correctly calibrated the pump, completed setting it up at the bedside, added the pain medicine, and gave Anderson the hand-held button with instructions on how to use it. The prescribed dose was three milligrams of a strong narcotic every two hours. The medication-holding chamber was loaded with a total of 18 milligrams, or six doses. Anderson's daughter was there, also.

Suddenly an emergency intercom message indicated a patient needed immediate assistance in the room next door. The nurse instructed Anderson to wait until she returned to push the button and stepped next door to assist with the other patient, leaving Anderson alone with only the daughter in the room. The pain was becoming unbearable and Anderson pushed the button.

The valve in the chamber malfunctioned and opened completely, delivering all 18 milligrams of pain medicine into Anderson's blood stream. Anderson stopped breathing and the daughter screamed for help. Other staff rushed in to help and within seconds, Anderson's heart stopped. Cardiopulmonary resuscitation (CPR) was begun and included several shocks with a defibrillator, but after approximately 15 minutes of CPR, Anderson was pronounced dead.

As part of the investigation, you reviewed the pump calibration log and the chamber that malfunctioned with the equipment manufacturer representative. The nurse correctly calibrated the pump. However, the flow-controlling mechanism was locked in the fully open position.

Discussion Questions

1. What are the management issues to address in this case?
2. What are the liability issues to address in this case?
3. Was it reasonable for the nurse to have left Anderson to attend to the patient next door?
4. If your answer is yes, what might the nurse have done differently?
5. What actions would prevent this from happening in the future?

Additional Resources

Caplan, R. A., Vistica, M. F., Posner, K. L., & Cheney, F. W. (1997). Adverse anesthetic outcomes arising from gas delivery equipment: A closed claims analysis. *Anesthesiology, 87*(4), 741–748.

Centers for Disease Control and Prevention. (n.d.). *Adverse drug events in adults.* https://www.cdc .gov/medicationsafety/adult_adversedrugevents.html

The Joint Commission. (n.d.). *Joint Commission resources.* https://www.jointcommission.org /performance-improvement/joint-commission-resources/

The Joint Commission. (2013, April 8). *The Joint Commission sentinel event alert 50: Medical device alarm safety in hospitals.* https://www.jointcommission.org/resources/patient -safety-topics/sentinel-event/sentinel-event-alert-newsletters/sentinel-event-alert -issue-50-medical-device-alarm-safety-in-hospitals/

U.S. Department of Health and Human Services. (n.d.). *Adverse drug events.* https://health.gov /our-work/health-care-quality/adverse-drug-events

U.S. Food and Drug Administration. (n.d.). *Examples of reported infusion pump problems.* https:// www.fda.gov/medical-devices/infusion-pumps/examples-reported-infusion-pump-problems

Weiss, A. J., Freeman, W. J., Heslin, K. C., & Barrett, M. L. (2018, January). *Adverse drug events in U.S. hospitals.* Healthcare Cost and Utilization Project. https://hcup-us.ahrq.gov/reports /statbriefs/sb234-Adverse-Drug-Events.pdf

Young Richiutti Caldwell and Heller, LLC. (n.d.). *What is an infusion pump and what can go wrong?* https://www.yrchlaw.com/blog/2016/11/what-is-an-infusion-pump-and-what-can-go-wrong/

CASE 86

Has Dr. Traveler Abandoned Patients? Part I

Nancy H. Shanks

Shady Acres Nursing Home (SANH) is a for-profit skilled nursing facility located in central New Jersey. The residents are predominantly covered by Medicaid, and the facility struggles to make ends meet. It has always been short-staffed, thus making it difficult to maintain quality.

Tree is a registered nurse employed at SANH and is often stressed while trying to care for a high patient load. Typically, over 25 patients reside on the wing where Tree works. There is always a lot to do, dispensing meds, documentation, providing care, and supervising the certified nursing assistants (CNAs) and other employees. Tree has grown fond of many of the residents, although several problems have arisen recently.

Many of the residents for whom Tree cares have spinal cord injuries and are on heavy duty medications, including oxycontin, oxycodone, and other controlled substances. Dr. Traveler is the physician who oversees the care of these patients and orders their medications. Tree has not seen Dr. Traveler for a quite a while, but that's not unusual because there are other nursing homes with residents to see.

Tree runs into two of the spinal cord patients, J and C, in the hallway. Both of are upset and give Tree an earful.

J says, "I haven't gotten my correct medication for days! What's up with that?" And, C chimes in in agreement.

Before Tree can reply, J adds, "Dr. Traveler hasn't been in to see me in weeks or done an evaluation of my status and my medications in months. My meds are important to me, and I pay close attention to what I am supposed to be taking. I think the doctor changed my medication dosages because what I'm being given is not the same dosage as it's been for years, not the same color or size. Dr. Traveler never discussed anything about changing my meds with me. Now, I'm having trouble controlling my pain and the spasticity in my legs, and Dr. Traveler is never here to assist me. I even tried calling and emailing, with no reply!"

C is also upset about potential medication changes. "My medications are also not the same. I've seen on the news that the government is cracking down on the use of these opioid meds and wants to decrease dosages that people are being given. But, it's just not right to just change someone's medications without discussing it with them."

Tree is shocked. This is the first-time hearing of this problem. "Let me check into this and reach out to Dr. Traveler. I promise I will get back to you asap."

Back at the nurses' station, Tree learns there have been several calls from angry family members of other residents about these same kinds of concerns. Before this problem turns into a facility-wide crisis, Tree heads downstairs to talk to Joyful, the director of nursing (DON).

Joyful is happy all the time, but sometimes doesn't follow through. When presented with this case, Joyful pats Tree on the hand, says there is nothing wrong, explains that Dr. Traveler will be back, and asks again to not worry about this.

Tree is now really confused and tries to call Dr. Traveler, but the voice mail box is full, and they can't leave a message. What should Tree do? Can you provide any advice?

Discussion Questions

1. What is going on here? What is the definition of abandonment? Do you think that Dr. Traveler has abandoned these patients?
2. What types of specific mistakes were made in this case by Dr. Traveler?
3. Do these mistakes fit the definition of abandonment?
4. What rights do nursing home patients have with respect to their care?
5. Have these patients' rights been violated?
6. What has the federal government done to decrease the prescribing and use of opioids?
7. What do you think Tree should do next?

Additional Resources

Babitsky, S., & Mangraviti, J. J. (2005). *The 10 biggest legal mistakes physicians make that lead to claims of patient abandonment* [Blog post]. SEAK, Inc. https://seak.com/blog/uncategorized/10-biggest-legal-mistakes-physicians-make-lead-claims-patient-abandonment/

Centers for Medicare and Medicaid Services. (n.d.). *Your rights and protections as a nursing home resident.* https://downloads.cms.gov/medicare/Your_Resident_Rights_and_Protections_section.pdf

Nicholson, K. M. (2021, June 15). The opioid crackdown is hurting people in pain. *Washington Monthly.* https://washingtonmonthly.com/2021/06/15/the-opioid-crackdown-is-hurting-people-in-pain/

Pozgar, G. D. (2016). *Legal aspects of health care administration.* Jones & Bartlett Learning.

CASE 87

Has Dr. Traveler Abandoned Patients? Part II

Nancy H. Shanks

The saga of Shady Acres Nursing Home (SANH) doesn't end with merely Dr. Traveler's caregiving issues. As mentioned in the previous case, SANH is a for-profit nursing care facility in central New Jersey. The residents are predominantly covered by Medicaid, and the facility struggles to make ends meet. It has always been short-staffed, thus making it difficult to maintain quality.

J, one of the patients who complained about Dr. Traveler, has numerous other issues. J is a man in his 40s who experienced spinal cord and head injuries in a skiing accident when he was 17. When J was well enough, he went on to finish high school and graduate from college with two degrees. J has had more than 15 surgeries for his condition. In addition, he has a baclofen pump in his stomach that is catheterized to his spine to supply medication to control the spasticity in his legs, and he has been moved from several facilities because of poor quality. J was able to walk with a cane for many years, but without regular physical therapy he is now confined to a wheelchair. However, he has been estranged from his family for several years and really has no support from his parents, his siblings, or other relatives. J is alone except for college friends who keep in touch.

When J first was recruited to move to SANH, he was promised many things, such as regular access to medical care, physical therapy (PT) several times a week, high-quality and nutritious food, access to physical exercise and yoga, and a holistic approach to care. This all sounded great to him, and he agreed to the transfer.

Unfortunately, most of what J was told was a come-on to get new residents into the facility. The promised things never materialized. He hasn't received PT; he has lost a lot of weight mainly because the food is horrible, often cold, and to J inedible; there are no exercise programs—the problems go on and on.

B, a resident who has been moved around the facility after not getting along with roommates, has now become J's new roommate. J wasn't asked about this; the staff just moved B in. This change has been difficult, as B stays up all night watching television with the volume turned up so loud that J can't sleep. B screams, swears at, and is abusive to the aides who come in. J has tried to discuss these concerns with B, as well as the administration, but has gotten nowhere. When J asked to be moved, the request was turned down.

The bottom line is that J is not getting the correct medications, now weighs 115 pounds, isn't getting therapy, is in poor physical shape, and is now confined to a wheelchair. Because of these disabilities, J is covered by Medicare and Medicaid. J has a Medicaid case manager (MCM) who has received J's complaints. Unfortunately, the MCM is aligned with SANH administration and hasn't been willing to do anything. J has talked to friends and others, but thinks there is nowhere to turn for help, except that J's Aunt Nin has often offered to help if asked.

Aunt Nin and her husband are watching TV when the phone rings and J's name and number come up on the television screen. It's been nine years since she has heard from J. Now she assumes something must be very wrong with him. She answers the phone and listens to the scenario. Wanting to be supportive, Aunt Nin is asking for your help about what to do next.

Discussion Questions

1. What are the responsibilities of nursing homes with respect to patient care? (Hint: The Centers for Medicare and Medicaid Services (CMS), particularly cms.gov/nursing-homes, may be a good resource for you.)
2. What rights do patients have with respect to their care?
3. Have J's rights been violated?
4. Can Aunt Nin just call up the nursing home and get information about J? Can she talk to J's Medicaid case manager? Why or why not?
5. What does J need to do to allow Aunt Nin to get involved?
6. What do you think Aunt Nin needs to do to try to help J?
7. What resources can she draw upon to help her? Should she contact the New Jersey State Health Department? Are there other resources that might be helpful?

Additional Resources

Centers for Medicare and Medicaid Services. (n.d.). *Your rights and protections as a nursing home resident.* https://downloads.cms.gov/medicare/Your_Resident_Rights_and_Protections_section.pdf

New Jersey Statutes. (2020). *30:13-3: Responsibilities of nursing homes.* https://www.lawserver.com/law/state/new-jersey/nj-laws/new_jersey_laws_30_13-3

Nursing Home Abuse Guide. (2021). *Nursing home regulations.* https://nursinghomeabuseguide.com/legal-action/nursing-home-regulations/

Pozgar, G. D. (2016). *Legal aspects of health care administration.* Jones & Bartlett Learning.

Has Dr. Traveler Abandoned Patients? Part III

Nancy H. Shanks

Our friend, J, is in a somewhat better situation since Aunt Nin came to the rescue and facilitated a move to a smaller facility, called The Chateau. It's a new facility in a renovated large house that is only going to house 15 residents. This initially seems like a better solution for J.

The Chateau is owned by G, a developer who, after trying to care for his own parents, could not find a nice, high-quality facility to care for them. G seems to think he knows enough to become a nursing care facility administrator. There is little staff initially—an Assistant Administrator (AA), two aides, a licensed practical nurse (LPN), and a cook.

G opens The Chateau to residents starting in January 2020, just before the start of the COVID-19 pandemic. This timing is very unfortunate and makes things exceedingly difficult.

J was injured in a skiing accident in 1996 and has had many surgeries to try to address the spinal cord injuries and to place a baclofen pump in his belly and catheterize it to the spine. J has been on many medications over the years and was put on opiates following the last surgery seven years ago. J has had trouble getting pain medications and getting adequate medical care ever since. G and the AA assure J that they will be able to help and will take good care of him.

J is one of the first residents to move into the facility. J knows that new doctors are needed to work with prescription medications, physical therapy (PT), and pain management. G and the AA get J scheduled with a new physician and a new therapist, but that all comes to a screeching halt with the onset of the changes relating to the coronavirus crisis. The doctors decide that they won't be taking any new patients, because their offices are now shut down, the PT facility they refer to is also closed, and they don't want to try to establish a relationship with a new patient when it can only be done virtually. This would be particularly problematic with J because he is on opioids and the doctors know the federal government is now concerned that overprescribing of opioids has become a crisis. The government is monitoring and trying to crack down on physicians who prescribe opioids.

J feels abandoned, again, but as you know from your prior assessment of abandonment in the first two cases, this can only happen when a doctor already has an established relationship with the patient.

Months go by, and the AA finally gets in touch with a pain management doctor, Dr. Burdened, who will take J on as a patient, but has an initial goal of getting J off the opioids. Dr. Burdened has many patients and doesn't have time to visit J in person or explain the process. Dr. Burdened merely tells the facility management team that J's medications will be changed, and they will begin the process of weaning J off the opioids. An appointment will be scheduled with J when this process has been completed.

J is left to go through withdrawal alone without caregivers who know anything about the process, what to expect, what to do, and when. J is basically alone and doesn't know where to turn and what to do. Can you help?

Discussion Questions

1. What is the federal government doing to address the opioid crisis?
2. What does the literature tell us about the process of going through withdrawal from opioids?
3. What is the definition of abandonment? Do you think that Dr. Burdened has abandoned J?
4. What should G and the AA be doing to assist J? Do they have any expertise in this area?
5. What do you think should be done to help J?

Additional Resources

Babitsky, S., & Mangraviti, J. J. (2005). *The 10 biggest legal mistakes physicians make that lead to claims of patient abandonment* [Blog post]. SEAK, Inc. https://seak.com/blog/uncategorized/10-biggest-legal-mistakes-physicians-make-lead-claims-patient-abandonment/

Barnett, M. L. (2021). Opioid prescribing in the midst of crisis – Myths and realities. *New England Journal of Medicine, 382*(12), 1086–1088.

Felbab-Brown, V., Caulkins, J. P., Graham, C., Humphreys, K., Pacula, R. L., Pardo, B., Reuter, P., Stein, B. D., & Wise, P. H. (2020, June). *The opioid crisis in America. Domestic and international dimensions.* Brookings Institution. https://www.brookings.edu/research/overview-the-opioid-crisis-in-america/

Nicholson, K. M. (2021, June 15). The opioid crackdown is hurting people in pain. *Washington Monthly.* https://washingtonmonthly.com/2021/06/15/the-opioid-crackdown-is-hurting-people-in-pain/

Pozgar, G. D. (2016). *Legal aspects of health care administration.* Jones & Bartlett Learning.

Rose, S. (2021, June 5). *What does opioid withdrawal feel like?* [Podcast]. Steve Rose PhD podcast. https://steverosephd.com/what-does-opioid-withdrawal-feel-like/

U.S. Department of Health & Human Services. (2021, February 19). *What is the U.S. opioid epidemic?* https://www.hhs.gov/opioids/about-the-epidemic/index.html

How Did My Patient Get to This Unit?

Nancy H. Shanks

Elaine is a cardiac care nurse at Carefree Metropolitan Hospital (CMH). She is working with Certified Nursing Assistant (CNA) Teaser, who tends to joke with her patients. It's Friday, January 29, 2021, after the 7:00 p.m. shift change, and a new 75-year-old patient, Jimmy, has been admitted to the cardiac care unit (CCU) from the emergency department (ED). While there, he had two liters of fluid drawn from his lungs, and the ED doctors think he is having heart failure. His wife, Amanda, comes in to see him, but Jimmy is exhausted after being prodded and poked for the last seven hours.

Amanda speaks briefly to a cardiology doctor. The cardiologist explains what they think is going on and indicates that they will be doing many tests over the weekend and will know more later. Amanda explains that Jimmy has never had heart problems and is in the advanced stages of cancer treatment but is rebuffed by the physician.

Elaine and Teaser reassure her. "Don't worry, Jimmy is in good hands."

The weekend passes uneventfully. Amanda visits Jimmy on Saturday and Sunday, and he seems to be holding his own. As is typical on weekends, not much has happened and the test results are not back yet. When she is getting ready to leave on Sunday afternoon, Jimmy is very fidgety, wanting to get out of bed and sit in a chair or walk around the floor. Amanda mentions this to the nurses and aides who are on the afternoon shift and is again assured all will be fine.

Monday morning arrives, and Amanda goes in to see Jimmy. She meets Teaser as she comes out of Jimmy's room.

Teaser asks, "Who is this guy? This isn't the same person I've been joking around with all weekend."

Amanda enters the room and is shocked to see Jimmy tied down to the bed with boxing gloves on his hands. "What the heck has happened here? He was anxious when I left, but this is over the top."

Elaine comes in and explains, "Jimmy got combative last night and was fighting with all of the nurses and aides and had to be restrained." She then asks, "What do you think is going on?"

Amanda thinks about this for a moment and immediately says, "I'm not a doctor or a nurse, but I think he's in withdrawal."

Shocked, Elaine says, "What?"

"Jimmy is a cancer patient," Amanda explains. "He's been in extensive treatment for the last year and has been in a lot of pain. He's been on very heavy-duty pain killers for the last couple of months, including morphine, oxycodone, and gabapentin. I gave that list of medications to the folks in the ED. They wouldn't let me in the ED because of COVID-19, so I couldn't be there to advocate for Jimmy and explain things about his condition. Hasn't he been given anything for his pain since he's been here?"

Elaine responds, "He hasn't, but we will get this figured out." She wonders why this patient is in the cardiac care unit. *I think we may have made a big mistake.*

Although Elaine gets Jimmy some pain meds, he takes a turn for the worse and dies the following evening.

Discussion Questions

1.   What do you think went wrong in this case?
2.   What could have been done differently that might have changed the outcome? For example, would the communication, the care, and the outcome possibly have been different if Amanda had been allowed in the ED, and if Jimmy had been admitted to the cancer unit? That is, was there an error in the handoff from the ED to the CCU?
3.   Do you think that this problem was exacerbated by the fact that this scenario took place during the COVID-19 epidemic?
4.   Should the nurses, aides, and doctors on the CCU have recognized that Jimmy was in withdrawal? Is this something they should have been taught in school?
5.   What is involved in a malpractice suit? Do you think Amanda should sue the hospital for malpractice? Why or why not?

Additional Resources

American Cancer Society (ACS). (2019, January 3). *Opioids for cancer pain.* https://www.cancer.org
    /treatment/treatments-and-side-effects/physical-side-effects/pain/opioid-pain-medicines-for
    -cancer-pain.html

Fliesler, N. (2014, November 18). *Safer patient handoffs. Better communication, fewer medical errors
    with I-PASS.* https://hms.harvard.edu/news/safer-patient-handoffs

Pozgar, G. D. (2016). *Legal aspects of health care administration.* Jones & Bartlett Learning.

Smith, D. J., Britigan, D. H., Lyden, E., Anderson, N., Welniak, T. J., & Wadman, M. C. (2015).
    Interunit handoffs from emergency department to inpatient care: A cross-sectional survey of
    physicians at a university medical center. *Journal of Hospital Medicine, 10*(1), 711–717.

Zipperer, L. (2020, July 30). *COVID-19: Team and human factors to improve safety.* Patient Safety
    Network. https://psnet.ahrq.gov/primer/covid-19-team-and-human-factors-improve-safety

CASE 90

Why Were the Paramedics Charged?

Nancy H. Shanks

In the last three years there has been an excessive number of deaths relating to police involvement in the arrests of Black men. One such case was that of Elijah McClain, a resident of Aurora, Colorado. *The Denver Post* (2021) published the following explanation of the arrest on August 14, 2019:

> Elijah McClain, 23, was walking home from a store around 10:30 p.m. on a Saturday evening when authorities contacted him near Billings Street and Colfax Avenue. Someone called 911 to report a "suspicious person" who was wearing a ski mask and waving his arms. McClain routinely wore masks when he was outside because he had anemia—a blood condition—and became cold easily, according to his family. Aurora police said McClain refused to stop walking when they asked him to, and he battled when they attempted to take him into custody. After a struggle, McClain was handcuffed, and officers requested medical assistance. Aurora Fire Rescue injected him with ketamine to sedate him, police said. He suffered cardiac arrest during the ambulance ride to a nearby hospital. (para. 1)

Elijah McClain died several days later, after being declared brain dead.

Initially, the Aurora Police Department (APD) indicated no charges would be filed in this case. After an extensive public outcry and numerous public protests, however, the state convened a grand jury to evaluate the evidence in the case. More than two years after the incident occurred, the grand jury returned its findings on September 1, 2021. Colorado State Attorney General Phil Weiser announced that the three involved police officers and two paramedics had been indicted. It was not surprising that charges were brought against the officers. What was shocking was the fact that charges were brought against the paramedics.

"The two paramedics who administered the sedative ketamine to McClain each face charges of manslaughter and criminally negligent homicide, as well as three counts of assault and six sentence-enhancing charges" (Phillips & Schmelzer, 2021, para. 5).

As several authors pointed out, these charges are rare and may be difficult to prove. Please help me understand what this all means.

Discussion Questions

1. What is a grand jury indictment?
2. What is ketamine and what is it used to treat? What is the standard of care for administering ketamine? (Hint: The Porter article may provide some clues about the standard of care.)
3. What is meant by the terms "manslaughter" and "criminally negligent homicide"?
4. What is required to find negligence in a legal case like this? That is, what is required to show the elements of negligence?
5. Why are the charges against the paramedics considered to be rare?
6. Although most of us are not lawyers, what is your best guess about what the outcome will be in terms of the charges against the paramedics?

Additional Resources

Denver Post Newsroom. (2021, September 1). Elijah McClain timeline: What happened that night and what has happened since. *Denver Post.* https://www.denverpost.com/2020/06/26/elijah-mcclain-timeline-aurora-police/

Fisher, A. D. (2015). 3 reasons to use ketamine for prehospital analgesia. *EMS1.* https://www.ems1.com/pain-management/articles/3-reasons-to-use-ketamine-for-prehospital-analgesia-cBc4tznjJW1AkJe0/

Phillips, N., & Schmelzer, E. (2021, September 2). Three Aurora officers and two paramedics face 32 combined counts in 2019 death. *Denver Post.* https://www.denverpost.com/2021/09/01/elijah-mcclain-grand-jury-aurora-police

Porter, K. (2004). Ketamine in prehospital care. *Emergency Medicine Journal, 21,* 351–354.

Pozgar, G. D. (2016). *Legal aspects of health care administration.* Jones & Bartlett Learning.

Tabachnik, S. (2021, September 2). Experts: Case against officers, medics comes down to intent. *Denver Post.* https://www.denverpost.com/2021/09/02/elijah-mclain-charges-manslaughter-negligent-homicide/

Wolfberg, D. M., & Wirth, S. R. (2021). Legal analysis: What the paramedic criminal charges in the Elijah McClain case mean for EMS. *EMS1.* https://www.ems1.com/legal/articles/legal-analysis-what-the-paramedic-criminal-charges-in-the-elijah-mcclain-case-mean-for-ems-wlPxkOn0Hn4ToKVk

CASE 91

The Butterfly Case

Gregory James Smith

Columbine General Hospital (CGH) is a safety net general hospital in the metropolitan area of Denver, Colorado. Several years ago, a committee was created to guide the product selection process at CGH. The committee is charged with protecting the integrity of its product selection process, making the best choices among the numerous products for operations and patient care, and promoting the good stewardship of the limited financial resources of CGH. The committee routinely vetted all incoming products in most, but not all, of the departments of the hospital. Some departments insisted on having their own system of accomplishing this task and had enough clout with CGH's administration to remain independent of the committee.

The committee conducted its own investigation of any product proposed to be purchased for CGH, including reviewing published product evaluation studies. Some time ago, the committee was asked to evaluate a handheld ultrasound device designed to take the place of the traditional stethoscope, but with many more functions. These devices essentially placed many of the resources of a radiology department in the hands of the examining clinician for an almost instantaneous and highly accurate views of bones, muscles, and circulatory and other organ systems. This device spared the patient from trips to radiology for x-rays or other expensive and time-consuming imaging processes. The physicians in the emergency department (ED), especially Dr. Excited, were very interested in acquiring these devices to examine the patients who presented at the ED. The advantages of the device were obvious, even though it was more expensive than a stethoscope.

The committee's research revealed that there were four possible devices that might fill this need, manufactured by companies A, B, C, and D. Since "trials" of devices under consideration for purchase can be very time-consuming and confusing for the clinicians at CGH, two brands were obtained for evaluation. For the comparison, sample devices were obtained from companies A and B. After a reasonable period of evaluation, those involved in testing the devices favored the one made by company A, but some members of the committee were troubled because Dr. Excited was also a paid consultant for company A. In addition, the doctor was pressing the committee hard for a quick decision in company A's favor, even though some committee members wanted to look at the devices made by companies C and D as well. Others at CGH gave input to the committee, including the chief compliance officer (CCO) who advised the committee to follow Dr. Excited's recommendation, as did another official with the title of director of innovation (DOI). A cost comparison of the devices from companies A and B yielded little difference. Purchasing devices from either manufacturer would represent a significant investment of CGH's cash resources.

After consideration of all these factors, the committee voted to purchase the device made by company A, called the "Butterfly," even though some committee members felt the conflict of interest related to Dr. Excited tainted the process.

Discussion Questions

1. After reviewing this summary of the facts involved in this case, do you believe the committee made the right decision to select company A's device? Provide a rationale for your decision.

2. Should the committee have excluded the device made by company A because of the financial relationship of company A with Dr. Excited, regardless of whether company A's device appears to the best one for the tasks at hand and is available at a competitive price?

3. Should the committee be influenced by the recommendations of other executives at CGH in making its choices or should other executives (if not committee members) stay out of these procurement decisions?

4. Should CGH require that all departments in the hospital use the committee process? Provide a rationale for your decision.

5. What other steps should CGH take in its procurement process to avoid the conflict of interest problem that arose in this case? For example, if published evaluation studies do not recommend the first choice being recommended to the committee by anyone at CGH, should the published studies take precedence in the committee's decision-making?

Additional Resources

Buchbinder, S. B., Shanks, N. H., & Kite, B. J. (2021). *Introduction to health care management* (4th ed.). Jones & Bartlett Learning.

Mayo Clinic Board of Governors. (2012). *Conflict of interest policy*. https://www.mayoclinic.org/documents/mc0219-09-pdf/DOC-20078760

Muth, C. C. (2017). Conflict of interest in medicine. *JAMA, 317*(17), 1812. https://jamanetwork.com/journals/jama/fullarticle/2623608

Pozgar, G. D. (2016). *Legal aspects of health care administration*. Jones & Bartlett Learning.

The Joint Commission. (n.d.). *Conflict of interest policy*. https://www.jointcommission.org/about-us/policies-and-financials/conflict-of-interest/

PART 8

Crossing the Line/ Fraud

CASE 92

Malady or Malingerer?

Dale Buchbinder

Mr. Robinson, a 42-year-old male, presented to Dr. Jones's office with a history of bilateral leg swelling and pain. The physician evaluated Mr. Robinson and found a mild venous insufficiency in both legs. Dr. Jones started him on a trial of compression stockings. However, after three months he was not getting any benefit from the stockings. Further evaluation, which included an invasive intravascular venogram, demonstrated bilateral hemodynamically significant iliac vein stenosis (i.e., narrowing of the vein). Dr. Jones treated the stenosis with bilateral iliac vein stenting (i.e., the placement of a metal tube into a vein to keep it open).

Mr. Robinson returned for a follow-up visit. He complained of constant pain to Dr. Jones; however, the physician and his staff noted the patient walked into the office with no apparent difficulty and laughed and flirted with the staff. Mr. Robinson requested Dr. Jones to complete disability forms for him. Instead, Dr. Jones referred him to physical therapy and to his primary care doctor, as it was impossible to determine if Mr. Robinson actually had a disability.

Mr. Robinson began calling the office, threatening the staff and the physician with legal action. Mr. Robinson was hospitalized and claimed it was because his stents clotted. However, upon review of his case with the doctors at the hospital, it turned out his stents were fine, and he had a hernia. At this point, Dr. Jones discharged Mr. Robinson from his practice and provided him with a list of vascular surgeons and their contact information for follow-up.

The practice did not hear from him for over a year. One day, Dr. Jones's office received a call from a disability company asking for verification of a disability form Mr. Robinson submitted. After reviewing the form, Dr. Jones saw it was not his handwriting. It was evident the patient had forged the doctor's signature, and the practice provided this information to the disability company.

Discussion Questions

1. Was it appropriate for the practice to discharge the patient after he threatened the staff and the doctor?
2. What are the legal implications of forging a physician's signature on a disability form?

3.   If you are the practice manager in this case, should you report this action to legal authorities?
4.   What are the steps for reporting suspected disability fraud?

Additional References

Office of Inspector General, Social Security Administration. (n.d.). *Do you suspect fraud, waste, or abuse?* https://oig.ssa.gov/

Office of Inspector General, Social Security Administration. (n.d.). *Making false statements on claims.* https://oig.ssa.gov/fraud-reporting/making-false-statements/

Ruffing, K. (2015, September 21). *Disability insurance has many safeguards against fraud and abuse.* Center of Budget and Policy Priorities. https://www.cbpp.org/blog/disability-insurance-has-many-safeguards-against-fraud-and-abuse

Scott, J. (2021, March 29). Former postal carrier from Montgomery County sentenced for disability fraud. *Fox 5 News.* https://foxbaltimore.com/news/local/former-postal-carrier-from-poolesville-sentenced-for-disability-fraud

Social Security Administration (SSA). (n.d.). *The faces and facts of disability.* https://www.ssa.gov/disabilityfacts/facts.html

CASE 93

A Gun in the ED

Sharon B. Buchbinder

Nurse Ryan has been working in the Emergency Department (ED) of Hillside Hospital (HH) for over a decade. Located in an affluent county in Maryland, HH enjoys an excellent reputation and serves a wide range of patients from newborns to octogenarians. While Ryan's job ranges from tedious to frantic on a good day, she has never felt unsafe. In fact, the security guards are off-duty county police officers, one on each shift, so she and the other ED staff know they are well-protected.

Late one evening as Ryan is just about to leave for the day, a sleeping man is brought in by a well-dressed woman via wheelchair. Ryan immediately recognizes Mrs. and Mr. Greenback, mega-donors to HH. Mr. Greenback is a former athlete and has been the face of many HH fundraising campaigns.

"He passed out after drinking a quart of vodka," Mrs. Greenback says with a little sob. "Maybe *this* time he'll be ready for rehab."

Shouting at the in-take clerk to get a doctor, Ryan knows she must get Mr. Greenback out of the waiting room before anyone else recognizes him. Moving as fast as she can, Ryan motions to Mrs. Greenback to follow her and wheels him into a private room. She and a muscular orderly lift him onto a gurney. Mrs. Greenback takes a seat in the corner, covers her bruised face, and sobs.

Knowing intoxicated patients can be unpredictable, she asks the orderly to stay with her as she sets up a Ringer's Lactate IV. There have been rumors of domestic violence swirling around the wealthy duo, but looking at this beautiful couple, who would believe that? After all, she tells herself, people are jealous of celebrities—they make things up all the time. Even if Mrs. Greenback has a black eye, there *must* be an innocent explanation.

Just as Ryan inserts the butterfly into the patient's arm, Mr. Greenback wakes up screaming.

"What the hell do you think you're doing?"

"You're in Hillside Hospital Emergency Department, Mr. Greenback. You passed out, and your wife was concerned."

He sits up, his face twisted in rage.

"You witch," he shouts and rips the needle out. "I'll show you who's in charge."

A big black gun is pointed straight at Ryan.

Mrs. Greenback screams, "Honey, no, please don't—"

The gun goes off, nearly deafening Ryan. Chaos erupts, everyone is screaming, and Ryan can't believe the bullet missed her. She whirls to run for the exit just as Mrs. Greenback falls back into the chair, a crimson stain blossoming in the bosom of her white designer dress.

Discussion Questions

1. What is going on in this case?
2. Identify the main organizational problem in this case.
3. What are three factors contributing to this problem?
4. Provide three possible solutions to the problem you identified.
5. Provide your reflections and personal opinions as well as your recommendations for addressing this problem.

Additional Resources

Blando, J. D., Cramer, R. J., & Szklo-Coxe, M. (2019). Hospital security programs and policies related to guns and other weapons. *Journal of Healthcare Management, 64*(3), 157–166.

Buchbinder, S. B., & Kite, B. J. (2021). Special topics and emerging issues in health care management. In S. B. Buchbinder, N. H. Shanks, & B. J. Kite (Eds.), *Introduction to health care management* (4th ed.) (pp. 416–424). Jones & Bartlett Learning.

Edmonson, C. (2019). Practitioner application: Hospital security programs and policies related to guns and other weapons. *Journal of Healthcare Management, 64*(3), 166–168.

Hays, D. A. (2019, November 22). "Caring for our caregivers:" House passes unprecedented workplace violence prevention bill. *National Law Review.* https://www.natlawreview.com/article/caring-our-caregivers-house-passes-unprecedented-workplace-violence-prevention-bill

CASE 94

I'm Calling About Your Test Results

Sharon B. Buchbinder

The phone rang for the tenth time, and 75-year-old Rose Wolf could no longer ignore it. Her husband yelled from the TV room that it was probably just another scammer trying to sell non-existent car warranties. *What if it was someone important, like her doctor's office?* She had some blood drawn, and they always called if something was wrong.

She grabbed the phone. "Yes?"

"Mrs. Wolf," a man said. "I'm so glad we caught you. It's important."

"Is it about my blood tests?"

"Yes—yes, that's exactly what it's about. Your tests came back with some abnormal results."

"Oh." She clutched the phone. "Should I get my husband? He's just in the other room."

"It's pretty serious, so yes, go get him. I can wait."

"Joe," Rose shouted. "Come to the phone."

"What?" *Why doesn't he just wear the darn hearing aid?*

"I've got abnormal blood."

Joe clicked the remote and silenced the TV. "Abnormal what?"

"Blood. My blood is abnormal."

"Give me the phone." Her husband made his way to the kitchen with the help of his walker. "Let me talk to them."

Tears blurred her vision. *What if it's cancer? Who will take care of Joe?*

"Yes, okay. I see." Joe frowned. "How soon can we do this test? Today? We'll be there."

She clutched the back of a chair. "Test for what?"

Joe patted her hand. "Cancer."

Her stomach dropped. "Where do we need to go?"

"To the other coast, Boca Raton."

"We don't know any doctors in Boca Raton. Why do we have to go so far?"

"This guy said he's the best oncologist in the State of Florida. He can do genetic testing to see if you're eligible for immunotherapy." He patted his pockets and pulled out his car keys. "Don't worry, it's free. Medicare pays for it."

© Willyam Bradberry/Shutterstock.

261

Now it was Rose's turn to be suspicious. "What doctor's office did he say he was calling from?"

"Your usual guy, Dr. McKeon."

"My doctor's name is *McKesson*." She picked the phone up and began to punch the numbers. "This sounds fishy. I'm calling his office right now."

Discussion Questions

1.   What is going on in this case?
2.   Identify the main problem in this case.
3.   What are three factors contributing to this problem?
4.   Provide three possible solutions to the problem you identified.
5.   Provide your reflections and personal opinions as well as your recommendations for addressing this problem.

Additional Resources

Association of Certified Fraud Examiners. (2021). Elderly fraud scams: How they're being targeted and how to prevent it. *The Fraud Examiner*. https://www.acfe.com/fraud-examiner .aspx?id=4294997223

Breckenridge, E. (2021). Health care regulation and compliance. In S. B. Buchbinder, N. H. Shanks, & B. J. Kite (Eds.), *Introduction to health care management* (4th ed.) (pp. 391–409). Jones & Bartlett Learning.

Federal Bureau of Investigation (FBI). (n.d.). *Elder fraud.* https://www.fbi.gov/scams-and-safety /common-scams-and-crimes/elder-fraud

Federal Bureau of Investigation (FBI). (2020). *Elder fraud report.* https://www.ic3.gov/Media/PDF /AnnualReport/2020_IC3ElderFraudReport.pdf

Sabatini, P. (2021, September 13). Hi, it's Medicare calling with free genetic testing services. In this case, it's best to be rude and hang up. *Pittsburgh Post Gazette.* https://www.post-gazette.com/business /money/2021/09/13/Medicare-Becky-robocall-scam-fraud-free-genetic-testing-Covid-AARP /stories/202109120042

U.S. Department of Justice (DOJ). (2021, May 3). *Three Florida men charged in $46 million health care fraud, kickback, and money laundering conspiracy.* https://www.justice.gov/opa/pr /three-florida-men-charged-46-million-health-care-fraud-kickback-and-money-laundering

U.S. Department of Justice (DOJ). (2021, September 17). *National health care fraud enforcement action results in charges involving over $1.4 billion in alleged losses.* https://www.justice.gov/opa/pr /national-health-care-fraud-enforcement-action-results-charges-involving-over-14-billion

CASE 95

Patient Dumping

Christina Cottrell

The newspaper and television headlines scream: *"Independence Hospital leaves patient outside to freeze." "Caught on video: Man dumped outside of hospital wearing only a hospital gown." "Boston hospital tosses patient to cold streets."*

Independence Hospital, based in inner city Boston, is part of Revolutionary Health System, which owns and operates over 25 hospitals along the east coast. A 767-bed urban hospital, Independence's general patient population consists of low-income and uninsured individuals. The majority of this population utilizes the emergency department for either primary care or behavioral health—mental health and substance use disorders—services. In some cases, individuals are homeless and looking for respite in a warm and comfortable environment.

During a cold February night, a patient wearing only hospital socks and a gown is slumped over and sobbing on the curb outside of the Independence emergency department (ED). A passerby notices the person in distress and asks if they need help. The passerby is so shocked by the situation, they use their cell phone to record the incident and call 911.

Within hours, the video goes viral on social media and the news media takes notice. Upon investigation, reporters determine the patient, 33-year-old Birch Woodland, walked into the ED during the afternoon of the incident with a broken nose. Once Birch received treatment and their discharge papers, they are resistant and reportedly combative. Hospital security intervenes and removes the wailing Birch to the sidewalk, holding them up upright by the arms. The security guards laugh, calling Birch "crazy." Further research reveals the patient suffers from schizophrenia.

Neither Independence Hospital nor the Revolutionary Health System make any type of statement within the first week of the incident, despite national media attention and public outcry. No press conferences. No promise of improvement. They do not respond to any media requests from the press or even from the Woodland family. The president and chief executive officer (CEO) of Revolutionary Health finally hold a public press conference. The hospital acknowledges the incident and apologizes, but places blame on Birch's combativeness. The CEO states, "The security officers and the ED staff were simply doing their jobs."

Internally, there is finger pointing but no accountability. Security blames the ED providers. The ED providers blame the behavioral health team. The behavioral health team blames administration. Administration is blaming no one—except Birch. Like its delayed and limited statement to the public, hospital leadership sends out no communication about the incident to its team members and providers until a week after the occurrence.

Discussion Questions

1. What is going on in this case?
2. Did you make any assumptions while reading this case regarding race, ethnicity, gender or gender identity, sexual orientation, socioeconomic status, or culture?
3. Were these assumptions focused at the individual/staff level, clinical/program level, or organizational/administrative level?
4. How do these assumptions affect cultural awareness, cultural knowledge, behaviors, and/or skill development?
5. Provide three possible solutions to the problem you identified.
6. Provide your reflections and personal opinions as well as your recommendations for addressing this problem.

Additional Resources

Buchbinder, S. B., Shanks, N. H., & Kite, B. J. (2021). *Introduction to health care management* (4th ed.). Jones & Bartlett Learning.

Center for Substance Abuse Treatment. (2014). *Improving cultural competence.* Substance Abuse and Mental Health Services Administration. https://www.ncbi.nlm.nih.gov/books/NBK248428/

Centers for Medicare and Medicaid Services (CMS) (2012). *Emergency Medical Treatment & Labor Act (EMTALA).* https://www.cms.gov/Regulations-and-Guidance/Legislation/EMTALA

Holm, A. L., Gorosh, M. R., Brady, M., & White-Perkins, D. (2017). Recognizing privilege and bias: An interactive exercise to expand health care providers' personal awareness. *Academic Medicine, 92*(3), 360–364.

Kendi, I. X. (2019). *How to be an anti-racist.* One World.

Kennedy, M. (2018, March 21). Federal regulator cites Baltimore hospital after patient left at bus stop in gown. *NPR.* https://www.npr.org/sections/thetwo-way/2018/03/21/595628103/federal-regulator-cites-baltimore-hospital-after-patient-left-at-bus-stop-in-gown

McGregor, B., Belton, A., Henry, T. L., Wrenn, G., & Holden, K. B. (2019). Improving behavioral health equity through cultural competence training of health care providers. *Ethnicity & Disease, 29*(Suppl 2), 359.

Meyer, H. (2018, March 20). CMS cite University of Maryland hospital for EMTALA violations. *Modern Healthcare.* https://www.modernhealthcare.com/article/20180320/NEWS/180329990/cms-cites-university-of-maryland-hospital-for-emtala-violations

Office of Minority Health. (2020). *Think cultural health. What is CLAS?* https://thinkculturalhealth.hhs.gov/clas/what-is-clas

Pozgar, G. D. (2016). *Legal aspects of health care administration.* Jones & Bartlett Learning.

Effective Communication During Difficult Times

Stephen Duarte

After a long week at the Brewster County Pain Management Group (BPMG), Lee, the billing and coding supervisor, finally had a chance to relax and reflect on the week's events. Lee felt both overwhelmed and frustrated with how things were going at BPMG, but also knew it was not business as usual. The practice had been recently acquired, and with that acquisition came a new, inexperienced administrator. Lee knew the effects of those changes would eventually subside, but to have it all take place during the COVID-19 pandemic made things much more complicated.

For the most part, BPMG ran smoothly, but as people began to work from home, many of the daily operations were being overlooked. It was expected that not everything would run smoothly under the circumstances, but Lee felt that many important issues were not being addressed. One situation troubled Lee more than the others, and could result in the practice being accused of Medicare fraud.

Brewster County Pain Management Group

The BPMG is in the Brewster County area of North Dakota and has been serving the surrounding communities since 1985. Its reputation is good, but had been better in the previous years. The practice has had frequent management and employee turnover and has gone through numerous acquisitions over the years. Recently, BPMG has been operating as an independently owned physician practice, but in 2020 BPMG was acquired by Oaktree Health, a national health care system. Since the acquisition, many changes occurred, including Oaktree's placement of Taylor as the BPMG Practice Administrator.

Taylor

Taylor started working at Oaktree as a customer service representative (CSR) while attending college. Taylor enjoyed working in health care and at Oaktree and ultimately decided to get a master's degree in health care administration with the hopes to transition to a hospital setting one day. Taylor had a long history with Oaktree Health and eventually had participated in Oaktree's administrator training program and had been identified as one of Oaktree's promising future administrators.

BPMG consisted of seven doctors, all of whom specialized in orthopedics and pain management. Dr. James Harsh had been the practice medical director and liaison to St. Pius Hospital (a local hospital) and Oaktree Health for many years. His career began as an orthopedic surgeon, but as retirement neared, Dr. Harsh stopped performing surgeries and transitioned to pain management specific to orthopedic traumas. With over 40 years of experience, Dr. Harsh was well respected by peers, who jokingly considered Dr. Harsh the "Elder" of the local pain management community and a valuable resource.

Dr. Harsh had a "my way or the highway" approach to practicing medicine. In a recent interview, Dr. Harsh was quoted as saying:

> I do not quite understand why anyone would question someone such as myself. I have decades of experience and pretty much have seen everything. Just do as I say, and both of our lives will be much simpler.

Everyone was aware of Dr. Harsh and the preferred approach, even the office staff, who stay as far away as possible out of fear of retaliation.

Lee

Lee has worked for BPMG for over 30 years and has held multiple positions and is familiar with all aspects of the practice's daily operations. At one point, Lee had served as the interim administrator of the practice, but eventually settled into the current position as the billing and coding supervisor. Despite being a few years away from retirement, Lee takes this job seriously and takes pride in doing it well.

As part of Lee's responsibility for the oversight of all the practice's billing and coding, a primary responsibility is to assure that the physicians' dictation of the patient visits and all associated current procedural terminology (CPT®) codes match the billing submission to the insurance companies for reimbursement.

During the coronavirus pandemic's initial stages, BPMG re-evaluated its current business practices to determine what adjustments were needed to accommodate local and federal requirements while keeping their employees and patients safe. After much deliberation, BPMG shut down most of its operations and many employees worked from home. Lee was one of those employees. During that time, it was challenging to communicate with everyone inside the organization. As a result, important information sometimes did not get disseminated correctly.

The COVID-19 pandemic changed a lot of the billing process. Insurance companies began allowing for telemedicine to accommodate the stay-at-home orders issued by the Governor of North Dakota. Insurance companies had two reimbursable telemedicine categories: audio/visual and teleconference. During an audio/visual visit, the physician used a webcam to see their patient in the comfort and safety of their home. For a teleconference, the physician would only use the telephone for patient visits and consultations.

During the initial stages of the COVID-19 stay-at-home order, Medicare did not reimburse for either telemedicine category. However, a few months later, Medicare announced that it would cover both telemedicine categories for visits with patients, but these would be reimbursed at different rates. Audio/visual was reimbursed at a higher rate than telephonic communication with the patient. According to Medicare guidelines, each telemedicine category had a specific CPT code and they could not be used interchangeably.

Although neither Taylor nor Lee sent any official emails regarding the Medicare changes, Dr. Harsh had heard of the Medicare changes to its telemedicine policy through another physician. Dr. Harsh began using audio/visual and telephonic communications for Medicare patients, assuming Lee was aware of the changes though the new Medicare policy was never discussed or confirmed with Lee. After all, it was reasoned, the coding and billing department was Lee's responsibility.

Working from home, Lee reviewed the physicians' dictations and compared them to the CPT coding and billing information to be submitted for Medicare reimbursement. During the process, Lee noticed that Dr. Harsh dictated that visits were being conducted via teleconference, which suggested that everything was done over the phone and no audio/visual was used. When comparing the billing CPT codes, Lee noticed that Dr. Harsh used the audio/visual CPT code. Lee was confused about why Dr. Harsh dictated teleconferences but submitted reimbursement CPT codes for audio/visual. Was this a mistake? Lee knew it was the physician's responsibility to dictate the patients' visit and identify the appropriate CPT code. Lee's role was to ensure they matched.

If Lee submitted Dr. Harsh's bills as coded to Medicare, in an audit, it could be considered Medicare fraud. Based on past experiences and Dr. Harsh's "my way or the highway" demeanor, Lee was hesitant to speak with Dr. Harsh directly. However, the matter needed to be addressed. After much deliberation, Lee sent Taylor an email explaining Dr. Harsh's discrepancies, an alert that submitting these services under their current CPT codes for reimbursement would not be appropriate. Lee indicated the only way to correct the problem was for Dr. Harsh to review each dictation and corresponding CPT code to verify their accuracy. Lee estimated that Dr. Harsh would have to review approximately 100 patient files, a significant amount of re-work for Dr. Harsh. Lee concluded the email by asking Taylor to help correct the situation.

The next day when Lee logged onto to the work account, there was an email from Taylor. While reading it, Lee noticed that Taylor had forwarded the entire email directly to Dr. Harsh and copied Lee on it. In the email, Taylor wrote, *"Dr. Harsh, Lee has some concerns about discrepancies between your dictated Medicare patient visits and the CPT codes indicated for billing. Please read Lee's email below and correct any discrepancies."*

Lee's stomach turned and heart started to beat faster. Why would Taylor forward the entire email to Dr. Harsh? Taylor knows Dr. Harsh is challenging to work with, and now it's going to be impossible.

Dr. Harsh responded, *"They were all done audio/visual, and I am not going to change anything. That's Lee's job."*

Based on Dr. Harsh's response Lee suspected Dr. Harsh used a combination of both telemedicine categories and did not want to go through all the records to correct the situation, blanketing all the consultations as audio/visual. In doing so, this raised two concerns. First, the practice would not be billing appropriately, and if billed inappropriately for services not rendered, it could be committing Medicare fraud.

Lee took a moment and reread the email multiple times. Lee hesitated to interject any thoughts to the administrator. Because Lee's relationship with Dr. Harsh was not good, there was also concern about confronting Dr. Harsh. That would not be an easy discussion.

Lee was in a tough spot. Should Lee question Dr. Harsh about the dictation and billing practices, or should he do what the doctor says and switch all the consultations to the audio/visual category? Lee knew switching everything to audio/visual was not the right thing to do. In addition, it was the physician's responsibility to identify the appropriate code and dictate accordingly. Because Taylor was new and most likely did not want to create tension between the doctors, Lee did not feel supported.

Discussion Questions

1. Identify all the major issues concerning Lee's situation. How would you solve them?
2. Should Lee talk to Taylor about forwarding the email to Dr. Harsh?
3. What should Lee do about Dr. Harsh and their relationship going forward? Should Taylor be a part of the process? Who should lead the effort?
4. What role did the pandemic and stay-at-home order play in creating Lee's dilemma?
5. Based on how Taylor managed Lee's email, how would you assess Taylor's readiness to be an administrator? How could Taylor have managed the situation differently?
6. If Lee complies with Dr. Harsh's orders, could that be considered culpable of committing Medicare fraud—or would Lee be let off for "just following orders"?
7. Does Lee bear some responsibility for staying on top of changes in Medicare billing and reimbursement policies, especially since telemedicine became a major issue during the pandemic?
8. In the bigger picture of operations of BPMG, should Taylor address the problem of employees' fear of Dr. Harsh?
9. Did you make any assumptions while reading this case regarding race, ethnicity, gender or gender identity, sexual orientation, socioeconomic status, culture, or other protected class? Were these assumptions focused at the individual/staff level, clinical/program level, or organizational/administrative level? How do these assumptions affect cultural awareness, cultural knowledge, behaviors, and/or skill development?

Additional Resources

Center for Substance Abuse Treatment. (2014). *Improving cultural competence*. Substance Abuse and Mental Health Services Administration. https://www.ncbi.nlm.nih.gov/books/NBK248428/

Dukes, T. (2021, September 9). Latest COVID surge stressing hospital staff, space across North Carolina. *News & Observer.* https://www.newsobserver.com/news/coronavirus/article 254099708.html

Harte, J., & Bernstein, S. (2021, September 17). Some U.S. hospitals forced to ration care amid staffing shortages, COVID-19 surge. *Reuters.* https://www.reuters.com/world/us /some-us-hospitals-forced-ration-care-amid-staffing-shortages-covid-19-surge-2021-09-17/

Marcozzi, D. E., Pietrobon, R., Lawler, J. V., French, M. T., Mecher, C., Baehr, N .E., & Browne, B. J. (2021). The application of a hospital medical surge preparedness index to assess national pandemic and other mass casualty readiness. *Journal of Healthcare Management, 66*(5), 367–378.

Masson, G. (2021, September 30). Cleveland health system implements new staffing strategies amid COVID-19 surge. *Becker's Hospital Review.* https://www.beckershospitalreview.com/hospital -management-administration/cleveland-health-system-implements-new-staffing-strategies -amid-covid-19-surge.html

Medina-Craven, M. N., & Ostermeier, K. (2021). Investigating justice and bullying among healthcare workers. *Employee Relations, 43*(1), 31–44. https://doi.org/10.1108/ER-04-2019-0195

Perry, N. (2021). When telehealth went viral: How the COVID-19 pandemic influenced the rapid move to virtual medical treatment, and what non-rural providers not treating COVID-19 patients should do about it. *Journal of Health Care Finance, 47*(4).

Schumaker, E. (2021, August 13). Short-staffed hospitals battling COVID surge after opting not to staff up. *ABC News.* https://abcnews.go.com/US/short-staffed-hospitals-battling-covid-surge -opting-staff/story?id=79360422

CASE 97

Asking to Make Someone Dead

Sarah Hess and Kristen Dugan

Carie had been an EEG (electroencephalography) technician (tech) for almost three years at Westside Regional Medical Center (WRMC). She had obtained her national registry credential and was considered top in her class. Carie loved her job. She loved performing EEGs on all age groups and was known for her gentle bedside manner. In her position at the hospital, she performed several different modalities of testing, including EEGs, nerve conduction velocity (NCV) tests, evoked potential (EP) tests, epilepsy monitoring, and other operating room (OR) monitorings. Many times, Carie would be in the operating room all day recording and monitoring patients' waveforms to make sure they did not wake up with neurological deficits following procedures. She was admired by her peers and the physicians who read and conducted studies within their department. Many of the neurologists would call Carie while performing the procedures to get her opinion of the waveforms so they would not have to come to the hospital and read the records until the following day. They bragged about how Carie could save them a trip, and would call in orders for the patient according to what she saw on the recordings. All the doctors she worked with valued her clinical opinions and interpretation of the recordings.

WRMC was well known in the state for their successful open-heart surgeries and quality neurological care. It was not at all unusual for patients to be airlifted or transported to WRMC for traumas and invasive procedures from other small medical centers. Carie felt she was a valued team member and was proud of her accomplishments.

One Thursday, Carie had been in the OR monitoring for subarachnoid hemorrhage clamping. This was the fourth time she had a long case in the OR that week. The OR case did not go as expected, and issues arose. The case took four hours longer than the original five hours planned. After nine hours of constant monitoring in the OR with no breaks, Carie was ready to go home. She cleaned her equipment and entered the lab to complete her charges and saw an order on the printer for a STAT (immediate) EEG in the neurointensive care unit (Neuro ICU). Carie called the floor to determine whether the patient needed to be assessed for any brain activity. Carie knew she was already past the allotted time she was to be there. The memo she received last week stated clearly there was to be no more overtime allowed—and no exceptions. However, because Carie was the only registered tech there that week, she was going to have to be the one to perform the procedure to determine electrocerebral silence (ECS), also known as electrocerebral inactivity (ECI), on the patient. She rushed to gather supplies and equipment and hurried to the patient's room.

Carie entered the Neuro ICU and started hooking the patient up. She was exhausted, knew the clock was ticking, and was trying to move as fast as she could. Carie knew she would be cutting it close to get out on time. The last thing she felt she needed was to explain why she stayed late to her new supervisor. They had already written up four people for overtime. When it was time to begin the record, the channels were not responding appropriately. Oh NO! In Carie's haste, she had forgotten to hook up the additional leads required for an ECS/ECI. Moving rapidly, Carie added the additional leads, constantly watching and fearing the clock.

After the record ran for a few minutes, Carie was able to see the waveforms were indeed flatlining on the majority of the record. However, there were small diffuse intermittent waveforms with measurable amplitude in two channels. These were representative of the left parieto-occipital area. Carie had run the record for about 25 minutes at this point. She had just completed painful stimulation on the patient to try and elicit some brain activity in the other channels, when she heard the nurse call her name. The nurse brought Carie the mobile phone with a call from the patient's neurosurgeon, Dr. Marchin. This was the same physician with whom she had been in the OR all day.

Dr. Marchin asked what she saw on the recording. He was tired and might not make it back to the hospital since he had already left. Carie informed him the recording was mostly flatline. However, there were some low amplitude, but recognizable waveforms in the left parieto-occipital area. Dr. Marchin asked Carie if she elicited a response from the patient following painful stimulation.

Carie said, "No."

Dr. Marchin asked if the waveforms could be an artifact.

Carie explained she had hooked additional electrodes to the bed, ventilator, and IV pumps to prove these were not physiological findings compared to brain-wave physiological findings, as their ECS/ECI protocol dictated. Again, she stated the findings on the record were not artifacts, but biological waveforms. They were minute and small across the double distance montage, but there was minimal activity in two channels.

Carie could tell by Dr. Marchin's response he was not pleased with this news. If the patient was not in ECS/ECI, then he was going to have to come and do an evaluation. Dr. Marchin asked Carie to look in the chart and see if the patient was an organ donor. Carie checked and confirmed the patient was an organ donor. Dr. Marchin told Carie the patient had suffered multiple myocardial infarctions and was oxygen deprived for a long time. It was his professional opinion that the patient would expire in the night. However, he was hoping the record would show ECS/ECI so they could go ahead and pull the plug.

Dr. Marchin then shared this patient did not have insurance, and he would not get reimbursed if he saw them. Not to mention, if Dr. Marchin was coming to see the patient, he would want Carie to continue to monitor them, and that would make her late leaving. Dr. Marchin explained if they removed the patient from life support, many lives could be saved by harvesting the patient's organs before any went into failure. Carie was glad to hear the patient was an organ donor because her uncle had needed a donated kidney the year before. However, as she told Dr. Marchin, this patient did not show ECS/ECI.

The doctor paused for a few seconds. He asked Carie if she turned her filters down on the EEG machine, would the waveforms go away? Carie replied yes, they would, but it was protocol to turn the settings up so the maximum number of waveforms could come through. Dr. Marchin then asked if Carie would turn the filters down to show the record as ECS/ECI since the patient was more than likely going to expire that night anyway. That way, she could unhook the electrodes and go home. After all, he said, no one would know the difference except Carie and Dr. Marchin, who were both exhausted.

Discussion Questions

1. What are the facts of this case?
2. What are the ethical dilemmas you recognize?
3. What legal ramifications can you find within the case study?
4. What should Carie do? What should Dr. Marchin do?
5. What are other potential issues and concerns can you find within the case?

Additional Resources

Jackson, E. (2015). The relationship between medical law and good medical ethics. *Journal of Medical Ethics, 41*(1), 95–98.

Kovner, A. R., & Knickman, J. (2015). *Jonas & Kovner's health care delivery in the United States* (Vol. 11). Springer Publishing Company.

Lewis, M. A., & Tamparo, C. D. (2007). *Medical law, ethics, & bioethics for the health professions* (6th ed.). F. A. Davis Company.

Pozgar, G. D. (2016). *Legal aspects of health care administration.* Jones & Bartlett Learning.

Cheating the Government: Medicare Fraud

Madison Price

Windsor is a 24-year-old medical assistant (MA) employed in an outpatient endocrinology clinic. Windsor enjoys this job because it provides the opportunity to work alongside and learn from various licensed health care professionals including physicians, physician assistants (PAs), and nurse practitioners (NPs). Windsor also loves interacting with the patients, most of whom are over the age of 65.

One day while cleaning up after clinic, Windsor notices two nurse practitioners and a physician, Dr. Walley, secretly conversing in one of the exam rooms. Windsor catches bits and pieces of their conversation, though not enough to fully understand what they are discussing. All that is clearly heard is something about "Medicare patients" and "reimbursement practices." Though this piqued Windsor's interest, work must resume to avoid getting caught eavesdropping.

On the drive home that night, Windsor's mind wanders back to the conversation that was overheard. Recently there were rumors that the clinic was struggling financially. Windsor surmises the providers' conversation must have been about their financial concerns around reimbursement. "Well, that's not my problem," Windsor says out loud, and gladly pushes their conversation to the back burner.

Over the next few months, Windsor does not notice any more secretive meetings in the clinic and thinks maybe imagination played a role in this scenario and the providers were not trying to be secretive at all. Before long, Windsor starts to notice a troubling trend when going through some of the patients' records.

"Ka? Did Dr. Walley see Mrs. Allen yesterday or was it the NP?" Windsor asked the MA.

"If memory serves me right, it was the NP. Yes, I know it was because I was asked to order labs for Mrs. Allen," Ka states.

"Alright, thanks Ka," Windsor responds, and walks away thinking, "I wonder why only Dr. Walley's signature is on the patient's clinic note?"

As Windsor starts to look back over the last few weeks of notes, the realization that Dr. Walley is the only one signing the clinical notes for many of the patients that only the NP saw is glaring. Windsor knows despite the doctor's signature being on the charts, Dr. Walley was not consulted to assist in those patients' care at all during any of their appointments. Windsor has never noticed this before, and an uneasy feeling sets in. Not knowing whether to say anything, Windsor decides to confide in Ka again after clinic is over. After explaining the discrepancy, Ka agrees that it is indeed odd that Dr. Walley's signature is the only one on the notes. What is even more odd is this is only happening for patients who have Medicare. They cannot decide if they should take this concern to their practice manager or wait to see if the issue resolves itself.

Dr. Walley ends up going on vacation for the next two weeks, so Windsor decides not to pursue the issue until then. However, after arriving at work a couple of days later, Windsor notices the NP and the practice manager sitting in the conference room with individuals dressed in professional suits. Windsor learns from other coworkers that the individuals are lawyers representing the clinic. Though management tries to keep the issue hush-hush, it eventually makes it around the office that the clinic got audited by the government and discrepancies were recognized. Chief among those discrepancies is that the clinic has an abnormally large number of reimbursement claims for physician visits, yet a relatively small number of reimbursement claims for NP and PA visits. Upon further investigation, it became known that the clinic had been billing Medicare the physician rate for office visits even when patients were only seeing a PA or NP during their visit.

Upon learning this information, Windsor understands now why Dr. Walley's signature was appearing on all the notes, despite the NP being the one who actually saw the patients in clinic. Afraid of getting in trouble, Windsor does not say anything about noticing the signature discrepancies and advises Ka to do the same. It finally dawns on Windsor, though, what the providers had been up to all those months ago during their secretive meeting. They had been designing a scheme to increase the clinic's revenue by submitting fraudulent claims on their Medicare patients. Windsor cannot help but wonder if mentioning this months ago could have helped or whether the issue could have been avoided all together. Now they can only hope that the thousands of dollars the clinic must repay Medicare does not end up costing them their jobs.

Discussion Questions

1. What are the first indications in the case study that suggest medical fraud was occurring in the practice?
2. If you had been in Windsor's shoes when the discrepancies between what provider was seeing the patient and what provider was signing the notes, would you have confided in a colleague or would you have taken the concern to management? Explain your rationale.
3. If you took a concern like the one Windsor had to your practice manager and they ended up dismissing it without investigating it, do you believe you would have an ethical responsibility to report the suspicious activity to an objective third party? Who might you be able to report such an issue to outside of your practice?
4. Do you think the providers or clinic in this case are going to face legal consequences beyond having to pay back the money they owe to the government?

5. What do you believe were the primary motives driving the providers to engage in this type of fraudulent activity? Do you believe their behavior put their patients at undue risk? Explain your rationale.

6. According to the American Academy of PAs (2018), Medicare covers services that PAs provide in all practice settings at 85% of the physician fee. If you were a practice manager, would you attempt to overcome that 15% reduction by scheduling a large number of patients with the PA in a given day? Or would you have the PA assist the doctor with charting in order to free up the doctor to see more patients that could be charged the full fee? Elaborate on your choice.

7. Did you make any assumptions while reading this case regarding race, ethnicity, gender or gender identity, sexual orientation, socioeconomic status, culture, or other protected class? Were these assumptions focused at the individual/staff level, clinical/program level, or organizational/administrative level? How do these assumptions affect cultural awareness, cultural knowledge, behaviors, and/or skill development?

Additional Resources

American Academy of PAs. (2018, April). *Third-party reimbursements for PAs.* https://www.aapa.org/wp-content/uploads/2017/01/Third_party_payment_2017_FINAL.pdf

Baker, L. C., Bundorf, M. K., Devlin, A. M., & Kessler, D. P. (2016). Medicare advantage plans pay hospitals less than traditional Medicare pays. *Health Affairs, 35*(8), 1444–1451. https://www.healthaffairs.org/doi/10.1377/hlthaff.2015.1553

Borkowski, N. (2011). *Organizational behavior in health care* (2nd ed.). Jones & Bartlett Learning.

Center for Substance Abuse Treatment. (2014). *Improving cultural competence.* Substance Abuse and Mental Health Services Administration. https://www.ncbi.nlm.nih.gov/books/NBK248428/

Lopez, E., Neuman, T., Jacobson, G., & Levitt, L. (2020, April 15). *How much more than Medicare do private insurers pay? A review of the literature.* https://www.kff.org/medicare/issue-brief/how-much-more-than-medicare-do-private-insurers-pay-a-review-of-the-literature/

Weldon, D. (2014, May 28). Non-physician providers: An unexpected route to revenue increases. *Healthcare Finance.* https://www.healthcarefinancenews.com/news/non-physician-providers-unexpected-route-revenue-increases

PART 9

Health Policy

CASE 99

How Do I Do This?

Monika Piccardi

Potter, the program manager (PM) working for the state's children's health program, received a call from Shaw, the director. Shaw had gotten a call from the department's policy analyst and legislative liaison. Legislation was in the process of being passed that would require them to gather a workgroup. This group was tasked to discuss congenital anomalies, describe current processes to educate providers and the public, make educational materials available from the department, and put together parent education recommendations. In addition, they were required to draft a report to the legislature regarding the recommendations.

Shaw asked Potter not only to be a part of this workgroup but to chair it as well.

Potter, who had never been asked to take part in a legislative workgroup, yet alone chair one and be responsible for the resulting report, was both thrilled and nervous. With some trepidation, Potter agreed to take on this new responsibility. After several weeks, Potter received word the legislation did indeed pass with a directive of who should be on the workgroup. Shaw advised Potter to gather the group as soon as possible as the report to the legislature was due in four months.

As Potter was to chair it, the first thought that came to mind was, "How do I do this?"

The legislation that put in motion the workgroup and report was brought to the state's legislature by a religious group, several national and local organizations that worked with children and families of those with congenital anomalies, and concerned members of the public. These same groups were legislated to be part of the workgroup. Potter knew it would be necessary to represent the program and the overall public health interest, while other members would probably have opposite points of view. Potter needed to gather the workgroup in short order and *had* to produce a plan to keep the meetings on track and civil. Potter had a lot of expectations about the workgroup participants and what the final report should look like.

Potter thought back to previous groups and how other chairpersons handled things, both positively and negatively, and created a plan. Potter would:

- Have a detailed agenda at every meeting.
- Allow for introductions during the first meeting that include why the person is there and their goals.
- Set up ground rules and norms for discussion and deliberative decision making.

- Acknowledge the legislative goals of the workgroup and agreed upon deliverables.
- Formally acknowledge and express respect for opposing views but remind the workgroup that the goal was to benefit all residents.
- Assign roles and responsibilities as needed.
- Set deadlines.

Potter set up the first meeting of the workgroup and implemented the plan. With a few hiccups along the way, the participants produced a comprehensive report that took all perspectives into consideration.

Discussion Questions

1. What is happening in this case?
2. What leadership or teaming skills would be useful in this situation?
3. How would you navigate this situation to put out a report or product that is factual yet considerate of everyone's perspective and serves the public health interests?
4. What else might Potter have done to ensure a successful workgroup?
5. Should the office director have done anything different to support Potter? If so, what?
6. Did Potter have any internal biases that might have affected the reaction to the workgroup composition or how the workgroup was approached? If yes, what were they?

Additional Resources

Booher, D. D. (2013). *Leading effective meetings: 72 tips to save time, improve teamwork, and make better decisions.* Booher Research Institute.

Buchbinder, S. B., Shanks, N. H., & Kite, B. J. (2021). *Introduction to health care management* (4th ed.). Jones & Bartlett Learning.

Center for Substance Abuse Treatment. (2014). *Improving cultural competence.* Substance Abuse and Mental Health Services Administration. https://www.ncbi.nlm.nih.gov/books/NBK248428/

Hicks, D. (2002). The promise(s) of deliberative democracy. *Rhetoric & Public Affairs, 5*(2), 223–260.

Maltzman, R., & Stewart, J. (2018). *How to facilitate productive project planning meetings: A practical guide to ensuring project success.* Maven House.

Watkins, M. D. (2016). Leading the team you inherit. *Harvard Business Review, 94*(6), 60–67.

An Exercise in Comparing Health Systems: Spain

Nancy K. Sayre

Managers in the U.S. can learn from the administration of health systems around the world. One example is to explore policies, practices, data, and attitudes regarding the health system in Spain. What are the pros and cons of the Spanish health system? What practices of the Spanish health system could be "borrowed" by a health policy expert or administrator in the U.S.?

The Spanish health care system is public and private. Social welfare, based on tax payments, provides universal, free medical care for all, with the option to contract with an insurer and to pay to access private physicians and hospitals. In 1942, a law in Spain created a system of obligatory health insurance based on a percentage tax linked to employment. The Spanish constitution of 1978 mandated protection of health as a right of all citizens. Reinforced in 1986 via Spain's General Healthcare Act, all Spanish nationals are guaranteed universal coverage and free health care access, regardless of employment status or personal wealth. The Ministry of Health and the Health Councils were established to oversee health in Spain and comprise the Spanish National Health System (NHS). Their role is to propose and execute government policy on health planning and regulation and to assure citizens the right to health protection (HealthManagement.org, 2010).

The country of Spain has 17 autonomous communities, and since 2002, each has a regional health department and their own policies and practices. Although this gives each region the ability to determine local health priorities and allocate resources as needed, it also has drawbacks such as that the availability and quality of health services may vary by region. Also, if you are a Spaniard, you are automatically registered into an electronic health record. However, a fully centralized and normalized electronic patient record with a complete clinical history does not exist; each region has its own system architecture, implementation, and interoperability standards. Beneficial features like information sharing between clinicians and pharmacies are common.

The efficiency of care in Spain is world class. For example, most cancer care is provided in big university hospitals owned and funded by the central government. Anyone living in Spain has full access to any proven treatment, complex surgery, or expensive cancer treatment medication (Cubedo, 2020). To aid in cancer care, Spain has a nationwide cancer registry that helps analyze and determine effective prevention and treatment. The best option for most chronic conditions such as cancer, Alzheimer's disease, or heart disease is the public health system in Spain, called INSALUD or Seguridad Social. Also, Spain is number one worldwide in the rankings of organ donations, proof of the belief that health is a common goal for the entire nation (Miller, 2014). Blood donation is also viewed as a collaborative endeavor to help all Spaniards. All hospitals share in the collection and distribution of blood, and buses go into the communities to solicit donations.

Each autonomous community has an integrated emergency medical system. These can be publicly managed with government employees or outsourced to private companies. It is a two-tiered system with advanced life support with physicians and nurses and basic life support with technicians. There is a 112 phone number, the equivalent of 911 in the U.S., and an emergency number for medical services, 061, available in several regions. If a noncitizen of Spain or the European Union goes to the public health care system, that person will receive the urgent care required. The health system will try to charge him or her, and/or the government of the patient's country.

Cost containment is a focus but balanced against the public's need for services. For example, in Madrid, ambulances rush to hospitals and howl through the streets all day and night. However, Spanish citizens must pay a fee if they are deemed to use the service for less than a true emergency. One physician in Spain suggested that a nominal or symbolic fee could be placed on urgent services so that people do not go there for trivial problems.

Another example of how Spain contains health care costs is through pharmaceuticals. Drugs must be purchased in pharmacies, not grocery stores like in the U.S., but a 20 pack of generic acetaminophen costs about 98 cents. Pharmacists are often used as substitutes for physicians for minor ailments and recommend products to consumers. In 2019, Spain's national health authority reduced prices on 16,000 types of medications including over the counter, prescription and hospital dispensary drugs which will save the public around $135 million a year. The consumer now pays less for ibuprofen, paracetamol, antibiotics (which need a prescription), lorazepam, and other commonly used medications (Bay Radio, 2019). The Spanish National Health System monitors and controls pharmaceutical prices, particularly those reimbursed by the NHS.

In general, people are happy with the public health system in Spain because it provides good quality services overall and is affordable and free in most cases. According to anecdotal interviews with Spaniards, personal attention is provided by caregivers. This is evidenced by the statistic that less than 15% of citizens enroll in the private voluntary system despite the fact that private insurance is far cheaper than in America, at around $200 per month for an individual (Costa-i-Font, 2016; Wise, 2020). Many European Union (EU) countries offer their citizens a European Health Insurance Card that provides emergency medical treatment insurance when visiting, and Spain has become a top spot for medical tourism within the EU.

Spanish citizens view health care as a right rather than a privilege. In general, they believe that a good health care system requires universal coverage, government regulation, and freedom for the patient to choose. The positive national health ranking of Spain and the long-life expectancy support the fact that the health system is working well (Espana Global, 2019). Perhaps this is because people live without the worry of expensive medical bills, and they feel supported by their government for their health needs.

Waiting times are the biggest problem in the public system, less so in the private system. When you are sick, you might need to wait four days to see a primary care doctor. Primary care doctors are the gate keepers to specialists. If you need to see a specialist, you might need to wait two to four months. And if you need surgery or other specialty care, it may take another three months of waiting. Some specialists and services may be in shorter supply in some autonomous communities. For example, dental care is not covered by the public system, creating unmet needs, particularly for low-income people. Spanish citizens believe more funding should be allocated to the public health system. This would enable hiring more physicians and other medical personnel to lessen patient waiting times. Also, greater funding for salaries for medical staff is needed. Individuals sometimes study medicine in Spain and then go into the private system or abroad where salaries are higher, creating a "brain drain." Clinical research may be another area worthy of greater funding. Because of the engrained belief in health care as a fundamental right, not a business, most citizens do not support privatization of services. Overall, the Spanish people truly benefit from a sound health care system, as well as good weather, a Mediterranean diet, and a culture that believes in a convivial and communal society.

Exercise: Health Metrics

To explore the health of each country in greater detail, complete the following chart with health metrics of the United States and Spain.

	United States	Spain
Population		
% of GDP spent on health care		
Life expectancy		
Infant mortality per 1000 live births		
Smoking prevalence in adults		
Obesity in adults		
Number of physicians		
Number of dentists		
# CT scanners per million population		
# Hospitals		
Health ranking (varies by source)		

Discussion Questions

1.   Did you find differences when comparing the health metrics of each country? Were you surprised and why?

2.   Why is the U.S. the only developed nation without some level of free care offered to its citizens?

3.   Recognizing the governmental and public policy support for universal coverage in Spain, explore the historical perspectives of policies regarding universal coverage in the U.S. Conduct some research on when U.S. policy makers first explored establishing universal health coverage. Can you locate an *early* U.S. universal health care proposal on the Internet? Can you find a *current* U.S. universal health care proposal on the Internet?

4.   Understanding the public commitment to universal health care in Spain, what did people think about universal health care in the United States in the 1950s, 1980s, and other earlier decades? What attitudes prevent the U.S. from moving forward now?

5.   Does the lack of a universal health system in the U.S. create stress among its citizens? Can one compare the stress of people with universal coverage to those without? What are the limitations of a comparative analysis?

6.   Examine health systems in other countries and conduct some secondary research. What insurance and health funding approaches and policies do these countries use to support the health of their population? Examine Switzerland, Taiwan, Canada, and Germany. What aspects of their solutions would you advocate? Consider the contrast of the U.S. and Spanish health care systems with these countries.

7.   Examine the trend line of the portion of GDP allocated to health in various countries with different health systems, beginning in 2010.

8.   Survey friends and family to learn what they know about health systems in other countries and how they would compare it to the United States. Compile the responses.

Additional Resources

BayRadio. (2019, September 20). *Prices slashed for 16,000 OTC and prescription drugs in Spain.* https://www.bayradio.fm/prices-slashed-for-16000-otc-and-prescription-drugs-in-spain/

Costa-i-Font, J. (2016). *Voluntary health insurance in Europe: Country experience.* https://www.ncbi.nlm.nih.gov/books/NBK447723/

Cubedo, R. (2020, February 6). *Cancer in my community: How Spain is caring for an increasing number of people with cancer.* https://www.cancer.net/blog/2020-02/cancer-my-community-how-spain-caring-increasing-number-people-with-cancer

Espana Global. (2019, May 8). *Spanish health, the best in the world.* https://www.thisistherealspain.com/en/citizenship/spanish-health-the-best-in-the-world/

HealthManagement.org. (2010). *Overview of the Spanish healthcare system.* https://healthmanagement.org/c/hospital/issuearticle/overview-of-the-spanish-healthcare-system

Miller, K. (2014, May 10). *Which country has the highest organ donation rates?* https://www.pbs.org/newshour/health/country-highest-organ-donation-rates

Wise. (2020). *Getting health insurance in Spain: A complete guide.* https://transferwise.com/gb/blog/health-insurance-spain

CASE 101

Medicaid After the Pandemic

Nancy H. Shanks

The coronavirus pandemic had a huge impact on the U.S. economy as a whole and, in particular, on the health care industry and health insurance coverage. As a result of job and income loss, many people became eligible for public health insurance coverage, with the number of Medicaid enrollees increasing from 71.3 to 80.5 million people between February 2020 and January 2021 (Galewitz, 2021). This came only six years after many states had already expanded their Medicaid programs in response to changes enacted as part of the Affordable Care Act (ACA). As pointed out by Galewitz (2021), "at the end of 2020, 14.8 million newly eligible adults were enrolled in Medicaid because of the ACA" (para. 6).

Those earlier changes to Medicaid were quite beneficial to the states that expanded Medicaid, bringing significant financial resources to those states. This was not true for the 12 states that did not expand, however. (Note that two states, Missouri and Oklahoma, did not initially expand, but were in the process of doing so as a result of 2020 ballot initiatives.) According to Garfield et al. (2021), there is a coverage gap of 2.2 million low-income individuals, 97% of whom reside in the South, many of whom are people of color who already experience health disparities.

The challenges to the ACA have been resolved with the U.S. Supreme Court's decision to dismiss the suit brought in *California v. Texas* (Jost, 2021). Since the non-expanding states are still eligible to expand their Medicaid programs, the question is should they do so now? Those states include Alabama, Florida, Georgia, Kansas, Mississippi, North Carolina, South Carolina, South Dakota, Tennessee, Texas, Wisconsin, and Wyoming. Select one of these states to address the discussion questions.

Discussion Questions

1. What are the requirements under the ACA for states to expand Medicaid and how will this work?
2. Who will be covered and for what benefits and services in your selected state?
3. What is the rationale for your selected state not opting into expansion?

4. Do the same issues exist for your state now in terms of political, social, and economic issues?
5. Are there other differences that resulted from the coronavirus legislation and the recent Supreme Court decision that should be considered?
6. Do you recommend that your selected state expand or not? Explain your recommendation.

Additional Resources

Buchbinder, S. B., Shanks, N. H., & Kite, B. J. (2021). *Introduction to health care management* (4th ed.). Jones & Bartlett Learning.

Corallo, B., & Rudowitz, R. (2021, June 17). *Analysis of recent national trends and CHIP.* https://www.kff.org/coronavirus-covid-19/issue-brief/analysis-of-recent-national-trends-in-medicaid-and-chip-enrollment/

Galewitz, P. (2021, June 17). *Pandemic swells Medicaid enrollment to 80 million people, a 'high-water mark'.* https://khn.org/news/article/medicaid-enrollment-record-80-million-pandemic/?utm_campaign=KHN%3A%20Topic-based&utm_medium=email&_hsmi=134662865&_hsenc=p2ANqtz-9ZnswJLF-p_p68bT6Wn8vNhK89IECgFhFsn4EDqOpAWuxXFsfEF8LowOEjT2HQiZuJILBJHgzt8eVsiIQ9kQGqc2s0pg&utm_content=134662865&utm_source=hs_email

Garfield, R., Ortega, K. & Damico, A. (2021, January 21). *The coverage gap: Uninsured poor adults in states that do not expand Medicaid.* https://www.kff.org/medicaid/issue-brief/the-coverage-gap-uninsured-poor-adults-in-states-that-do-not-expand-medicaid/

Jost, T. S. (2021, June 21). *The Supreme Court throws out the ACA lawsuit, not the ACA* [Blog post]. Commonwealth Fund. https://www.commonwealthfund.org/blog/2021/supreme-court-throws-out-aca-lawsuit-not-aca

CASE 102

Never Give Up on ACA Repeal

Nancy H. Shanks

The U.S. Supreme Court ruled to keep the Affordable Care Act (ACA) (also known colloquially as Obamacare) in June 2021, when the justices decided that those who had brought the suit in 2017 had no standing to do so. As several articles point out, not many Republicans have had much to say about this outcome (Hogberg, 2021; McFall, 2021). Minority leader of the House of Representatives, Kevin McCarthy, was an exception, stating that the ruling "does not change the fact that Obamacare failed to meet its promises and is hurting hard-working American families" (Hogberg, 2021, para 3).

Your governor agrees with McCarthy and is joining with other Republicans who have supported the ACA's repeal ever since it was passed in March 2010 during the Obama administration. He sees this as an infringement on states' rights and as cost-inducing for his state. And, while many efforts have been made to repeal parts of it and to have it thrown out by the courts, it is still on the books, and your governor is dead set on trying once more to have it repealed.

You are a health policy intern in the governor's office who has been tasked with preparing a position paper brief on the topic for the governor's consideration. You need help with researching the following issues.

Discussion Questions

1. What have been the key Republican issues relating to repealing the ACA?
2. Are those issues supported by the facts and the data? That is, has the ACA "failed to meet its promises" and is it "hurting hard-working American families?"
3. Who has benefitted from the ACA? Explain how and why.
4. Republican lawmakers have constantly said they want to repeal and replace the ACA. Have they ever had a plan to do this? Do they now?
5. What is the public's position on Obamacare? What do opinion polls show about the ACA?

6. What has changed since the earlier attempts to get rid of the ACA? Have changes been made since subsequent administrations took office?
7. Where do the Republican states stand on these issues?
8. Do you recommend that the governor continue to focus on this issue? Provide your rationale for your response.

Additional Resources

Bagley, N. (2021). California v. Texas – Ending the campaign to undo the ACA in the courts. *New England Journal of Medicine, 385,* 673–675. doi:10.1056/NEJMp2110516

Buchbinder, S. B., Shanks, N. H., & Kite, B. J. (2021). *Introduction to health care management* (4th ed.). Jones & Bartlett Learning.

Cohn, J. (2021, March 22). The real reason Republicans couldn't kill Obamacare. *The Atlantic.* https://www.theatlantic.com/politics/archive/2021/03/why-trump-republicans-failed-repeal-obamacare/618337/

Hogberg, D. (2021, July 2). GOP quiet about Obamacare repeal following third Supreme Court decision upholding law. *Washington Examiner.* https://www.msn.com/en-us/news/politics/gop-quiet-about-obamacare-repeal-following-third-supreme-court-decision-upholding-law/ar-AALHh4d

Jost, T. S. (2021, June 21). *The Supreme Court throws out the ACA lawsuit, not the ACA* [Blog post]. Commonwealth Fund. https://www.commonwealthfund.org/blog/2021/supreme-court-throws-out-aca-lawsuit-not-aca

Keith, K. (2021, May 17). *The Affordable Care Act in the Biden era: Identifying federal priorities for administrative action.* Commonwealth Fund. https://www.commonwealthfund.org/publications/issue-briefs/2021/may/affordable-care-act-biden-era-federal-priorities

McFall, C. (2021, June 18). Decade of defeats: The Republican failure to take down Obamacare. *Fox News.* https://www.foxnews.com/politics/decade-of-defeats-how-republicans-failed-to-take-down-obamacare

Sanger-Katz, M., & Kliff, S. (2021, June 17). Obamacare is here to stay. Brace for new health care battles. *The New York Times.* https://www.nytimes.com/2021/06/17/upshot/obamacare-supreme-court-decision.html

Appendix A

Health Care Management Case Studies and Guidelines*

Sharon B. Buchbinder, Donna M. Cox, and Susan Casciani

Introduction

A case study is the presentation of an organizational scenario. The case will usually present a description of the organization and its market, as well as the major players in the organization and their interactions regarding a specific situation. The objective in analyzing a case study is to develop and test a proposed "solution" to address the described situation. "The case method is not only the most relevant and practical way to learn managerial skills, it's exciting and fun" (Hammond, 2002, p.1). Hammond states further:

> Simply stated, the case method calls for discussion of real-life situations that business executives have faced. Casewriters, as good reporters, have written up these situations to present you with the information available to the executives involved. As you review their cases, you will put yourself in the shoes of the managers, analyze the situation, decide what you would do, and ... [be] prepared to present and support your conclusions. (Hammond, 2002, p. 1)

Case studies are thus widely used as learning methods in the education of health care managers and administrators. Cases require the student to think, reason, develop critical thinking and analytic skills, identify underlying causes of problems, use creative abilities, make decisions, and, in the case of group work, deal with personality conflicts and change. Generally, health care management utilizes two types of case

---

* Note: This Appendix was originally published as "Healthcare Management and Case Study Guidelines" in *Introduction to Health Care Management, 2nd Edition*, by Sharon B. Buchbinder and Nancy H. Shanks. This version has been adapted.

studies: **diagnostic** and **descriptive**. In a **diagnostic case study,** a major issue or problem will need to be identified and addressed. A **descriptive case study** usually presents a theme or describes a situation or series of events. There is not necessarily a major problem presented, and thus the objective is more of discussing the theme in terms of management challenges. Regardless of the type, case studies can be daunting at first and a good strategy for how to tackle the case study is needed.

Case Study Analysis

Based on over two decades of experience using the case study method in the classroom and in faculty workshops, we recommend that students work in teams and use the following guidelines for case studies.

- Read (or watch) the case carefully several times. The first time you read it, read it quickly, trying to pick up the high-level issues and players. In successive readings, become absorbed in the situation in such a way that you see yourself intimately involved with the personalities, problems, and conflicts.

> **TIP** Highlight sentences that may be important in identifying the main issue or theme of the case, as well as strike out those sentences that are "nice to know" but not critical to the issues in the case. This will help you to filter out the "noise" in the case.

- As the case starts to become more familiar to you, begin to ask yourself the following types of questions and jot down your thoughts:
  - What is *really* going on in this case? Generally speaking, what types of managerial issues are there (e.g., human resources, leadership, legal, confidentiality, quality control, conflict management, etc.)? Can you describe *in one sentence* the major issue/problem? Make a list of all of the problems you can identify. Analyze this list to see if you can determine how these problems interrelate to each other. Are some problems the *cause* of other problems? If so, highlight the causal problems to see if a pattern develops. For example, a problem that is usually rather easy to identify is a loss of revenue, but you must dig deeper—*why* is there a loss of revenue? What is causing it?
- This will lead you to begin to understand the secondary, or underlying, issues. It is important to note here that you may end up with more than one "major" problem; your challenge is to identify the one that has the greatest potential to alter the situation for the better if addressed successfully.

> **TIP** Sketch out the relationships between your major and secondary problems in a flowchart-like manner. Apply reasoning to how and why the problems developed; always answer the question "WHY?" While we only know what the case tells us, we need to think about underlying motivators while we read. Play "devil's advocate" to test these causal relationships to help ensure you are on the right track.

- Conduct some initial research on your identified major problem/issue. The research will likely help frame the major problem and reinforce its relationships to your potential secondary problems. For example, if the problem you have identified deals with employee supervision, research what types of things need to be considered when supervising employees (e.g., performance reviews, hiring/firing processes, related potential legal issues, discrimination and/or diversity issues, mentoring, confidentiality, etc.). Be sure to consider any potential diversity issues and the impact they may have. Only by gaining an understanding of the relevant management issues surrounding the major problem can you begin to develop potential solutions.

> **TIP** Utilize the academic and trade journals as the major focus of your research. Websites can only get you so far, and academic/trade journals will provide you with more in-depth and directly relevant **information!**

- **IMPORTANT NOTE:** If you are working in teams on the case study, we highly recommend you complete all of the above steps *individually*, and then come together as a group to compare notes. This will help to ensure you have done the best job of analyzing the case.
- Now that you have identified the major problem, decide on what management level you want to "solve" the problem from. Is the problem best addressed from a departmental perspective (e.g., supervisor, director, manager), a senior executive perspective (e.g., vice presidents), an organizational perspective (e.g., CEO, Board of Directors), or perhaps is it best dealt with from an outside perspective (e.g., consultant)? Note that in order to best make this decision, you *must* understand the roles and responsibilities of each of these levels as they relate to the problem, and identify the strengths and weaknesses of each approach.
- Identify at least two, but no more than three, potential alternative "solutions" to address the major problem *from the management level you have selected*. This is where you are being asked to "think outside of the box." Were there possibilities not suggested by the text? How would each of these solutions improve the situation, and to what degree? Identify the strengths and weaknesses of each approach. The best choice may not be affordable; as managers we have to "satisfice," i.e., make the best choice available at that time. Is one more cost-effective than the other(s)? Would one of them take too long to implement before experiencing the needed results? Do you have the expertise and resources to implement the solution? In developing your alternative solutions, keep in mind the strengths and weaknesses of the organization *as they relate to the major problem*. Having a great community reputation, for example, will likely have little bearing on whether or not you should fire the head of surgery. However, significant financial reserves may be very relevant in trying to increase access for patients in outlying areas. Remember, there is no one right or wrong solution, only better or worse solutions. The difference will be in how you analyze and present them.
- Select the best alternative solution to implement. In the step above you analyzed each potential alternative in terms of the strengths and weaknesses of each. Through this process it should have become evident which alternative has the best chance of successfully addressing the major problem. Your final challenge is to identify *how* and *when* you will know whether your proposed alternative solution worked. To do this, you must identify ways to evaluate your solution. For example, if the desired outcome of your solution is increased revenue, when will this occur, and to what degree? Increased revenue will be one of your evaluation metrics, but you will need to outline specifically what you expect to happen. A sufficient response in

this example could be, "increase revenue by 5% by end of third quarter." Note that regardless of which metrics you choose, you need to be able to *measure* them. At this point in the case it may be necessary to "assume" some things. For example, if a desired outcome is increased patient satisfaction, you can assume the organization already measures this and simply state your expected quantitative improvement and timeframe (e.g., "improve patient satisfaction by 10 percentage points within six months"). However, be sure to *state any assumptions* you are making "We assume the organization already tracks patient satisfaction, and it is currently at 30%").

Case Study Write-up

Prepare a written report of the case using the following format:

Background Statement

What is going on in this case *as it relates to the identified major problem*? What are (only) the key points the reader needs to know in order to understand how you will "solve" the case? Summarize the scenario in your own words—do not simply regurgitate the case. Briefly describe the organization, setting, situation, who is involved, who decides what, etc.

Major Problems and Secondary Issues

Specifically identify the major and secondary problems. What are the real issues? What are the differences? Can secondary issues become major problems? Present analysis of the causes and effects. Fully explain your reasoning.

Your Role

In a sentence or short paragraph, declare what role you will address the major problem from, whether you are the chief administrator in the case or an outside consultant called in to advise. Regardless of your choice, you MUST justify in writing WHY you chose that role. What are the advantages and disadvantages of your selected role? Be specific.

Organizational Strengths and Weaknesses

Identify the strengths and weaknesses that exist *in relation to the major problem*. Again, your focus here should be in describing what the organization is capable of doing (and not capable of doing) with respect to addressing the major problem. Thus, the identified strengths and weaknesses should include those at the managerial level of the problem. For example, if you have chosen to address the problem from the departmental perspective and the department is understaffed, that is a weakness worthy of mentioning. Be sure to remember to include any strengths/weaknesses that may be related to diversity issues.

Alternatives and Recommended Solution

Describe the two to three alternative solutions you came up with. What feasible strategies would you recommend? What are the pros and cons? State what should be done—why, how, and by whom. Be specific.

Evaluation

How will you know when you've gotten there? There must be measurable goals put in place with the recommendations. Money is easiest to measure; what else can be measured? What evaluation plan would you put in place to assess whether you are reaching your goals?

> **TIP** Write this section as if you are trying to "sell" your proposed solution to the organization. Convince the reader that your proposed solution is the best available, and that it will work as planned. Make sure that the goals you identify are worth the effort required to achieve them!

Team Structure and Process for Completion

We recommend that teams select a team leader and a team recorder, although *all* should take notes. The team should decide how to divide up the tasks to be accomplished. In our classes, we expect to see written responses to the aforementioned questions, and the written, typed case studies to be a minimum of five pages long. Teams should indicate who had responsibility for different tasks/sections on the written materials that are handed in.

Team findings should be presented in no more than 10 minutes to the rest of the class. Individual grades are given for each student's designated sections and a group grade for the case study as a whole from peers on the presentation, plus teammates are required to grade each other's efforts and teamwork within the group. The average of the three grades becomes each individual's case study grade. Copies of forms utilized for each (individual sections, group presentation, and teamwork) are provided in this chapter (**Figure A.1**, **Figure A.2**, and **Figure A.3**).

Guidelines for Effective Participation

1. Attend all team sessions. Eighty percent of life is showing up. It's important here too!
2. Prepare before coming to team sessions and take careful notes. Think about the project and be prepared for each session.
3. Help establish the purpose of the session and the direction to be followed by the group.
4. Have an open mind and be willing to modify your conclusions. Welcome the stimulation of having your ideas challenged.
5. Strike a balance between your speaking time and that of others.
6. Be respectful, considerate, and tactful of the feelings of others—especially when you disagree.
7. Present the substance of your thinking concisely and to the point.
8. Help the team reach some conclusions within the allotted time.
9. Really pull your weight on the team. Assist in accomplishing the work of the team by putting the needs of the group ahead of your own needs.
10. HAVE FUN!

	A Level	B Level	C Level	D Level
Introduction (10 pts)	The section introduction ■ Was well organized ■ Smoothly pulled the reader into the topic ■ Presented the main focus of the case study section ■ Included adequate content ■ Was written for the correct audience	The section introduction had one limitation: ■ Disorganized ■ Not smooth ■ Did not present the main focus of the case study section ■ Too detailed or too sketchy ■ Rocky first sentences	The section introduction had two of these limitations: ■ Disorganized ■ Not smooth ■ Did not present the main focus of the case study section ■ Too detailed or too sketchy ■ Rocky first sentences	The section introduction had three or more limitations listed at left or required major changes
Content (20 pts)	The content of the case study section ■ Was clear ■ Had a unified focus ■ Focused on important information ■ Adequately explained concepts ■ Was correct	The content of the case study section had one of these limitations: ■ Hard to understand ■ Included irrelevant or too much detailed information ■ Failed to explain concepts ■ Had a disjointed focus ■ Incorrect information	The content of the case study section had two of these limitations: ■ Hard to understand ■ Included irrelevant or too much detailed information ■ Failed to explain concepts ■ Had a disjointed focus ■ Incorrect information	The content of the case study section was not clearly written and difficult to understand OR had three or more limitations listed at left
Paragraph organization (20 pts)	Paragraphs in the case study section ■ Had clear topic sentences ■ Were about a single topic ■ Were organized at the paragraph level ■ Had transitions from one paragraph to another	Paragraphs in the case study section had one of these limitations: ■ Poor topic sentences ■ Run-on paragraphs or paragraphs were too brief ■ Lacked organization within the paragraph ■ Lacked transitions from one paragraph to another	Paragraphs in the case study section had two of these limitations: ■ Poor topic sentences ■ Run-on paragraphs or paragraphs were too brief ■ Lacked organization within the paragraph ■ Lacked transitions from one paragraph to another	Paragraphs in the case study section had three or more of the limitations at left
Case study section organization (20 pts)	The case study section's organization ■ Was easy to follow ■ Was presented in a logical manner ■ Integrated information ■ Summarized information when needed ■ Used headers	The case study section had one of the following limitations: ■ Organization was not logical ■ Information was not consistently integrated together ■ Information was not summarized when needed ■ Headers were missing	The case study section had two of the following limitations: ■ Organization was not logical ■ Information was not consistently integrated together ■ Information was not summarized when needed ■ Headers were missing	The case study section was disorganized and illogical OR had three or more of the limitations listed at left.
Writing style (10 pts)	The style of writing is professional ■ Easy to understand ■ Uses appropriate vocabulary ■ Shows mature syntax style	Writing is affected by one of the following limitations: ■ Jargon ■ Wordiness ■ Redundant phrasing ■ Awkward syntax structures ■ Choppy sentences ■ Run-on sentences ■ Incorrect use of vocabulary	Writing is affected by two of the following limitations: ■ Vocabulary jargon ■ Wordiness ■ Redundant phrasing ■ Awkward syntax structures ■ Choppy sentences ■ Run-on sentences ■ Incorrect use of vocabulary	Writing is affected by three or more limitations occurring three or more times
Writing mechanics (10 pts)	The case study section is free of spelling, grammar, and punctuation errors.	The case study section has fewer than 5 errors in spelling, grammar, or punctuation.	The case study section has 6–10 errors in spelling, grammar, or punctuation.	The case study section has more than 10 errors in spelling, grammar, or punctuation.
APA (10 pts)	All APA rules are followed for citations, numbers, quotes, references, headers, etc.	The case study section has fewer than 5 APA rule errors.	The case study section has 6–10 APA rule errors.	The case study section has more than 10 APA rule errors.

Figure A.1 Detailed Rubric for Grading Written Case Studies

PEER EVALUATION CRITERIA FOR CASE STUDY PRESENTATIONS SCORING SHEET	
Presentation Title and Author's Name	**Your Name**
Use a scale of 1 to 10, where 1 is poor and 10 is excellent. **(You must explain any scores below 3 and above 8.)**	
How well did the presenter:	**Points**
Indicate the purpose of the presentation and its relevance to the course?	0
Ensure the presentation was relevant to the current state of health care?	0
Demonstrate knowledge about the *case study*?	0
Contribute to peer knowledge?	0
Use proper grammar, punctuation, and vocabulary?	0
Adhere to length constraints (*10 slides maximum*, excluding references)?	0
Use current references and cite properly in presentation?	0
Provide appropriate main points?	0
Use legible fonts with appropriate colors/background and clip art?	0
Accomplish the stated objectives?	0
TOTAL	**0**

Figure A.2 Peer Evaluation Criteria for Group Presentations

CONFIDENTIAL TEAMMATE EVALUATION CRITERIA			
Use a scale of 1 to 10, where 1 is poor and 10 is excellent. (Do NOT evaluate yourself.)			
How well did your teammates:	**Name**	**Name**	**Name**
Attend all team sessions?	0	0	0
Prepare for each session?	0	0	0
Work collaboratively to identify and meet session goals?	0	0	0
Actively participate in group discussions?	0	0	0
Keep an open mind or modify opinions or conclusions to keep the project moving?	0	0	0
Present ideas concisely?	0	0	0
Submit assigned work on time?	0	0	0
Interact with teammates in a respectful, considerate, and tactful manner?	0	0	0
Fulfill responsibilities as agreed?	0	0	0
Work actively to achieve group consensus on issues/problems?	0	0	0
TOTAL	0	0	0
Would you be willing to work with this teammate again on another team? (YES or NO)			
(You must evaluate ALL teammates and explain any scores below 3 and above 8.)			

Figure A.3 Confidential Teammate Evaluation Form

Reference

Hammond, J. S. (1976, April 16). *Learning by the case method*. Industry and Background Note 9-376-241. Harvard Business Publishing.

Index

A

Abandonment, 243–244, 245–246, 247–248
Abuse, 91–92, 271–274
ACA. *See* Affordable Care Act
Academic medical center, 71–72, 227–228
Access to care, 9–12
Accountable care organization, 31–34
ADA. *See* Americans with Disabilities Act
Adverse drug reaction, 241–242
Affordable Care Act
    legal challenges, 289–290
    Medicaid expansion, 287–288
    preventive screenings, 183–184
    repeal, 289–290
    Section 1557, 187–190
Allergy screening, 55–56
Ambulatory care, 3–4, 43–46, 77–80, 83–86
Americans with Disabilities Act, 43–46,
    187–190
Assault, 259–260
Audits, 153–156, 275–278
Authoritarian leadership, 19–22

B

Bariatric Care, 147–148, 149–152
Behavioral health care, 19–22, 237–240,
    262–264
Bias
    cognitive, 225–226
    gender, 17–18, 171–174
    mental health, 263–264
    racial, 119–122, 207–210
    sexual orientation 201–202, 203–204,
    205–206
Black Lives Matter, 119–122
Board of Directors
    conflict with management, 17–18
Bullying
    employee, 35–36, 49–50, 133–136,
    253–254, 265–270
    patients, 55–56, 83–85, 87–90, 105–106,
    137–138
Butterfly, 253–254

C

Cancer care, 9–12, 249–250
Cardiac care, 57–58, 143–146, 249–250
Caregiver issues, 59–60
Case study guidelines
    analysis, 292–294
    grading rubric, 296
    group presentations, peer evaluation criteria
    for, 295
    guidelines for effective participation, 295
    peer evaluation criteria, 297
    purpose of, 291
    team evaluation criteria, 297
    team structure and process for completion,
    295
    types of, 291–292
    write-up, 294–295
Centers for Medicare and Medicaid Services
    reimbursement for telehealth, 47–48,
    77–80
Certified nursing assistants
    staffing issues, 13–16, 39–40
Children's hospital, 123–124
Chronic care, 47–48
Chronic pain, 243–244, 245–246, 247–248
Civility, 63–66
Claims denials, 147–148, 149–152
Climate change issue, 115–116
Colonoscopy, 83–86, 87–90, 137–138
CMS. *See* Centers for Medicare and Medicaid
    Services
CNAs. *See* Certified nursing assistants
Colorectal screening, 31–34
Common sense care, 107–108
Communication
    between physicians, 249–250
    with parents, 99–100
    with patients, 93–94, 95–96, 97–98
    with staff, 3–4
Community outreach, 31–34
Conflict of interest, 223–224, 253–254
Conflict resolution
    abandonment, 243–244, 245–246,
    247–248